Best Walks in Ireland

Best Walks in Ireland

David Marshall

REVISED EDITION

Frances Lincoln

Frances Lincoln Ltd
4 Torriano Mews
Torriano Avenue
London NW5 2RZ
www.franceslincoln.com

This revised edition published by Frances Lincoln 2006
First published in Great Britain 1996 by Constable and Company Ltd
Copyright © Frances Lincoln 2006
Original text © David Marshall 1996
Photographs © Rob Beighton 2005
Revised edition designed by Kevin Brown at park44.com

British Library Cataloguing in Publication data
A catalogue record for this book is available from the British Library.

Printed and bound in Singapore

ISBN 07112 2420 X

9 8 7 6 5 4 3 2 1

frontispiece: Coumfea from Nire Valley, Walk 17

Publisher's note: For this edition, the routes and information summaries for each
walk have been updated, as have the Appendices at the end of the book. Local
transport suggestions that appear in the text have been checked where possible,
but routes and timetables are liable to change: be sure to check with local operators before setting out. The route diagrams throughout the book are meant to be
used alongside an up-to-date map of the areas through which the walk passes.
Walkers should make sure they take the appropriate maps with them.

Contents

Acknowledgements

How do you thank the people of a nation and a province? The staff in tourist offices, the innumerable farmers, the old man who told me of his childhood on Achill? I don't know. But this is a start:

In a kind of geographical order, going anti-clockwise from Dublin I would like to say thank you to these people: Berni Isabelle and JB, my family in Raheny who gave me a second home in Ireland; Katie and Jimmy Murphy (formerly of COSPOIR) and everyone in 'The Elderberries' walking gang; a special thank you to Helen Kehoe of Bord Fáilte (Irish Tourist Board) in Dublin, and to her many generous colleagues in offices in London and across Ireland; Eddie McGrane of An Óige, especially for reminding me about Captain Boycott; Bernard Ryan of 'The Brotherhood of The Lug', reputedly the oldest walking club in Ireland; Frank Fahy of COSPOIR; Dave Fadden of the Office of Public Works; to Joss Lynam for his company one lunchtime and for not telling me not to write the book; Margaret Hayes and her staff at the Dublin Library in the ILAC centre; staff at the Irish National Library; Catherine Keane at Howth Library; Ms Ward and her staff at Louth Co. Library, Dundalk; Anthony McGeehan, James McEvoy and Gerard Carr at the Mourne Countryside Centre; Jenny and Melvin Spiers at the YHANI hostel, Newcastle, especially to Melvin for inviting me to his fortieth birthday bash and to Jenny for being a friend; Billy and Ann Montgomery at the YHANI hostel, Cushendall; the staff at the National Trust, Giant's Causeway Visitor Centre, and at the Causeway School Museum; members of the Forestry Service (NI); staff at Glenariff Forest Park; staff at the Northern Ireland Tourist Board, particulary Janet McIver and Phillipa Reid; library staff at Ballymena, Cushendall,

Newcastle, Newry, Omagh and Castlederg Libraries; Newcastle Technical College; Ordnance Survey of Northern Ireland; wardens and staff at the Glenveagh National Park; much appreciation to John Boyd of Bunbeg; staff at the Dunlewey Lakeside Centre; Mary Monaghan, Co. Donegal Library Services; staff at the Glencolmcille folk village; Sean in Derrylahan; Lorainne Duffy of NW Tourism, Sligo; Fran Heggerty of Sligo Co. Library Services; the librarian at Westport; Sarah Smith and Paul Keogh of Clifden Library, especially to Sarah for making sure I got back from the Twelve Bens safely; staff at the Connemara National Park Visitor Centre, including the café where I enjoyed such a lovely cup of tea; staff at the Galway libraries, City and Island House; everyone on Inis Oírr who treated me like an old friend; particular thanks to Aer Árann for giving me the chance to see the Aran Islands and Roundwood Bog from the air; the *Happy Hooker* for the diversion to see the minke whale; Michael Costelloe of Kerry Co. Library Services, who must have thought I was researching the *Encyclopaedia Britannica* (sorry it ended up so short, Michael, I just ran out of room); the branch library at Dingle; Dennis at Paddy Macs of Tralee for promising to teach me everything he knows about Brandon; the farmers at the foot of Brandon for telling me the stories of the *Great Carrabuncle* and giving me dire warnings about the best ways up and down the mountain; staff at the Killarney National Park, Killarney Library and Muckross House; Brian and Marc O'Sullivan and everyone in the village of Eyeries; the staff of Cork and Kerry Tourism, in all their different offices; Paddy and Margaret Fenton of Molanna dairy farm; Tipperary Tourism; Tipperary branch library; the family in Glencoshabinnia; Niall Caroll of Powers The Pot hostel of Clonmel; Midlands East Tourism; Portlaoise Library; stacks of local authorities and district councils; Terry Doherty and the other staff of the Wicklow Mountains National Park; Sealink Ferries; the Garda Síochána, from the Dublin headquarters to stations and gardaí across the country; the Royal Ulster Constabulary for not locking me up when I lost my tax disc; the Meteorological Service, don't we love them! Loads of walkers, ramblers, climbers, cavers, cyclists, boatmen and tourists everywhere I went. A very special thank you to each and all of the landowners, tenants and farmers that I met and shared some of the day with, their warmth and hospitality are rightly legendary. And a few people and places in England: Arnold and Sutton-in-Ashfield Libraries in Nottinghamshire; all the staff at the Nottinghamshire County Library in Kirkby-in-Ashfield, who supplied ninety per cent of the preliminary research material. Thanks to friends and family for their help and support including colleagues in the NUJ; Maureen Richardson of Notts CC; my sister Carol Farmer and my long-time close friend Pauline Marshall, and finally my partner Natasha Isabelle.

I'd also like to add a thanks to Psion (UK) plc, who supplied the MC400 notebook computer on which the entire book was written, in libraries, in cafés and bars, amid ruins, on beaches, by rivers, some of it on the tops of mountains and on at least one occasion sitting, rather wet, in the middle of a Sperrin bog. I took it everywhere.

And finally my thanks to everyone I ever met in every bar, by every strand, on every hilltop … I think that's all!

I would also like to acknowledge the use of the following books as reference material: Joyce, P. W., *A Child's History of Ireland*, Longman, 1898; *The Statesman's Yearbook,* ed. Brian Hunter, Macmillan Press, 1992, 1993, 1994; Bence-Jones, Mark, *A Guide to Irish Country Houses,* Constable, London, 1988; Webb, D. A., and Scannell, Mary J. P., *Flora of Connemara and the Burren,* Royal Dublin Society and Cambridge University Press, 1983; Danaher, Kevin, *Ireland's Traditional Houses,* Bord Fáilte; Delaney, Frank, *Legend of the Celts,* Hodder & Stoughton, 1989; Feehan, John, *The Landscape of the Slieve Bloom,* Blackwater, Dublin, 1979; *A World of Stone,* The O'Brien Press, Dublin, 1972; Rohan, P. K., *The Climate of Ireland,* Dublin Stationery Office, 1975; Donleavy, J. P., *A*

Singular Country, Ryan Publishing, 1989; Hickey, D. J. and Doherty, J. E., *A Dictionary of Irish History 1800–1980,* Gill & Macmillan 1980; Watson, Philip S., *The Giant's Causeway: a remnant of chaos,* HMSO Belfast, 1992; the Irish National Committee for Geography, *Atlas of Ireland,* Royal Irish Academy, Dublin, 1979; Mitchell, Frank, and others, *Book of the Irish Countryside,* Blackstaff Press, 1987; Sheehy, Maurice, *Discovering the Dingle Area on your Feet,* and several other booklets, published by the author, 1979 onwards; Sanger, Andrew, *Exploring Rural Ireland,* Christopher Helm, 1989; Room, Adrian, *A Dictionary of Irish Place Names,* Appletree Press, 1986; Robinson, Tim, *Stones of Aran: a pilgrimage,* Lilliput Press, 1986; Robinson, Tim, *Connemara,* Folding Landscapes, 1990; Rafferty, Barry, *Trackways Through Time: Archaeological Investigations on Irish Bog Roads 1985–89,* Headline Publishing, 1990; Pochin-Mould, Dorothy, *The Mountains of Ireland,* Gill & Macmillan, 1955,1976; O'Keeffe, Peter, and Simington, Tom, *Irish Stone Bridges,* Irish Academic Press, DoE, 1991; Mersey, Richard, and Thee, Bernd, *The Hills of Cork and Kerry,* Gill & Macmillan, 1987; Marshall, J. D. C., *Forgotten Places of the North Coast,* Clegnagh Publishing, 1991; Loudan, Jack, *In Search of Water: being a history of the Belfast water supply,* 1940; Poucher, W. A., *Ireland,* Constable, 1986; Holland, C. H., *A Geology of Ireland,* Scottish Academic Press, 1981; Gailey, Alan, *Rural Houses of the North of Ireland,* John Donald Publishers, 1984; Bellamy, David, *The Wild Boglands: Bellamy's Ireland,* Christopher Helm, 1986; Gilmore, Desmond, *The Irish Countryside,* Wolfhound Press, 1989; Harbison, Peter, *Guide to National and Historic Monuments of Ireland,* Gill & Macmillan, 1972, 1975, 1992; Doran, Sean, and Greenwood, Margaret, and Hawkins, Hildi, *Ireland: The Rough Guide,* 1990 onwards; three volumes of the New Irish Walk Guides edited by Joss Lynam, Gill & Macmillan, 1991: McCarthy, Miriam Joyce, and Herman, David, *East and South;* Whilde, Tony, and Simms, Patrick, *West and North;* Ó Suilleabháin, Sean, *Southwest;* Crowl, Phillip, A., *The Intelligent Traveller's Guide to*

Historic Ireland, Gill & Macmillan, 1990; Evans, Phil, and Pollock, Eileen, *Ireland For Beginners,* Readers and Writers, 1983; Lynam, Joss, ed., *Irish Peaks,* Constable, 1982; Neville, Peter, *A Traveller's History of Ireland,* Windrush Press, 1992; O'Connell, James, *The Meaning of Irish Place Names,* Blackstaff Press, 1979 onwards; Joyce, P. W., *Irish Local Names Explained,* Fitzhouse Books, 1990; Brennan, Éilis, ed., *Heritage – A Visitor's Guide,* Office of Public Works, 1990; Doherty, J. E. and Hickey, D. J., *A Chronology of Irish History since 1500,* Gill & Macmillan, 1989. And not least, McLoughlin, John, *Discovering Ireland's Woodlands,* Coillte, 1992.

Introduction

These twenty key walks are here to help you to discover the joy of walking in Ireland, the landscape and the people. Route descriptions help you find your way and the narrative and THE COMMENTARIES are there to entertain and inform. Each of the key walks has several variations or alternatives to suit your mood, your experience, the time you have available or the desire to take children. There are more than one hundred suggested walks in all, so there should be something here for every walker.

CHOOSING YOUR WALK

The book provides you with differing ways to select a walk. The map on page 14 will help you find the key walk in a particular area. You can then choose to walk it, or one of the VARIATIONS, or all of them. Or follow up the suggestions for other walking in the area. The list of walks graded according to difficulty (see p. 16) will help you find a particular kind of walk: something easy, moderate or strenuous. There are long walks, short walks; mountain or coastal walks; walks suitable for the family; walks to famous tourist spots; or wilderness walks for a day away from the crowds. And if you have difficulty deciding which area to visit, use the phone numbers in the listings section at the start of each walk to call one or two of the (all-season) tourist offices. They will be able to give you more information and help you plan your trip.

If you are new to walking, the choices will help you progress; if you are new to Ireland they will help you discover a land full of diversity, beauty, tranquillity and excitement. If you are an old hand at both, I hope you will enjoy this island through a different pair of eyes. Whatever, treat the walks as adventures of discovery; make them your own.

Using the Walk Descriptions

The walk descriptions are organised in a straightforward way. After a brief introduction to the area comes a paragraph or two entitled ADVICE AND GRADING. This describes the nature of the walk, indicates any difficulties and occasionally suggests where you might go for an overview of the walk or landscape. GETTING THERE gives the starting place for the walk, with a map reference and a route description of how to arrive from a prominent town or main road. And where an overview is not possible in ADVICE AND GRADING, then GETTING THERE may offer you a more descriptive route instruction, written to introduce you to the landscape.

THE WALK uses *italic* and roman typefaces to distinguish between commentary and a route instruction. For example:

> *Neither is it difficult to understand that these inspiring heights were once the haunt of the golden eagle, or that peregrines and merlins still soar ever skyward here.*
>
> Once you attain the summit of Rocky Cap with its pile of stones, do not go straight to **Slieve Snaght** as there is a very deep defile. Rather, head generally SW.

But anything of more than a few sentences of commentary is reserved for the section which follows: the bold type used to highlight words and phrases in THE WALK directs you towards a description or account of the item of interest in THE COMMENTARIES.

Compass and other directions: As a matter of good practice, whenever a change of route is indicated in the walk descriptions, a compass direction is generally given in brackets. The conventional abbreviations have been used to help the direction stand out from the body of the text: N, E, S and W for the cardinal points and

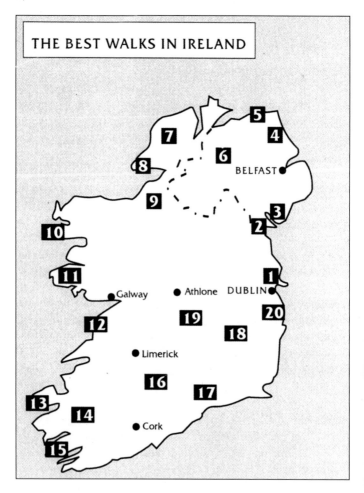

THE BEST WALKS IN IRELAND

NE, SW, WNW, ESE, and so on for composite directions. If there is ever any doubt about the route, the compass directions should then help to clarify your position, but they should never be used as a substitute for your own map or compass bearings. Compass directions for any purpose other than route finding are given in full, for example: 'The view to the north-east ...' Determining the left and right bank of the river, as used in this book, is quite easy. Stand with your back to the source of the river, facing downstream. The left bank of the river is then your left, and the right bank of the river, your right; and are known as the *true* descriptions.

Time: the listings section toward the beginning of each walk description gives essential information: for example, the maps you may need, the distance and time required for the walk, the level of difficulty and some useful telephone numbers. The time is always calculated according to *Naismith's Rule* because that is most widely understood. It assumes we walk at 5 km (3 miles) an hour and take another 30 minutes for every 300 m (1000 ft) that we climb. So it is reasonably generous but takes no account of either the terrain, or the desire to stop or dawdle (which I do all the time). So walks graded as *Easy* are likely to take less than the Naismith time, whilst walks graded as *Difficult* may take a little longer. It depends upon you and your companions. The best policy is to treat the Naismith as a minimum, and if you want to take a picnic, stop to chat or make a few detours, take all day instead.

Difficulty: In spite of various efforts there are still no international standards on difficulty. In an attempt to bring some consistency from walk to walk, I have used a computer to estimate the level of difficulty for each of the walks and variations. There are five grades: Easy, Moderate, Challenging, Strenuous and Difficult. If you are unused to walking, the walks of average difficulty, described as Challenging, are precisely that, you will know about it the following day. Finally, the level of difficulty can depend so much on the weather. A fit experienced walker will find the most difficult walks rewarding and fulfilling, but not especially testing, unless he or she chooses to walk in winter conditions or in mist and fog.

Emergency telephone numbers: Emergency telephone numbers, and those of the local police stations, are the most appropriate, as advised by the Garda Síochána (Guardians of the Peace) Headquarters in Dublin, and the Police Service of Northern Ireland.

The section of each walk description called VARIATIONS AND ALTERNATIVES offers suggestions for shorter, longer, easier or more adventurous routes, with information on times, distances and map references where appropriate. People differ. Some like walks with detailed route directions, some are happy with only a map. The key walks cater for the former whereas the alternatives tend to offer route description rather than instructions; for all but the simplest walks, say walking the East Pier on Howth (Walk 1B) or, more adventurous, climbing Knocknarae (Walk 9D), you are advised to study the map carefully and use your judgement as to whether you are happy to go with an outline of the walk and a map only, or whether you would prefer more direction.

The height of mountains: All mountain heights are given first in metres then in feet. All moutains and heights are listed in Appendix 2.

THE WALKS GRADED ACCORDING TO DIFFICULTY

Easy

1A, 1B, 1C, 1D, 1E; 2C; 4D; 5, 5A, 5B, 5C, 5D; 6B, 6C, 6D, 6E; 7C, 7D; 8B; 9D; 10A, 10C, 10D; 11B, 11D; 12, 12A, 12B, 12C, 12D, 12E; 13C; 14A, 14C, 14E: 15A, 15B, 15E; 16C, 16E; 18, 18A, 18B, 18C, 18D (long); 19C; 20C, 20D.

Moderate

1; 2; 3D; 4A; 6B, 6D; 7B; 8, 8B; 9C; 10B; 11B, 11C; 13B; 14B, 14D; 15A, 15B, 15C, 15E; 16A, 16E; 17A, 17B; 19C, 19D; 20B.

Challenging

2A; 3A; 4, 4A, 4B, 4C; 7A, 7B; 8, 8A, 8B; 9, 9A; 10, 10B, 10E; 11B; 13A, 13B, 13D; 14; 15, 15D; 16; 17D; 18D (long); 19.

Strenuous

2A; 3B, 3C; 4E; 6, 6A; 7; 9B; 10B; 11; 13, 13D; 14D; 15D; 16; 17; 17C; 20.

Difficult

2B; 3, 3B; 4E; 7; 11A; 16B; 17+17C; 19A; 20A.

RAMBLING IN IRELAND

Getting Around

With a total population of only around five million, it is hardly surprising that Ireland has a limited public transport system. It is good close by, and between, the major cities, especially during the summer when tourist demand increases the provision. But frequently there are large areas not serviced at all, most especially those wilderness places where you are likely to want to go for a walk.

Nevertheless public transport is viable for travelling around the country and to the start and finish of some of the walks; in Appendix 4 I have included the addresses and enquiry lines of the main operators such as Iarnród Éireann (Irish Rail), Bus Éireann, Northern Ireland Rail and Ulsterbus. The individual listings sections give local bus company enquiry numbers where appropriate and some situations the tourist information office will be able to advise. The bus or train operators will also advise on the facilities they have for carrying a bicycle, to cycle to the start of a walk.

All of the key walks include GETTING THERE directions for walkers travelling by car, motor cycle, moped or bicycle, and some give specific public transport information. For example Walks 1 and 18 are day walks from Dublin, by DART, bus or train. Some of the variations of Walk 20 can be done in a day from Dublin, by bus. But the full walk probably needs longer and you would need to overstay the night in the area. Walk 14 is a short trip from Killarney. Walks 3, 4 and 5 or their variations are accessible by bus, depending on the season. With Walk 6 bus service varies depending on whether schools are in session or on holiday. The start of some walks may be reached by walking from a main bus route, but the distance may be several kilometres, for example, from Grange for Walk 9 and from Recess for Walk 11. Then again, it is possible to start some routes at a different spot than that given in GETTING THERE. For example Walk 13 could be started on the Slea Head Drive (R559) at Kilvickadownig. Some routes, such as Walks 15 and 17, start deep in the heart of the mountains and in quiet rural areas.

All are accessible by hitch-hiking, especially in the summer. This is a traditional means of getting around in the Republic. It's quite common to see people hitching to and from work or college. The rural nature of much of the country and the limits of the public transport system make it necessary. However you have to recognise that getting there will take a little longer and some caution is necessary even in Ireland. But it is possible and for example Walk 16, starting in the Glen of Aherlow, is easily reached by hitching during the summer months. It's not so easy in the North, but then most of these walks are accessible by bus in the summer.

Guessing the Weather

Guessing the weather is easy. Whatever the season you can guarantee that the weather will be *variable*. Which is why they say Ireland has no climate, only weather, and lots of it. Actually it is fairly equable. Mild winds from the south-west, warmed by the temperate waters of the Gulf Stream, make temperatures almost uniform across the whole country, so you would never know you are at the same latitudes as Labrador or Siberia. Watch a few TV weather forecasts and you will see the isotherms (temperature contours) showing up as large oval shapes roughly echoing the shape of the coastline and circling around the Slieve Bloom Mountains near the centre. In winter they show the Midlands cooler than the coast and the reverse in summer, although the differences are minor with variations of only a few degrees Celsius. It's when you begin to walk upwards that you start to notice a difference.

The sunniest month of the year is May with almost 6.5 hours (average) of sunshine every day. June comes a close second, but the warmest months are July and August at an average of 14–16°C. And if you didn't know already, January and February are the coldest months of the year. However, this is not all gloom as mean temperatures range between 4 and 7°C, which might mean snow on the hills and clear roads for driving, if you're lucky.

Whilst the temperature may not vary much, the rain does, and Ireland can get a lot of rain. It is at its lowest along the eastern coastal strip, with 30–44 inches in the Midlands and as much as 60 inches in the low-lying areas in the west, and even more on the hills in the north-west. In 1969 Donegal was lucky enough to receive eleven times as much rain as Wexford. But you can relax – although it seems to rain on the majority of days of the year, in the spring and summer months it often tends to be for short periods only and frequently brightens up afterwards.

I think it's fair to say that overall it is a pleasant walking climate, just very difficult to guess, especially for ramblers going into the hills. So the answer is to get a forecast from someone with better practice at guessing, and who better than the Irish Meteorological Service, and the British Meteorological Office. Both publish regional forecasts on their respective websites and can deliver them to some mobile devices.

For the Irish Republic:
  General forecast office: 01 806 4255, website: www.met.ie

For Northern Ireland:
  Telephone: 0870 900 0100, website: www.metoffice.com
  Weathercall (for prerecorded forecasts for Northern Ireland:
    09014 722077

Additional premium rate voice or fax forecasts are also available for each country. For these numbers consult the respective website.

Local radio stations are also a good source of weather forecasts. Unfortunately both the phone lines and the radio forecasts are regional and generally for lowland areas. With that in mind, this quote from the sign on the Saint's Road at the foot of Mount Brandon offers good advice:

> Going climbing? Are you prepared for tough ground, wind and rain, cold, mist, accidents, etc? You should have map, compass, whistle, torch, first-aid kit, stout boots, protective clothing and spare clothing, food and drink. It's 10°C cooler at the 3000 ft summit than here. A breeze here is a strong wind up there.

Therefore if you are going into the hills you should look for other sources of weather information. In National Park areas, call the park warden's office, or the visitor centre, and ask for advice. Failing that, seek advice from local walkers, or help at the nearest tourist information office.

Finding a Map

There are two main map-making bodies in Ireland and a number of smaller independents making maps of interest to you, the rambler.

Suirbhéireacht Ordonáis na hÉireann, or the Ordnance Survey of Ireland (OSi – meaning the Republic of Ireland), remains a government department which issues two main series of maps. The half-inch (1:126,720) scale series, for which the Irish cartographers now carry the can, were actually surveyed by the British in 1833. And together with lumps of coal found at primary survey sites, partially demolished ancient monuments and hills in the wrong place, they are an interesting insight into British army cartography. But certainly not something to go walking with, as anyone in the OSi will tell you. Fortunately for us, newer determination and technology have produced the 1:50 000 Discovery (previously called the Rambler) Series. Based on 1970s aerial photography and field investigation, the whole of the Republic is being remapped. A total of seventy-one maps from the Republic of Ireland and eighteen for Northern Ireland are available.

The OSi also produces a 1:25 000 scale sheet, as Sheet 51a, for the Aran Islands and useful for Walk 12. Maps can be ordered from www.irishmaps.ie or from The National Map Centre Ireland, 34 Aungier Street, Dublin 2, Ireland, tel. 01 476 0471 or via the OSi at www.osi.ie, tel. 01 802 5300.

The Ordnance Survey of Northern Ireland (OSNI), an independent business, separate from the Ordnance Survey of Great Britain, produces the Discoverer Series, around twenty sheets of a 1:50 000 scale map. The 1:25 000 Outdoor Pursuits Map, *The Mournes*, covers the area of Walk 3. You will find all of these are generally available from www.osni.gov.uk or from Map Sales, Colby House, Stranmillis Court, Malone Lower, Belfast BT9 5BJ, tel. 028 9025 5755.

In early response to the need for better scale maps than the old half-inch series, a number of independent map-makers, or sponsors, appeared in the Republic. Some sponsored only one map, such as Eileen Ryan for the Comeraghs for which details are given in the Walk 17 listings section; others have taken map-making into the realm of recovering heritage, like Tim Robinson of Folding Landscapes whose maps are usable in Walks 11 (Connemara) and 12 (Oileán Árann). And occasionally maps contained within leaflets produced by the Office of Public Works (OPW) may also be suitable for some walks, or single use. For example, the OPW leaflet entitled *Gleann dá loch* (Glendalough) contains a 1:25 000 scale colour map, quite suitable for helping you to walk safely. Some of these maps will only be available from local tourist offices (numbers are given in the walks), others from the Map Sales Offices of OSi and OSNI, or in England from Stanfords of London, and in Ireland from Easons of Dublin. Most of these bodies will be pleased to supply you by mail order. You will find the addresses of the map-makers, main map and guide-book suppliers, and main tourist offices in Appendix 4 and the phone number of the local (all-season) tourist office in the listings section of the walks that interest you.

Right of Way

Ireland, both the Republic and the Province, does not have the network of footpaths, bridleways or green lanes – public *rights of way* – that you might expect to see in England or other parts of Europe. When an Irishman or woman says *right of way*, they mean something different. They mean, I, or someone else, has walked this route since anyone can remember. They mean, I claim this right by natural justice, it's only fair. They do not mean, I have a statutory right, granted by an act of the Oireachtas (Parliament) or Houses of Parliament, to walk across your property.

But don't frown; no one has ever refused me passage across their land. Quite the reverse – I have been greeted warmly. Sometimes we have discussed the land or the livestock or the latest vagaries of the EU Common Agricultural Policy. Sometimes we've talked about the weather, that terrible snow in 1937, or the threat of global warming. And sometimes we may just have sat. I have been offered sweets, tea, beer, whisky, sandwiches and dinner. I have camped on the lea, by the river and near the copse; and I have always been given a warm welcome. I have heard tales, for example in the Sperrins, of arguments between ramblers and farmers, but I have never found the Irish landowner, tenant or farmer to be anything but very friendly and courteous.

It has always been accepted that people will walk across the land. All that most farmers ask is: **Don't take a dog. Respect livestock. Use gates, close gates, cross fences by stiles and stones, and don't damage them**. In other words, recognise that this is someone's work. They made the fences, fitted the gates, built the walls and raised the livestock. So respect the work they have put into it and I don't think you will ever have any difficulty.

Sometimes landowners are concerned about large crowds or gangs, and when I think this might be a problem I have said so in the text, so use your judgement. However, the main concern for landowners and tenants is the matter of public liability. Not that long ago, a court jury in the Republic settled a large sum of money for compensation on a juvenile who was injured whilst trespassing. Naturally this frightened many farmers, who feared that ramblers might sue them should they injure themselves on the farmers' land. This has been the main concern farmers have consistently voiced to me. I always explain that I carry my own rambling accident insurance, which usually brings a relieved response and a sage nod of the head.

The situation in Northern Ireland is similar, although there is not the same cause for concern about public liability.

The Walks: In general this concern only affects pastoral land. No one has a problem about open mountain, generally it is only your access and egress that need to be considered. But for peace of mind in researching these walks, I spoke to as many people as was practical. I walked up to farmers and farm workers in fields and asked their permission for my own walk, I went to farmhouses and knocked on doors, and I asked around wherever I could to check that there would be few, if any, difficulties. Of course I couldn't get to everyone; on a mile of moorland more than hundred people might have some say about grazing or turbary, or other privileges or rights. Then occasionally during my walking I have been asked not to take a particular route, or at least not to write about it. I have respected those requests.

So whilst you have no statutory rights of way, if you conduct yourself responsibly and courteously, you should have no difficulties. If you do encounter a refusal, explain where you wish to go and ask for an alternative suggestion (preferably off the road) to keep you on your way. But why wait until there's a problem – go have a chat anyway.

Insurance: The federations of mountaineering clubs in many countries will offer personal accident insurance to their members, and public liability insurance for the events they organise. This is true in the United Kingdom and Ireland. Membership of the Mountaineering Council of Ireland (MCI) and the British Mountaineering Council (BMC) allows you to purchase the BMC's personal accident, equipment loss and liability cover for the British Isles, and overseas if you want it. Residents in Ireland should join the MCI, whilst the BMC is appropriate for residents in Britain. The insurance cover is the same for both and the addresses and phone numbers are given in Appendix 4.

Rambling for the Disabled

In researching this book I tried hard to look for suitable walks and rambles for the disabled. Whilst I have friends who are either blind or deaf, I know they have strategies for undertaking the walks outlined in this book; others, for example those who are wheelchair-bound, will require different facilities. I regret that the matter was too complex for inclusion here; however, it remains something for the future and I would be pleased to hear from any disabled organisation through Frances Lincoln, the publisher.

Wildlife

Only a few species of well adapted plants, animals and insects would have survived the last Ice Age, between 10,000 and 15,000 years ago. More than two-thirds of the land mass was covered in ice: a névé tens of metres thick. Conditions on the peaks (nunataks), which stood like islands above the frozen sea, must have been so cold as to kill even many alpine species, while the line from the hymn 'Earth stood hard as iron, water like a stone' suggests how the rest of the land may have been. I suspect that this gives a natural, more Darwinian, explanation for the absence of snakes on the island.

As a result, most of Ireland's wildlife has to be descended from immigrants. Modern candidates are obvious: the feral mink, escaped from commercial mink farms, and rabbits escaped from twelfth-century 'commercial rabbit farms' introduced by the Normans. Some species of rat, squirrel and various insects would have stowed away on ships, but it is logical to suppose that most arrived earlier than these recent visitors and must have migrated across a land bridge from Britain or mainland Europe. Certainly the generally more equable climate may have encouraged migration westwards. But this land bridge theory may, in part, be the explanation for Ireland's lack of snakes and for the fact that it generally records only about two-thirds of the species found in Britain. So residents from Britain will recognise most of the rodents, the butterflies and the birds. Still, this doesn't explain some interesting connections between the flora and fauna of Ireland and those of the Iberian peninsula. For example, the Mackay's heath referred to in Walk 7 and 11 is known otherwise only in Oviedo in Spain. And the almost rare, but recovering,

Roseate Tern, which breeds on the island of Rockabill on the east coast, also migrates to Spain. Clearly there are no straightforward explanations as to the origins of the wildlife in Ireland.

Rocks

Unlike climate, Ireland has rocks. Lots of them. The farmers complain about them, walkers trip over them and geologists collect them. Occasionally we lose them, as when the bedrock for the Silent Dam (Walk 3) couldn't be found. Walkers, unlike climbers, don't *need* to know much about them, except that they can be slippery when wet, it can hurt if you fall on to one from a great height, and – worse still – they can sometimes fall on you!

But over the millennia, through the deposition of sediments in the sea, the extrusion of molten lava from within the earth or the intense folding of existing material, the incredibly varied bedrock of Ireland has been formed and transformed. During these walks you will encounter fragments of the landscape of Donegal, perhaps 700 million years old, formed at the time of the first multicellular organisms; the red sandstones of the Galty mountains, deposited when this land was actually a sea bed, at a time, perhaps, when the first plants began to appear on the land; the limestones of the Aran Islands and Benbulbin, laid down in the seas a little before the first reptiles began to walk on the land of the neigbouring continent. And after the extinction of the dinosaurs, but around the time of the development of grasses, yet more activity within the earth forced new extrusions which created the strange basalt columns at the Giant's Causeway, and the brash newcomers we call the Mountains of Mourne. Of course, all have been subject to different pressures and impacts, such as the folding and superheating of the volcanic rocks in the Sperrins; the relentless erosion by the sea of Slieve League and Croaghaun; and the final shaping and crafting by the actions of ice, that can be seen in the multiple sculpting of the corries of the Comeragh Mountains.

This variety strikes at everything you see; apart from obvious differences such as colour and texture, different rocks erode in different ways, or give rise to different soils and so to different vegetation, birds and other wildlife, which create at least part of the quality of a walk. And as a rambler you will experience the more intimate differences, the sharp angular quartzite on Bencorr, the grykes of the limestone slabs on Inis Oírr, the unyielding granite of Snaght. Each will teach you something different.

Heritage

When you discover that the site at New Grange is 500 years older than the great pyramid at Cheops, you begin to realise that Ireland gives a special meaning to the word 'heritage'. Whether you are walking in the unique landscapes of the Giant's Causeway (Walk 5), the Burren (Walk 12) or the wild areas of mountain blanket bog (several), or visiting significant sites like Tievebullagh (Walk 4), Glendalough (Walk 20) or Muckross House (Walk 14), at times it seems that every step brings you within sight of some natural phenomenon or human heritage. A rift valley, a clochan, a vauclusian spring, a dolmen, a nunatak, a rath … The list is endless; Ireland's heritage surrounds you.

And in spite of odd ups and downs, Ireland seems set to value its heritage. In Northern Ireland there are nine Areas of Oustanding Natural Beauty, including the Mourne Mountains and the Glens of Antrim; and Walks 3, 4, 5 and 6 will take you through some of them. In the Republic, the Office of Public Works manages the National Parks, aimed directly at protecting the natural heritage, landscape and wildlife. Glenveagh in Co. Donegal (Walk 7), the Connemara National Park, Co. Mayo (Walk 11), the Burren (Walk 12), Killarney (Walk 14) and the Wicklow Mountains National Park (Walk 20) all afford some access to visitors whilst attempting to conserve the landscape and wildlife population. Additionally regional initiatives are able to produce the Slieve Bloom Environment Park (Walk 19) and the

Ballyhoura Mountain Park (Walk 16). At a local level, visitor centres such as the Dunlewey Lakeside Centre (Walk 7) conserve a different kind of heritage, the human community; whilst a range of other interpretative centres give us insights into the evidence or the folklore of lives past.

All of these organisations will help you interpret and understand the landscape through which you are walking, and for added enjoyment there are thousands of leaflets and publications available from the various centres and tourist information offices. So whether you want to read about the geology, the wildlife or some special feature of the landscape, you can find the book or booklet you want. Enquire at the tourist information office.

| *'The Hill of Howth for Health and Heather'*

SHELMARTIN AND THE GNR CLIFF PATH

So sang the tourist slogan in the days of the GNR tram, beckoning the citizens of Dublin to enjoy their doorstep wilderness as generations before. For Howth has played host to the many and the famous: to the god giant Finn MacCool and the warrior hero Cuchulain, to literary giants like H. G. Wells, to legendary pirates in the mould of Grace O'Malley. And more than a few notables of Irish history have tarried here. St Colomba, Christian missionary and sixth-century monk, thought it a delightful place, and the poet W. B. Yeats first fell in love here.

Today Howth remains a favoured spot of many a Dubliner, whether they come to sail, to stroll or just to gaze. On a fine day this walk offers truly expansive views, northwards to the Cooley Hills and the Mountains of Mourne, eastwards to Snowdonia and Cader Idris in North Wales, south to the hills of Dublin and west across the distant plain of Moy Bra.

Maps: OSi 1:50 000 Discovery series Sheet 50, Dublin (1995). Howth Chamber of Commerce Map and Tourist Guide. The Howth association of An Taisce provides a usable map on the Heritage Trail leaflet. There are also some useful general maps of Dublin | Distance: 13 km (8 miles) | Ascent: 600 ft (183 m) | High point: 550 ft (168 m) | Naismith time: 3 hours | Difficulty: Moderate | Rescue services: 999 | Garda station: 01 666 4900 | Tourist information: 01 605 7700 | Miscellaneous: Dublin Bus 01 872 0000; DART 01 703 3592

ADVICE AND GRADING

A moderate walk full of character and interest with plenty to feed the imagination and curiosity. The variations provide for easy views, aimless ambling and rambles to suit any timetable or any family. There is much to interest the naturalist, especially among the seabirds and the coastal flora. The route is generally easy going although cliff walking always requires some caution, but if you stick to the cliff path proper there are no hazards to contend with. Underfoot it is generally firm for the whole walk, although it does tend to acquire a few puddles after rain and is occasionally slippy. Sometimes portions of the cliff path can become a little overgrown, but never impassable.

There is no place to gain an overview of the walk, but a taste of the coast path can be had from the car-park at Baily Green (east of The Summit), and I personally think that the most attractive view of Howth can be found a little further north, from the coast at Portmarnock. At twilight or even after sunset there is a very special view over Dublin from the summit of Shelmartin. Follow VARIATION C, take a torch and walk slowly.

GETTING THERE

The walk begins by the harbour at the village of Howth, on the northern side of the peninsula which shares the same name. Dublin's famous DART, the Dublin Area Rapid Transit, will carry you from the centre of Dublin city to the station at Howth in around twenty minutes. The 31 bus will take an hour, but both make a pleasant journey with no traffic worries. If you come by car follow the signs to Howth until you cross over the traffic lights in Sutton and approach the harbour along the Howth Road, pass the entrance to Howth Castle on your right and reach

The coast path near Casana Rock

the DART station on your left. Then take the first turn left on to the West Pier and almost immediately turn right into the free car-park.

THE WALK

Leave your car, or go out of the DART station and turn left (E) on to The Promenade to walk past the inner fringe of **the harbour** along Harbour Road toward a prominent bluff sporting a **Martello tower** and known locally as Tower Hill. As you pass Abbey Road running up the hill to your right, continue straight ahead to follow the signs to Balscadden. Then at the start of the furthermost (East) harbour pier, pass a modern toilet block on your left and continue on the Balscadden Road, which rises steadily as it bends to the right (S) at the start of Balscadden Bay.

Here in the bay, some time after World War One, was the Dalriada tea-shop catering to the genteel society of earlier times. In the small cove below was a neatly kept ladies' bathing beach, whilst in accordance with the proprieties of the day, the men's facilities were to be found further around the bay, away from the ladies, in a small cove with a little beach by the detached mass of rock called The Stag or sometimes The Stack.

Follow the road around to the left (E), turn past the houses above the bay, pass Kilrock Road on your right (south) to continue on (E) by **Balscadden House** on your left and into the end of a cul-de-sac.

The hamlet of Balscadden was the home of the fictional character Sebastian Dangerfield who, whilst attending Trinity College after the GI Bill of Rights, was living off his wits in a rented house, which he was forced to leave when it practically disappeared into the sea. Sebastian, heavily into drink and women, then moved into Dublin where he carried on in the same vein for many pages. Written by J. P. Donleavy, the book was quite a cause célèbre in the early 1960s when its content was considered too shocking for Dublin society.

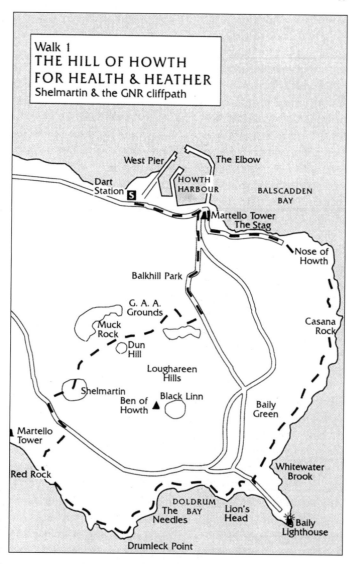

Walk 1
THE HILL OF HOWTH
FOR HEALTH & HEATHER
Shelmartin & the GNR cliffpath

West Pier

The Elbow

Dart Station

S

HOWTH HARBOUR

BALSCADDEN BAY

Martello Tower
The Stag

Nose of Howth

Balkhill Park

G. A. A. Grounds

Muck Rock

Dun Hill

Casana Rock

Loughareen Hills

Shelmartin

Black Linn

Ben of Howth ▲

Baily Green

Martello Tower

Red Rock

Whitewater Brook

DOLDRUM
The BAY
Needles

Lion's Head

Baily Lighthouse

Drumleck Point

Reach the end of the road and take the right (E) fork on to a sand and gravel track to walk up and away from the urban commotion. Ignore the various threads that head off to explore an assortment of nooks and crannies, and keep to the main tread.

'The Hill of Howth for Health and Heather' was the slogan broadcast far and wide in the first half of the twentieth century to encourage customers on to the trains and trams of the Great Northern Railway. And it is to that particular marketing exercise that we can say thank you for the Howth cliff path, for it was built by the railway company. The only evidence of this now remaining seems to be two sets of cast-iron squeezers further along the path, which themselves seem to be the remains of grand boundary fences. If I understand it correctly, in the path's infancy you could take a train to Howth, walk the path and get a lift back from John O'Brien, a farmer who lived on East Mountain and who would take you back to the station on a 'vis-à-vis', a kind of charabanc for fourteen passengers. I would imagine it was about as quick as driving around St Stephen's Green in the rush hour today, but rather more healthy.

Now the path quickly reaches the Nose of Howth and turns south to pass a variety of coastal features named by generations of fishermen, seafarers and smugglers. Pass the Brandy Banks and the Casana Rock, and a path leading uphill to your right (west).

Casana Rock was the site of a shipping disaster during a fearful snowstorm. A steamship, the Queen Victoria, was voyaging from Liverpool to Dublin when she crashed on to the rock at 3 a.m. on 15 February 1853. In the cold, dark and blinding snow, it must have been near impossible to understand what had happened. In a bid to save the stricken vessel, after several unsuccessful attempts, the captain cleared her of the rock, to reveal a gaping hole through which rushed the thousands of gallons of icy seawater that sank her. It seems the terrified passengers and crew would have stood a better chance had the captain let the ship sit on the rock until a rescue could be made, for incredibly, during the struggle to save the ship, eight passengers and crew were able to scramble up to the shore and make their way to the Baily light to give the alarm. It must have been a horrendous experience and although almost fifty were rescued by a passing steamer more than sixty people died, including the captain, the loss adding to the pressure to install a fog bell at the Baily light later that year.

As you begin to gain sight of the Baily lighthouse and the Wicklow Mountains beyond, continue on past numerous coastal features with their fascinating names, Green Ivy, Piper's Gut, Foxhole and Highroom Bed, to pass above the inlet of Lough Levan, regain a little of the urban sprawl and reach a major path junction.

The green lane now running off to your right zigzags back north-east toward the sight of the first Howth light at Baily Green on the cliff above you. The lane was built to connect the old Baily Cottage with the new **Baily lighthouse**, *visible on the prominent cape south of you.*

For VARIATION A1 turn right and follow the zigzag of the green lane up the hill to the car-park at Baily Green. Alternatively turn left (ESE) and follow the lane as it turns generally south, runs across a deep defile cut by the Whitewater Brook and goes through an old gateway to pass along the earthworks of the outer bailey of **Dún Criffan**.

Ahead now (south-south-west), is the irresistible panorama of the Dublin Hills across Dublin Bay and the curious conical shape of the Great Sugar Loaf, dwarfed at this distance by the power of the Wicklow Mountains. And on the distant shoreline is yet another Martello tower, this one made famous by James Joyce. But don't despair if you are in the embrace of a sea fret. Rather enjoy a rare seclusion experienced by only a few so close to the centre of a European capital city.

Reach the asphalt-coated Lighthouse Road. Walk directly across this and to the left of a modern house named Gale Point. Do not go straight on toward the sea, but at an indistinct fork in the path, turn right (ESE) around the back of the house, to keep a wooden garden fence on your right. Follow the path through thicket, bracken and veronica, as it wanders around the small bay to the Lion's Head promontory fashioned of quartzite, stained yellow and brown by the presence of iron oxide. Reach a more established path and turn left (W).

Coast path looking towards Baily Light

As the path works its way around Doldrum Bay, pass another right turn which offers VARIATION A2. Otherwise stay with the coast path as it turns S and then W past the shoreline rock pinnacles known as The Needles, sometimes called The Candlesticks, and turns S and W again around Drumleck Point.

There is much to connect the hero Finn MacCool with this elevated peninsula. The capstone of the cromlech (passage grave) found in Howth Demesne, which weighs ninety tons, was no more than a quoit to this giant,

who threw it here from the Bog of Allen way off to the west. It was here too that he received the vision of Ireland's future under the hand of the invader. But it seems that if the tales of heroes and gods are to teach us, then their lives must also be tainted and it is in the pursuit of the lovers Diarmaid and Grainne, and in Diarmaid's final demise (Walk 9), that Finn shows the darker side of his nature. But in Howth at least the lovers gained some respite as they rested in a cave near here and gained refuge from MacCool.

Pass around another steep defile and continue on to reach and cross the Balsaggart stream by the start of a wall on your right.

Nicknamed the Great Wall of Howth, this curious fence is made not of sandstone, as you might suppose, but of red limestone and the mussel shells that litter the southern shoreline of the peninsula.

As you continue toward the small but distinctive promontory of Red Rock the path descends briefly to a beach in a small cove as the Great Wall of Howth turns a sharp right (north-east). Seek out the path as it leaves the cove and almost immediately reach a path junction. For VARIATION A3 continue along the coast to reach Sheilmartin Road. But to remain on the walk, do not continue along the coastal path toward the Martello tower ahead, rather turn right (N) inland, to cross a drum, a long ridge of rock. The way climbs steeply to reach the concrete steps of an old cliff path which then runs to the left (west-north-west) of a pair of buff rock outcrops. Reach the crest of the ridge and descend N along a path to reach a damaged kissing gate. Go through the gate to Carrick-brack Road, cross the road to the safety of the pavement opposite and turn left (NW) for a short road walk, along the route of the once famous **Howth Tramway.**

Some distance down the road on the left is an old churchyard containing the remains of St Fintan's Church and holy well. There are disagreements over the age of the church, claimed as the smallest place of worship in Ireland, but there are those who still believe the well can cure ailment and illness if you leave an item of clothing there. (My old bit of clothing is still hanging on a willow, reputedly used by St Patrick, near Kells in Co. Kilkenny.)

After 200 m or so, reach 'open country' with the small but notice-able peak of Middle Mountain on your left (south-west) and the summit of Shelmartin on your right (north-east). Look for a small gap in the low concrete wall on your right. Turn right (NE) through the gap and follow the path to the **summit cairn of Shelmartin.**

From the summit you can see your route across the golf course and into a wooded dell. Descend N down the narrow path through the bell heather and fork right toward the small white cottage. At the corner of the cottage is a sign indicating that the right of way follows the white stones across the Howth golf course into a most delightful wooded dell. At forks in the path, keep to the main tread, first left, then right and over a path-crossing to veer right and emerge at the Deer Park golf course which you keep on your left. Arrive at a path junction by a hedge on your left and fork left (NE) across a field of rough pasture between areas of whin and bramble to reach a track by the playing field of Howth GAA club, at Balkill Park. Turn right (E) on to the track and walk around the head of the playing field to reach asphalt. Follow the tarmac NE through the entrance to the playing field and turn left (NNW) on to Balkill Road.

Descend with the tarmac road into the village of Howth. At the prominent church on your right (dedicated to the Assumption of Our Lady) reach Main Street. Continue to descend and fork right (N) down Abbey Street, passing **St Mary's Abbey** on your left to reach the Harbour Road at the foot of the hill.

The restored building on your left is Howth House. Built in 1807 to serve as the home of the chief engineer working on the harbour project, it was restored in 1993/94 after some local controversy about its future. Together with the Georgian terrace and the courthouse off to the left, I think it enhances the atmosphere of this characterful waterfront.

If your walk has been a pleasant one and you still have the desire to amble further, you may take a gentle stroll amid the seabirds and sailing craft with exotic names, along the piers of the harbour, perhaps to the **lifeboat sheds**. Otherwise turn left (W) to return to your car or the DART station.

THE COMMENTARIES

Martello Tower

When, in 1803, the Duke of York decided to have a series of towers

built along this Irish coast as a defence against possible invasion by Napoleon, he was behaving as all the previous occupants of Howth had done since the legendary Fir Bolg were conquered by first-century Gaels, who were in turn driven off by ninth-century Vikings, who themselves fell victim to Strongbow and the Norman invasion.

The name Martello is derived from the Mortella Point in Corsica, where in 1794 the British army found it very difficult to destroy an ancient watch tower. Then, as part of the cold war with Napoleon, it was decided to build a line of such towers along the coasts of Ireland and England. Work eventually started in 1805, the year the threat of invasion ceased, and was finally finished in 1812, leaving fifteen Martello towers along this coast. On this walk you may see one here on Tower Hill, now housing the undersea telephone cables, one on Ireland's Eye, another by Bottle Quay on the south-west side of the peninsula, restored after a fire in 1979 and now a private residence, and perhaps a number on the southern shores of Dublin Bay. One of these at Dalkey was made famous by the novelist James Joyce who, after spending only a week there in August 1904, was chased away by his host with a shotgun; he subsequently incorporated the place into the first chapter of his novel Ulysses. The tower is now the Joyce museum.

The towers were staffed by a corps of Sea Fencibles, but that's another story and you have to move on around the coast. But perhaps it is worth noting that at the time the population of Dublin, at 200,000 people, would have been similar to that of Amsterdam, Vienna, Moscow or Berlin, which says something about the continuing importance of the city in European life.

The prominent height of Tower Hill, which I believe is sometimes called The Height, was the site of the first Howth castle, which replaced the site of an even earlier castle on Ireland's Eye until this itself was abandoned in 1315 for the site of the present castle, off the Howth Road.

The Harbour

Fishing has flourished in Howth since the ninth century and people say there was a time when you could walk across the harbour on the fishing boats. But today overfishing of the shoals of herring, by the use of fine mesh diamond nets and by the boats of many nations, has largely destroyed the fleet here. Yet it is still a working harbour; trawlers still tie up at the West Pier to land their catches on a Thursday afternoon, and for longer during periods of bad weather.

A century ago the 'Molly Malones' would come here early every morning to bid for fish, after the commercial traders had bought what catch they wanted. Each woman would hope to pick up a bit of a basket at a bargain price and be selling it on Moore Street market (off Henry Street) in Dublin by 6 a.m. It was common to try to discredit the efforts of the women by claiming it as yesterday's fish in the hope that they would lower their prices. A statue to Molly Malone now stands in Grafton Street, Dublin.

The modern form of the harbour began to be fashioned 300 years ago. The first stone quay was constructed around 1700, principally to land coal for the light built in 1670 on Baily Green, which you will pass later. But in 1800, Howth was selected as the best place for a storm harbour and all-weather packet boat station, and the East Pier was built in 1807. The bend in the pier known as 'the elbow' was not an intentional design but a result of the foundations being shifted by a powerful gale while they were still under construction. The West Pier was begun in 1810 and in 1818 Howth became Ireland's mail station, although sailing to Holyhead still took about fifteen hours. This wouldn't be much appreciated by today's passengers, the fastest crossing now taking only 90 minutes.

Because of its status as a leading port, George IV landed here in 1821, much to the chagrin of the worthies of Howth's rival Dún Laoghaire (pronounced Doon Leary). The King was actually scheduled to land there and preparations had been made to rename it Kingstown upon his arrival. But perhaps it worked out better for them in the end, for he reputedly arrived in Howth drunk, whilst the worthies eventually got their wish when he departed via Dún Laoghaire presumably in a more sober state. As for Howth, the harbour quickly silted up and the port lost its primacy. Nevertheless the village kept its name and the King left his footprints in the cement in the jetty at the end of West Pier.

Ireland's Eye

Sometimes called Inis-Mac-Nessan, this is an interesting island of quartzite, and the home to a colony *of puffins and other auks. The reconstructed ruins that you may see on the south side are of Cill-Mac-Nessan, the Church of the Sons of Nessan, said to have been established by the three sons of Nessan, a prince of the Royal House of Leinster, around 570. During the nineteenth century an undated cist, containing human remains, was discovered.*

But the strangest story the island has to tell occurred in September 1852. William Kirwan and his wife Maria took a visit to Ireland's Eye and on his return William claimed that his wife had disappeared. Her body was found washed ashore on the island; no action was taken, but stories began to emerge of the couple quarrelling and of screams from the island heard by locals more than one and a half miles away on the day of the Kirwans' visit. In these bizarre circumstances the body of Maria Kirwan was exhumed thirty-one days after burial and although William always protested his innocence he was found guilty of murdering his wife on the island.

Balscadden House

Poet-to-be William Butler Yeats was only fifteen when he arrived with his family at Balscaddan Cottage (sic) in 1881 and began attending school in Dublin. The family had lived in London since 1867, but William's father, the Irish painter John Butler Yeats, suffered a significant drop in income, and it appears that their stay here may have been at the generosity of the owner. In any event in 1882 the family moved to Island View, a small house overlooking Howth harbour and Ireland's Eye. And it was in Howth that Yeats experienced the rejection in love that would shadow him for much of his life and which was probably the inspiration for the words on the plaque on this house. For it was during his time here that he fell in love with his cousin Laura Armstrong and began some of his first juvenile verse; Laura married another in 1884. The following year saw the first publication of Yeats' poetry, including The Island of Statues. *In the same year the family had to move again, this time into Dublin. During these years Yeats made his first visits to Sligo (Walk 9) and discovered, by the shores of Lough Gill, the Lake Isle of Inisfree, which in 1888 became the subject of a well-known and powerful poem of refuge. Later, in 1894, Yeats visited Paris and encouraged J. M. Synge to* make his memorable visit to the Aran Islands (Walk 12).

More of the story of Yeats' life, and the lives of other Irish writers, can be found in the Dublin Writers' Museum in Parnell Square, Dublin, which incidentally is next door to the Hugh Lane Municipal Art Gallery which exhibits a number of paintings both by John Yeats, William's father, and by Jack Yeats, his younger brother. Jack must be Ireland's greatest painter, and would have been ten years old when the family first moved here.

Baily Lighthouse

Not surprisingly, Howth has experienced its fair share of shipwrecks. So it was as early as 1670 that the first light, a cottage with a coal beacon, was built on Baily Green just below The Summit. But the problem of dense fog made the light all but useless when it was really needed and in an attempt to get a brighter light, a coal gas lantern was built on the same site in 1790.

Still in pursuit of greater brightness the present modern lighthouse was built in 1814. Various improvements have been made over the years, including the addition of a fog bell in 1853 in the wake of the wreck of the Queen Victoria. Getting too close to the modern horn in mist does tend to shake your innards around more than a little.

Dún Criffan

Howth is a Danish name from the word hoved, meaning head. In 1014, the Danes, fleeing their defeat at the Battle of Clontarf, recognised the natural defensive characteristics of this extreme end of the peninsula and used it as a refuge. But evidence suggests that its occupation goes back much further. Some older residents of Howth still call this finger of rock, pushing out into the Irish Sea, Dún Griffan, Crimthann or Criffan and claim it to be the fort of Criffan, a first century King of Ireland (or at least, this part of it) who drove out the legendary Fir Bolg (Walk 7). Looking down on to the cape from the vantage point of Baily Green it is still possible to see clearly the remains of an inner and outer bailey, a foss and other earthworks of a first-century promontory fort partially destroyed in the process of building the light. Excavating the foundations for the lighthouse, the engineers uncovered a 'midden', a first-century rubbish tip. And you may see that the green road connecting the old and new lighthouse sites was driven directly along the defensive earthwork of the outer bailey, unfortunately destroying much of it.

Howth Tramway

Running in a loop around the peninsula, alongside the Carrick-brack Road and through special tramway cuttings which now form parts of the Thormanby Road, the Howth trams were not quite the last in Dublin. The line was opened on 17 June 1901, after three years' construction. Local legend has it that the railway company used the Hill of Howth to wear out the carriages until they were all done. After forty years of service, the last tram left Howth at 11.45 p.m. on 29 March 1941. But the last tram in Dublin ran on the Dalkey route, south of the city, until 1949. Before the tram Ringsend Cars, a coach service, was the only public transport to Howth and a seat would have cost you 2s 2d (11p). So although rambling never seems to have caught on in Ireland the way it did in England, I have no doubt that you would have paid it happily for the chance of some fresh sea air and an invigorating walk.

Summit Cairn of Shelmartin

If the title Ben of Howth led you to think of a single peak, then this ring of small hills attended by vales, dales, heath, cairns, tumuli, dolmen and disused quarries dressed with a profusion and confusion of names, might be a curious surprise. More specifically, I am reliably informed that the name Ben of Howth now refers to the undulating tract of land that lies on the western lea of Black Linn. At 560 ft (171 m) it is actually the highest point on the peninsula, lies directly to the east of this summit and carries a cairn, perhaps a burial mound, from early Christian times. The complex web of paths from Howth Castle to the coast by The Summit and from Sutton House to Kilrock and East Mountain can provide you with endless hours of discovery and entertainment.

Shelmartin (sometimes spelt Sheilmartin) stands only 550 ft (168 m), but the force of the view speaks for itself and explains why it is believed that the cairn was built here to act as a sign for the last resting place of Criffan, said King of

Ireland, who lived on the promontory fort at the Baily light. He is said to be buried in the vale below you between Shelmartin and Dun Hill to the north-east. Dun Hill was once the site of a different kind of sign, a Post Office semaphore station, a function now echoed on the Loughreen Hills by an assembly of telecommunications antennae.

St Mary's Abbey

The west end of this building probably dates from early in the eleventh century to the thirteenth century, while the east end appears to be from the fourteenth and fifteenth centuries. After all that time in the building, it fell into disrepair around 1650. It was originally founded by Sitric (Sigtrygg), a Norse king of Dublin. The St Lawrence family, prominent in the history of Howth, placed their mark here, as may be seen from the carved tomb in the chantry chapel, and Sitric has to remain content with

giving his name to a seafood restaurant – albeit a famous one!

Lifeboat Sheds

There have been many wrecks at Howth, but perhaps the worst – and for that reason probably the best-known – is that of the Thérèse Emile Yvon, *a French trawler lost in February 1955. The wreck, nicknamed 'The Loch Ness Monster' by local children, is still visible off Claremont Strand behind Howth DART station. The drama is just one example of the courage of the local seamen. On this occasion, in the strong winds, one lifeboatman actually boarded the stricken vessel and transferred its crew one by one to the lifeboat.*

The first Howth lifeboat sheds date from 1816 and the buildings and commemorative plaques can be found at the end of the East Pier, now replaced by more modern facilities on the Middle Pier.

VARIATIONS AND ALTERNATIVES

A: COASTAL VARIATIONS: You may follow the route of the walk along the coast to any one of four different locations, numbered Variation A1 to A4, and then return to your start by 31B bus. Ranging from 2.5 km to 8 km, with very little climbing, all easy.

At VARIATION A1 turn right to follow the green lane northwest to the car-park at Baily Green and the short tarmac stretch of the Baily Green Road to the bus stop at The Summit. At VARIATION A2 turn right to follow the path to Cheanchor Road. At Carrickbrack Road, turn right, cross the road and follow it to the bus stop. For VARIATION A3 turn right on to Carrickbrack road and walk to the bus stop. Finally for VARIATION A4, continue on the coast path, past the Martello tower to reach the urban sprawl. Take the path from the cul-de-sac to St Fintan's Road and turn right to reach Carrickbrack Road and the 31B bus route.

It is, of course, possible to make any of these locations the start of a short circular walk. For example, bus or drive to The Summit, descend to the coastal path by VARIATION A1, follow the walk to VARIATION A2 and walk back to The Summit along Thormanby Road built along the route of the old Howth tramway.

B: AN EVENING STROLL: Try a walk along the East or West Piers of the harbour and perhaps take your binoculars to watch the seabirds or observe the delicate sculpture of Ireland's Eye. (About thirty minutes for the return walk along the East Pier. Easy.)

C: SHELMARTIN: Drive to Howth and at the traffic lights in Sutton turn right on to Greenfield Road, which soon becomes Carrickbrack Road. Pass the entrance to Howth golf course on your left and after a further 250 m find the gap in the low concrete wall which highlights the path to the summit. (Easy.)

D: WEST MOUNTAIN: The car-park at Baily Green displays a map of the footpaths around the central part of Howth known as the West Mountain, and the car-park at the end of the lane running from Howth Road to Howth Castle provides easy access to this urban wilderness described in the commentary on the **Summit cairn of Shelmartin**. (Easy.)

E: OTHER WALKING: Walkers in Dublin are really spoilt for choice. Within the city there are a number of town, heritage and canal trails. There are also a number of very attractive parks, and I have been happy to spend a day rambling around Phoenix Park, which offers a refuge to the American Ambassador, the Papal Nuncio, the Irish Ordnance Survey, and the Ashtown Castle Visitor Centre, among other interests. Marlay Park, start of the Wicklow Way, in the south of the city still offers some secluded strolling despite threats to build a ring road through a large part of it. Close by is St Anne's Park in Clontarf, previously the grounds of a mansion of the Guinness family, which makes for a pleasant stroll; its neighbour, Bull Island, offers the opportunity for a leisurely stroll or jog along the beach, and is a sanctuary for an interesting array of birds. It too has a visitor centre, and parking a car is never a problem. The DART will also spirit you away to the south where there are pleasant times to be had walking around Sandymount, Killiney or Bray Head.

| *Land of the Táin Bó Cúailnge*
BLACK MOUNTAIN AND THE COOLEY
HILLS

Stand where the mighty Cuchulain stood, walk in the footsteps of
Conchubar and the Red Branch Knights or yell your battle cry as
the champions of Queen Maeve before, when these most ancient
of Ireland's warriors fought in these hills for the possession of a
great brown bull. For this is the place of the Cattle Raid of
Cooley; a battle of chieftains, a struggle of gods, a contest
between good and evil. Yet the landscape appears in stark contrast
to the superhuman violence reputedly done here and provides a
subtle and truly pleasurable mixture: the intimacy of deeply
incised stream valleys with luxurious vegetation, slightly exotic
wildlife and great open vistas from the sites of Ireland's earliest
human habitation.

*Maps: OSi 1:50 000 Discovery Series Sheet 36. OSNI 1:50 000
Discoverer Series, sheet 29, The Mournes | Distance: 12 km/7.5
miles | Ascent: 450 m/1475 ft | High point: 510 m/1675 ft | Naismith
time: 3.5 hours | Difficulty: Moderate | Rescue services: 999 | Garda
station: Longford: 043 50540 | Tourist information:
Dundalk: 042 933 5484*

ADVICE AND GRADING

The route is straightforward, graded as Moderate, being almost
entirely on tracks, green lanes and a little tarmac. Although it can
sometimes be wet in places it is certainly suitable for properly pre-
pared children. Variations and alternatives provide for additional

adventure, a traverse of the mountain ridge and easy strolling, with gradings from easy to difficult.

From July to September the countless greens of plants, trees and grasses are complemented by the tiny splashes of colour from the wildflowers that thrive along the way. So if you have the time, take a wildflower guide as I did, or better still an expert friend; discover what fires the imagination of a botanist and perhaps learn the names of just a few of the flowers growing along the way.

GETTING THERE

The walk begins by Ravensdale post office (MR J 088131). Arrive by bus or car. By car drive from the direction of Dundalk (N) or Newry (S) along the N1/A1, and take one of a number of possible turns E to join the R174 to Ravensdale, which relaxes in the Flurry River valley on the south-west flank of the Cooley Mountains. Park your car off the road close to Ravensdale Bridge, or by the post office.

THE WALK

From the post office cross the road and go N toward the river to take the first right (NE) up a bohereen running toward the hill, Carrabane. Walk up the lane and at a Y-junction, stay right to continue on up the asphalt lane gently rising up the hill toward Anaverna.

In summer the walls are decorated with the tiny pink flowers of mallow and the diminutive yellow petals of tormentil. As you rise up the hill, pass a variety of other plants whose tiny white flowers spread out like a canopy and which the botanists call umbellifers; parsley, hogweed and angelica, close by the river, are prominent among the enchanting variety.

Stay with the bohereen as it bends first left, past a house on the left, and then begins to bend to the right. Here at the beginning of the bend look for a path on your left, running down to a stream and a small flat concrete bridge. This is the **Cadgers**

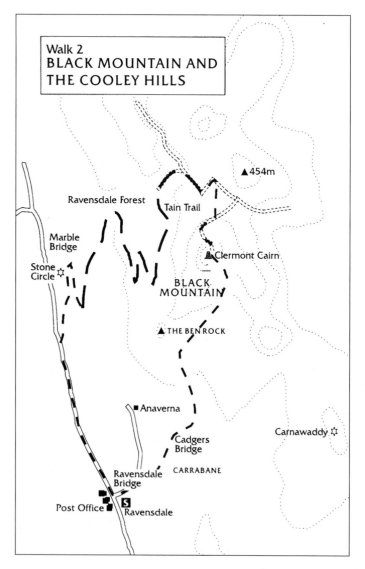

Walk 2
BLACK MOUNTAIN AND THE COOLEY HILLS

Ravensdale Forest

Tain Trail

▲454m

Marble Bridge

Stone Circle ☆

Clermont Cairn

BLACK MOUNTAIN

▲ THE BEN ROCK

Anaverna

Carnawaddy ☆

Cadgers Bridge

CARRABANE

Ravensdale Bridge

Post Office

S Ravensdale

Road. Follow the narrow path to quickly reach the small stone Cadgers Bridge. Cross the bridge, pass through the gate and ascend the hillside by the wall as the remains of the old green road become clear.

As you amble up this gentle ascent look for the low languorous flight of the heron, seemingly quite a common bird on the east coast and favouring these rich streams in their secluded valleys. Now the faint remains of the Cadgers Road give way to a bog road cut around 1940, presumably to give access to the turf on Black Mountain. Doubtless the route had been trodden for centuries before, for behind you now, on the slopes of Carrabane are the remains of a number of ring forts. One on the far side, excavated in 1940, was shown to contain more than a dozen small huts, and outside the fort are the traces of the early field system. In fact there are more than fifty prehistoric sites close to the route of this walk, and hundreds on the whole of the Cooley Peninsula.

Those wishing to follow VARIATIONS A and B will need to look out for the Cadgers Road fording of the stream shortly after the confluence of the two main tributaries. Otherwise reach a track junction and turn right (NNE); this easy track leads you alongside the lip of the deeply incised stream valley, around the flanks of Ben Rock and on to the summit of Black Mountain.

*As you rise up the track and near the summit of the mountain there are striking views generally to the east, of Carlingford Lough backed by the beckoning summits of the Mournes, the towns of **Warrenpoint and Omeath**, and the robust ridge and gabbro of Slieve Foye. Ahead of you the mast for the transmitter for the Irish state broadcaster RTÉ marks the summit. Its purpose is to provide reception for this station to the six counties of Northern Ireland and the wind singing through its structure may provide a suitably mystical musical accompaniment for your arrival at **Clermont Cairn**, the highest point on your walk.*

Here and there you may see people working in the bogs at the backbreaking work of turf cutting, tools may be left lying at the job, or a slipe (a traditional small wooden sledge) may be stacked with fresh cut turves.

Towards Northern Ireland from the Clermont Cairn

From the conspicuous cairn go right (NE) to the right of the TV mast and join the track which becomes a tarmac lane; follow it downhill and around a sharp right-hand bend and then fork left on to a turf cutters' green lane. Stay with this bog road until it regains the tarmac bohereen and turn left (SW). You are now on the route of the **Táin Trail**. Follow the road as it turns right and descends the hill towards the plantations. As you reach the first plantation look for the wide entrance to a forest ride on the left.

Turn left (S) and enter the plantation by a stile, so remaining with the Táin Trail. This is **Ravensdale Forest** and the route now makes a gentle ascent of the contours around Black Mountain and toward Ben Rock before making a series of zigzags, alternate left and right turns, down through the plantation and mixed woodland. The final left U-turn comes before you reach the Marble Bridge, and is the sixth in the series of zigzag bends. Make the turn (SW) and almost immediately on your right look to make a short detour W, down a steep narrow path, through the trees to view a small **stone circle**. From the circle return to the forest track and turn right (S) to continue downhill to reach the Ravensdale Park Road and turn left (SSE). When the park road joins the R174, continue SE and head back to the Ravensdale post office, the start of your walk.

Take care on this quiet road on which drivers seem to travel very fast. There are neat gardens and pleasant pastures. On the right (SW) is the Flurry river and its pleasantly wooded valley, and on the far bank one of many megalithic tombs in the area and the remains of a tower house.

THE COMMENTARIES

Táin Bó Cúailnge

This is the original Táin Bó or cattle raid. Now much embellished with the gory exploits of the warrior Cuchulain, versions of the tale are available in libraries and bookshops and well worth the read. The essence of the story concerns a struggle between two bulls, probably gods, with the main action carried out by humans and human warrior gods. A deal to borrow the much prized dún *(brown) bull, property of Dáire the local chieftain, is accidentally sabotaged by the drunken emissaries of Queen Maeve who desires the bull. Ostensibly Queen Maeve is seeking to gain possession of the brown bull in order to be even in wealth with her husband Ailill who owns the white bull of Connaght.*

As the deal falls through, Queen Maeve launches a most bitter and bloody attack on the sleeping men of Ulster (their sleeping being another story altogether), and after much battling by Cuchulain the brown bull is captured and taken to Connacht. But the bull is able to escape and returns to Cooley with the carcass of the white bull impaled on its horns, only to die shortly after, presumably from injuries sustained in the battle with the white bull.

Cadgers Road

Cadgers and jaggers were pretty much social outcasts right across the British Isles, and even today there really isn't a great deal of evidence about them, other than the routes they created and used to transport goods in trade. This route is shown in the first Ordnance Survey for County Louth of the 1830s, and local records show that it was used by the herring sellers from Omeath even in the late nineteenth century when they used trains of donkeys to carry their creels of fish.

Warrenpoint and Omeath

Omeath is a small town on the Carlingford Peninsula opposite Warrenpoint on the shores of Carlingford Lough. There used to be regular ferries from Warrenpoint to Omeath, because a few years ago tobacco and spirits were cheaper in the Republic than in Northern Ireland. Therefore people would travel over regularly from Warrenpoint to Omeath, bring their families and make a day's outing of it. One local told me that at the peak of the trade thirty years ago, it seemed that a ferry was leaving for Warrenpoint every ten minutes; so great was the traffic that Warrenpoint actually had a customs station. Times change.

Clermont Cairn

Lord Clermont is the former owner of the Ravensdale Park estate and seems to have given his name to a number of objects hereabouts, including this cairn and the neighbouring mountain to the north.

The circular cairn, though a national monument, is also graced with a triangulation pillar for the Ordnance Survey. Excavated by Lord Clermont, probably in the first half of the nineteenth century, this cairn contains the remains of a megalithic structure – a passage tomb, 21 m in diameter and over 4 m high, containing an opening 3.5 m long, up to 1 m wide, and corbelled for more than three-quarters of its length. There is also a circular structure near the centre of the cairn that the Office of Public Works reports may be the work of Lord Clermont.

But the cairn is interesting for a number of reasons. It lies at the centre of a stretch of land running north from Dublin where the earliest inhabitants of Ireland arrived over the land bridge with England that still existed prior to the last Ice Age.

Four lines of hills meet at Clermont, one from Clontigora and

Ravensdale Forest

the Fathom Hills above Newry, one from Feede and Slieve Gullion, another from Carnavaddy and the fourth from Slieve Foye across the Windy Gap, so it is considered by some that Clermont may have been a natural meeting point for mega-lithic cultures.

Táin Trail

A *táin is simply a raid, a reive in English epic language. This one of course refers to the Cattle Raid of*

Cooley, and the trail is a 30 km (19 mile), COSPOIR-sponsored circular route around the landscape of the táin. Mainly on the asphalt of minor roads, the route can be completed in a day. The Táin Way is 40km (25 miles) and is more off-road.

Ravensdale Forest (Gleann Na Bhfiach)

Coillte Teo, the Irish Forestry Board, report that many of the great variety of broadleaf trees and conifers were planted in the nineteenth century, and there are some fine old specimens to gaze at. The main species are Douglas fir, larch, Sitka spruce, oak, beech, sycamore, ash and cherry. In summer abundant colour is provided by bluebells and forget-me-nots, by the furze, bell heather, ericas and different varieties of thistle. Tiny highlights are provided by a wide range of other wildflowers, while the mixed woodland provides a habitat for a variety of birds, such as the jay and the goldcrest. The steep slopes of this wood also provide a home to squirrels, badgers and foxes.

Stone Circle

The eight regularly spaced stones,

surrounding an oval area 7 m by 4 m, were reputedly exposed by Lord Clermont around 1840. Sketches from different dates, ranging from 1890 to 1925, show the circle in different states of decay, and it seems that the stones have been reset in recent times. Close by are five stones concentric with the circle to the east, and apparently the sites of four standing stones lie 40 m south-west of the monument; this is unusual, as the area for standing stones tends to be further north in Co. Down. I'm afraid all this rather indicates that this is not a genuine monument but quite possibly a piece of romantic estate landscaping. Sorry!

VARIATIONS AND ALTERNATIVES

A: CARNAVADDY: This variation offers a longer route with a little tougher walking over open moorland and on boggy paths. If you are not yet free from the tyranny of the footpath, this would be a good route to practise wandering on to open mountain and moor, but take your time and pick a fine day in a dry month (well, as dry as they come, anyway!), as the route is wet. The rewards are solitude and airy views.

Follow the walk to the Cadgers Road, following it across the tributary shortly after the confluence of the two tributaries. Go E/SE across rough pasture to cross a second tributary. Then take a route across open mountain, perhaps making use of the remnants of bog roads into the saddle between Carrabane and Carnavaddy (MR J 104135). From here go E to an unnamed summit of the south-west spur of Carnavaddy, at MR J 112135, and NE across the saddle toward the old trig point for Carnavaddy and then N toward the prominent cairn. Reach a ridge path running from the Windy Gap to take a dogleg route along the ridge to **Clermont Cairn** to rejoin the walk. (14.5 km/9 miles, ascent 550 m/1800 ft, >4 hr, Strenuous.) Alternatively, return along the outward route of the walk, by descending the bog road alongside the tributary back to the Cadgers Bridge and Ravensdale, making a pleasant horseshoe. (9.5 km/6 miles, ascent 500 m/1640 ft, >3 hr, Challenging.)

B: THE RIDGE: If you can find a way to start at Carlingford and finish near Flagstaff this is the classic walk for the Cooley Hills and Carlingford Mountain (Slieve Foye). From the old town of Carlingford, climb Slieve Foye up its south-eastern slopes. Follow the ridge NW, then W via the Raven's Rock to the Windy Gap. Cross the road, and stay with the path via Carnavaddy to Clermont Cairn, Clermont and Anglesea, descending NW to Clontygora in Northern Ireland. (16 km/10 miles, ascent 1185 m/4000 ft, >5 hr, Difficult.) Two circular routes can be made of the ridge that use quiet lanes for the returns. The first circular route can be made from the Slieve Foye woods to Carlingford; then follow the ridge from Slieve Foye, past Carnavaddy to the Cadgers Road. Go E and descend by the Clermontpass Bridge and the Táin Way towards Omeath. Follow the road and then the Táin Way again back to the Slieve Foye woods. The second circular route starts at Clermont Bridge Pass. Walk along the road to Windy Gap, follow the ridge NW to Anglesea, descend to Clontygora and follow the lanes back to the bridge via Flagstaff.

C: SHORT RAMBLES: Take the service road to the RTÉ transmitter and park on the rough ground (MR J 100159). Either follow the ridge and summits to Anglesea or Carnavaddy (return the same way for both routes), or park in Carlingford, and climb Slieve Foye up its south-eastern slopes, from one of the tiny south-west-running streets in the town. (Up to 5 km/3 miles, ascent up to 100 m/300 ft, <1 hr, Easy.)

D: RAVENSDALE FOREST PARK: There is a pleasant 1 km waymarked trail which takes in some fine Douglas firs, the **stone circle** and the Marble Bridge. The walk begins from the Marble Bridge car-park (MR J 082157) and some parts are a little steep. A longer gentler walk can be made of the trail, forest tracks and the road back to the car-park. There is a description of the woodland in the commentaries. (Up to 4 km/2.5 miles, ascent up to 100 m/300 ft, <1 hr, Easy.)

E: OTHER WALKING: The Táin Trail described in the commentaries can be used as the basis of a number of walks. The Slieve Foye (Sliabh Féidh) Woods can be found on the R173 between Omeath and Carlingford, the forestry road rises up the hillside with exquisite views of Carlingford Lough and the Mountains of Mourne. Details of the Táin Way are available from COSPOIR (see Appendix 4).

| *'Where the Mountains of Mourne Sweep Down to the Sea'*
SLIEVE DONARD AND THE ANNALONG VALLEY HORSESHOE

The best-known feature of this range of hills, nestling almost secretly on the north-east coast, is recalled in the words of the memorable Percy French song: 'Where the Mountains of Mourne sweep down to the sea'. For although Slieve Donard, the highest peak in Northern Ireland, is only 850 m (2789 ft), it is the way that these great granite masses rise majestically from sea-level to surround an area of wilderness that gives them a fascination for everyone who views them.

Falcons fly above the tors of Bignian, ravens over the slabs of Lamagan. And clad in the white of winter, the countless greens of spring or the purples of summer and autumn, these hills provide both challenge and reward for the walker. In December 1986 they were declared an Area of Outstanding Natural Beauty.

Maps: OSNI 1:25 000 Outdoor Pursuits Map, Mourne Country. OSNI 1:50 000 Discoverer Series Sheet 29, The Mournes | Distance: 22 km (13.5 miles) | Ascent: 1835 m (6025 ft) | High point: 850 m (2789 ft) | Naismith time: 7.5 hrs | Difficulty: Difficult | Mountain rescue service: 999 | Garda station: Newcastle: 0845 600 8000 | Tourist information: Newcastle: 028 4372 2222 | Miscellaneous: Mourne Countryside Centre, Newcastle: 028 4372 4059, Ulsterbus (Mourne Rambler), Newcastle: 028 4372 2296

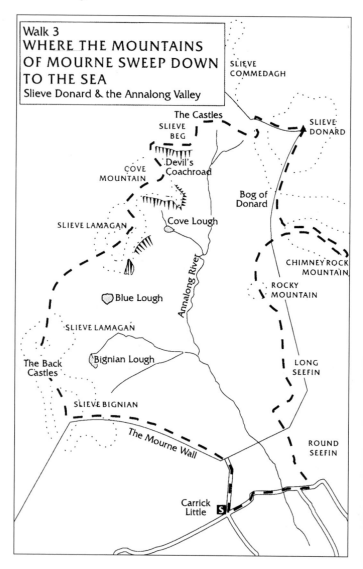

Walk 3
WHERE THE MOUNTAINS OF MOURNE SWEEP DOWN TO THE SEA
Slieve Donard & the Annalong Valley

SLIEVE COMMEDAGH

The Castles

SLIEVE BEG

SLIEVE DONARD

Devil's Coachroad

COVE MOUNTAIN

Bog of Donard

SLIEVE LAMAGAN

Cove Lough

CHIMNEY ROCK MOUNTAIN

ROCKY MOUNTAIN

Annalong River

Blue Lough

SLIEVE LAMAGAN

Bignian Lough

LONG SEEFIN

The Back Castles

SLIEVE BIGNIAN

The Mourne Wall

ROUND SEEFIN

Carrick Little S

ADVICE AND GRADING

Although it is graded as Difficult, the going underfoot is generally easy for mountain terrain. The profile of the hills, the Mourne Wall and the Annalong valley form important aids to secure navigation along with your compass and the OSNI *Mourne Country* 1:25 000 map. It does, however, require more endurance than most other walks in the guide. With 1835 m of climbing, there are few paths, and some of the descents – especially, for example, from the summit of Lamagan – require care. It should take a fit walker no more than seven and a half hours, but do it in summer, allow ten hours and give yourself the chance to enjoy the mountains in a variety of their many moods visible throughout a day. If the days are short, or you are building on your experience, enjoy the variations, graded from Moderate to Strenuous, until the opportunity for the whole walk arises.

GETTING THERE

From Newcastle take the coast road (A2) south toward Kilkeel. After 10 km (6 miles), at a point when you appear to be driving away from the mountains, turn right (NW) on to the Quarter Road, which is signposted to the Silent Valley (scenic route). Follow the road for 2 km (1.3 miles) to a sharp left bend (WSW), twisting down the Head Road into the Annalong Valley and over the Annalong River by the small granite Dunnywater (Dinnywater) Bridge. Follow the road out of the valley for 1 km (0.6 mile) until you reach the Old Town road on your left. Opposite is a minor lane, the Mourne Rambler bus stop and a small car-park. Park your car, or alight from the bus, here at Carrick Little (MR J 344219).

THE WALK

From the car-park set off back down the Head Road (ENE) to the lowest point on your walk, the Dunnywater Bridge. Cross the bridge and take the second turn on your left (NW) up the Dunnywater Lane, to walk toward Rocky Mountain directly ahead. Stay with the lane, as it begins to green, and continues NNW along the edge of a plantation, to pass through a gateway and between stone walls. Reach a pair of gates and immediately turn right (NE) to go through a single iron gate. Go along the edge of a wall to follow an obvious track which curves to the N along the western flank of Long Seefin and runs toward the **Mourne Wall** and the summit of Rocky Mountain.

The path rises to the saddle between Rocky and Long Seefin, when Chimney Rock Mountain comes into view, ahead on your right (NE). As you approach close to the Mourne Wall, leave the path to strike out NW toward the crest of the hill immediately ahead on your left, picking your way gingerly through the tussocks and boulders of the open mountain, or choosing one of the **long-abandoned tracks** scarring its face, to reach the summit of Rocky Mountain.

If you are blessed with clear weather at this first summit you will have a 360-degree panorama of the Mourne peaks, and an opportunity to survey almost the entire route of the walk.

Leave Rocky for Chimney Rock Mountain, by heading N parallel with the Wall as it turns towards the Bog of Donard. Head toward an outcrop of rock ahead of you and as you rise out of the col on to a small crest, look to take a gently curving line, over open mountain, above the Spences river valley, around to the E to reach a prominent tor north-west of Chimney Rock Mountain, crossing the Mourne Wall by one of the many jutting stile stones. If you wish to omit the summit of Chimney Rock, then at the Wall go N toward the Brandy Pad. Alternatively, reach the tor and follow the path past further large granite boulders to the summit which gives the Mountain its name.

Return toward the Mourne Wall by the summit path (NW) along the stretched spur of Chimney Rock Mountain, favouring the west to avoid the groughs leading into the Bloody Bridge valley running eastwards. Join the Wall and turn right (N) mainly keeping close to, or even on, the Wall to avoid the worst of the Bog of Donard. Cross the Brandy Pad and begin your climb of Northern Ireland's highest mountain.

At the summit of **Slieve Donard** pause by the tower. The route now turns left (WNW) and heads down by the Mourne Wall to join a path in the col between Slieves Comedagh and Donard, at the head of the Glen river valley. But first walk NE along the summit of Slieve Donard toward the **'lesser cairn'**. Now contour your way generally W/SW, through the boulders dispersed across the hillside, to return to the Mourne Wall and descend to the col (WNW).

As you descend enjoy the view of the rim of hills to the west: Bernagh, Meelmore, Meelbeg, Loughshannagh, Carn and Muck; with Doan and Ben Crom in the middle distance; and most especially of Slieve Comedagh, at 765 m almost 100 m less than Donard but still the second highest mountain in Northern Ireland. Finally, make sure you are not startled as you go down. The men who built the Mourne Wall were brave enough to face the hazards of granite slabs, atrocious weather and nights out alone on the mountains. But one recalled coping with all that, only to be frightened out of his wits, on this very hill, by an Irish hare!

At the col, join the path rising up from the north-east, along the Glen river valley. For Variation b to Newcastle turn right (NE), otherwise turn left (SW) and follow the path by the stile stones over the Wall. Now veer to your left and take a path which heads due S and crosses the flank of Donard to reach the **Brandy Pad**. Turn right (NE).

Follow the pad and look down the Annalong Valley at the classic glaciated 'U' shape and enjoy its mild tranquillity. Pass under the Castles of Comedagh and perhaps notice the way the jointing of the granite has given itself to the strangely eroded shapes, accompanied by the music of the streams as the water falls gently down the mountainside.

After you cross the final stream flowing from beneath the Castles of Comedagh, look for an intermittent path left (SW) to

Into the Silent Valley

take you above the edge of the buttress of Beg and to the Devil's Coachroad. Alternatively, you may make an easy return to your starting point by following a path (S) which leads down the valley almost from the foot of the Castles of Comedagh.

Your next objective is the summit of Cove, but, as is frequently said in Ireland, 'You wouldn't want to be starting from here'; the descent and ascent are both much too steep. Instead you need to head W toward the bare expanse of buff-coloured granite gravel on the saddle between the two hills, possibly following a vague path

which keeps above the wetter groughs. The closer you approach Cove from the crest of the saddle the easier will be your ascent.

At the gravel patch pass around the western end of an area of cotton grass and head SSE to ascend Cove over open mountain. The soil is poor and so the heather is short, and there are also plenty of small streams to help your tread, so that the going is not too difficult.

The British navy used the area as a firing range, with live ammunition, testing the products of the Belfast shipyards, during the early 1940s; this no doubt accounts for at least some of the craggy eastern profiles of these two peaks.

Reach the summit cairn of Cove and turn WSW and descend to the saddle between Cove and Lamagan, perhaps looking to your left (SE) for a glimpse of the still waters of Cove Lough. Take care if you choose to go south to peer over the edge of Upper Cove. Cross the saddle by a faint path and head almost due S to climb the northern spur of Lamagan, turning SW to ascend the spur to the summit.

*Here you can see **Ben Crom and the Silent Valley reservoirs,** and the western string of mountains from Muck to Meelmore. Let the fine view of the tors of Bignian inspire you now as you descend Lamagan and climb the North Tor. Bignian offers the closest approximation to a ridge walk in the Mournes, and I promise you will not be disappointed.*

There is no easy route down Lamagan, but head generally SW for the saddle below the North Tor of Bignian, picking your way carefully through the rocks and occasional ruts and gullies on the steep slope of Lamagan. Do not try to go south-east into the Annalong Valley; that way lies folly and the Lamagan slabs. If you wish to return to the start, meet a path which runs south-east from the saddle at the foot of North Tor and passes by the Blue Lough around the foot of Bignian to rejoin the route back to Carrick Little.

At the saddle pick up a path heading first SW and then SSW up the northern spur, and above the crags of North Tor. Do not be drawn into paths which contour around the east of the mountain and lead only to the Buzzard's Roost and the Blue Lough Buttress. Rather follow the path along the crest as it wanes occasionally but makes its way right (W) of the giant granite mass of North Tor.

How has your day gone? Do you have the time now to relax by this assertive tor with its strangely moulded shapes, or reflect above the attractive little tarn of Bignian Lough?

Pass to the left (E) of the Back Castles passing through a gap in a wall to follow the path and rise to reach the Summit Tor. Look for the faces of the stone monsters in these great granite rocks of **Slieve Bignian**. Now, at last, it is time to begin homeward. If you can drag yourself away, descend from the tor and retrace your steps (N) along the ridge until it becomes practicable to describe a large U-turn to the SE and head towards the Mourne Wall which runs eastwards from where it abuts the Summit Tor.

Descend the mountainside, keeping the Wall on your right and following a badly eroded path, which will take you to the floor of the Annalong Valley to reach a popular access track that runs to Carrick Little. Turn right (SW), pass over a stone stile by a gate and follow the lane S as it returns to the car-park and the start of the walk.

THE COMMENTARIES

The Mourne Wall

Our thirst for water sometimes seems unquenchable. More than a hundred years ago the Belfast Water Commissioners purchased 9000 acres of the Mourne Mountains with an annual rainfall of around 1760 mm (70 inches), and began a plan for the future supply of Belfast's water. Once they had the land they built a wall around the catchment area. No one seems to know what prompted this action. It seems difficult to believe that it was simply a means to control pollution. Some have suggested that it formed an important job creation scheme and developed and maintained local building skills with granite.

Construction began in 1904 and work was carried out during the months of March to October. It was eventually completed in 1923.

The Black Ditch, as the builders called it, is actually a double wall, and together with the three stone towers on top of Donard, Comedagh and Meelmore, it was built largely from granite rocks lying around the mountains. Around here any field boundary, except sheep wire, is called a 'ditch'. But as to the 'black', who knows? The staining of the lichen, common to see, or the mood it created in the builders? As you may see, it runs over the summits of twelve major peaks and is a tribute to the skill and courage of the men who built it.

The Mournes sweep down to the sea

Long-Abandoned Tracks

On this southern flank of the mountain there is much evidence of quarrying and the working of the granite, with a number of small bothys, built from 'spals' (waste stones) by the stonemen, to give them shelter. Here, until early in the twentieth century, they made the six inch square granite setts known locally as 'shoddies', so familiar in many an English market place, and destined for Belfast, Liverpool and the cotton towns of Lancashire. But by whatever transport they arrived at their destination,

they first had to be dragged down the mountainside, by hand or horse-drawn slipes. A Mourne slipe is a kind of sledge with runners, and sometimes with rollers, designed to stop it from sinking into bog — most especially when loaded with granite. That transport, I assume, is the origin of the many tracks on this side of Rocky and of the path you have just ascended. Once at the Head and Quarter Roads the shoddies would be loaded on to stone-carts and taken to Annalong to be shipped by schooner.

Granite from this area was used for the Albert Memorial in London,

*and as late as the 1960s, kerbstones
from granite quarried above Bloody
Bridge, and worked in
Glasdrumman, were used on Hyde
Park Corner.*

Slieve Donard

*The man-made features on the sum-
mit only hint at the stories to be told:
of prehistoric tombs; of the burial of
Slainge, son of Partholanus; of the
seclusion of Domangard and the
birth of a religious pilgrimage; of
Captain Maltby and Elizabeth I of
England; of Catholic persecution
and the secret celebration of Mass;
of the repeating vandalism of the
Ordnance Survey; of the hardships
of the men who built the Mourne
Wall tower; and of the evidence of a
passage grave, a well, a cell, an oratory and an altar, amid the piles of
stones now present.*

*The summit cairn, known as
Slainges Cairn, may have been his
passage grave and may also hold the
remains of a later oratory and a
makeshift altar of St Donard. But it
seems to me that an early OS account
that it also holds a well doesn't hold
much water! Everything is now
almost all obliterated by walkers and*

*others who have the habit of throw-
ing stones into a large heap.
Personally I've never understood this
practice; it's hardly environmentally
sensitive.*

The 'Lesser Cairn'

*Donard's cell? Who can tell? But
quite probably a prehistoric site. On a
clear day you can see Scotland, Wales
and the Lake District. Frequently,
though, it seems not to be clear
enough to see Slieve Comedagh! But
certainly if the weather is reasonable
you will have fascinating views over
the coastal lowlands to the north. The
inlet of Strangford Lough stands out
well, and even further north and a
little inland you may see Cave Hill
east of Belfast, whilst in the middle
distance, sporting its television mast,
is Slieve Croob.*

The Brandy Pad

*Smuggling has been a way of life
since the days of customs taxes. In
the Mournes small boats would land
at night on the open beaches between
Ballagh and Ballymartin. At times it
must have seemed as if the entire
local population would rush out to*

meet them, each to carry their share of the contraband burden. The cargoes of wines, spirits and tobacco, silks, spices, tea and coffee, and other exotic stuffs would be hidden in natural or manufactured caves and holes at the foot of the mountains. From there it would be packed on to the backs of small ponies called 'shelties' that with their twilight masters would follow a myriad of threads all winding eventually into the Bloody Bridge valley to form the Brandy Pad. The goods gave rise to the name Brandy and the repetitive thud of the shelties to the name Pad as they wove their way through the hills to the Trassey Burn below Hare's Gap and on to Hilltown, the chief distribution centre.

The Silent Valley and Ben Crom Reservoirs

Once in danger of becoming the Great Mourne Folly, the Silent Valley reservoir is 3.6 km (2.25 miles) long, 0.8 km (0.5 mile) at the widest point and with a water level 27.4 m (90 ft) above the old river bed. The project was ten years in construction. Begun in June 1923, it was not opened until May 1933.

Problems experienced during construction meant that new and untested building methods had to be used, taking four years longer than originally intended. The problem lay in the level of the bedrock below the level of the river. Original test bores showed the bedrock to be 50 ft (16 m) down, and work began, only for engineers to discover that the bedrock was actually more than 180 ft (55 m) below the river bed. Unbelievably, the original test drillings had all entered rock deposited during the last glaciation. The site was actually an area of terminal moraine of giant boulders and fine silt.

Slieve Bignian

Scramble to the top of the Summit Tor for truly inspiring views. The immediate fascination of views of the Silent Valley and reservoirs, the nearest mountains to the west and north, or the profile of Donard, compete with the views of Carlingford Lough, the Cooley Mountains and Slieve Foye. On a fine day you will see the eastern coastline of Ireland south to the Ben of Howth (Walk 1) on the northern fringe of Dublin.

VARIATIONS AND ALTERNATIVES

A: SLIEVE BIGNIAN Follow the walk in reverse order to Slieve Bignian, descending by the North Tor and turning right (SE) to join the prominent path past the Blue Lough to return to Carrick Little. (11 km/6.5 miles, ascent: 650 m/2130 ft, 3 hrs, Challenging.)

B: A MOURNE TRAVERSE: Take the Mourne Rambler bus from Newcastle to the car-park at Carrick Little and follow the walk to the col above the Glen river (MR J 350280). Turn right (NE) and follow the obvious path down the Glen river valley, toward Donard Park and Newcastle. (15 km/9.5 miles, ascent 500 m/1640 ft or 825 m/2700 ft, up to 4.5 hrs, Strenuous, bordering on Difficult.)

C: JUST DONARD: Start from the Bloody Bridge on the A2 (MR J 388270). Ascend to the Mourne Wall and turn right (NNE) to follow the walk over Donard and VARIATION B back to Newcastle. (10 km/6 miles, ascent 830 m/2720 ft, 3.5 hrs, Strenuous.)

D: ANNALONG VALLEY: Fairly flat easy walking with sensible footwear. Ideal for a rambler's summer evening or a family stroll. From the car-park at Carrick Little, follow the track N, over a stile by a gate, past the Annalong Wood on your right. Then keep forking left to the shores of the Blue Lough. Or take the first fork right to continue up the valley. Return the same way. (Blue Lough 8 km/5 miles, ascent 250 m/820 ft, 90 minutes return, Moderate.)

E: OTHER WALKING: Visit the Mourne Countryside Centre. The helpful staff there will advise you on the wealth of walking to be had in Co. Down, see the route instructions on page 61 for the telephone number.

The Glens of Antrim

GLENARIFF, LURIGETHAN AND THE FOREST PARK

For so many of us, each step into the future of our industrialised society means trampling on the traces of our own heritage; the evidence of our own past is destroyed by a new town development, a water construction scheme or a motorway. However, while Glenariff has seen 'development' – the coast road, afforestation, mineral exploitation and railways – so much evidence of natural and human heritage remains. Too much to include in this brief description, be it fairy folklore, the kelp harvest or the discovery of coal. And all within a designated Area of Outstanding Natural Beauty, the Glens of Antrim. Long inaccessible steep-sided valleys cut deep into wild uplands, and still shelter their secrets. Now is your chance to discover!

Maps: OSNI 1:50 000 Sheets 5, Ballycastle, and 9, Ballymena, Larne | Distance: 13 km (8 miles) | Ascent: 500 m (1640 ft) | High point: 380 m (1248 ft) | Naismith time: >5 hours | Difficulty: Challenging | Rescue services: 999 | Local police: Larne: 0845 600 8000 | Tourist information: Larne: 028 2826 0088 | Miscellaneous: Ulsterbus, Ballymena: 028 2565 2214 and Belfast; Glenariff Forest Park: 028 2955 6000

ADVICE AND GRADING

Graded as Challenging, after a short but steep climb this route runs on cropped grass, sheep treads and farm tracks, along a gently undulating escarpment and into a steep-sided valley with

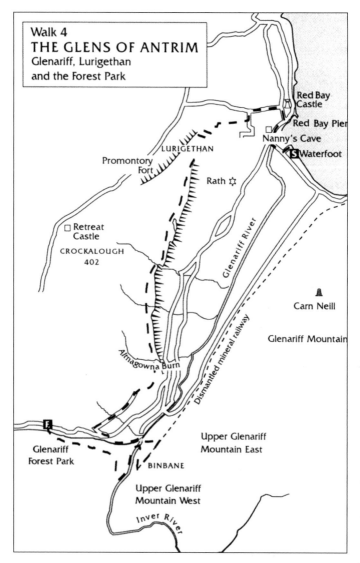

Walk 4
THE GLENS OF ANTRIM
Glenariff, Lurigethan
and the Forest Park

Red Bay
Castle

Red Bay Pier

Nanny's Cave

S Waterfoot

LURIGETHAN

Promontory
Fort

Rath ☆

Glenariff River

□ Retreat
Castle

CROCKALOUGH
402

Carn Neill

Glenariff Mountain

Dismantled mineral railway

Altnagowna Burn

F

Glenariff
Forest Park

Upper Glenariff
Mountain East

BINBANE

Upper Glenariff
Mountain West

Inver River

constructed paths. The variations, graded from Easy to Difficult, provide short cuts, a bus ride back to the start, a leisurely stroll down a metalled lane or adventurous walking along the route of an old mineral railway. Alternatives provide for short walks and family entertainment. Generally there should be no difficulty in route finding, but you will need to pay careful attention to the route instructions, especially for the easiest way along the escarpment – I've tried to make them as clear as I can. And please remember to close all the gates.

GETTING THERE

Take either the A43 from Ballymena, or the coast road (A2) N from Larne, to the small village of Waterfoot situated in Red Bay, at the mouth of Glenariff. Park in the village car-park, well signposted to the right (NE) off Main Road (MR D 242256). Your return is by one of the Ulsterbus services, which run along the A43 from the Glenariff Forest Park upper gate, past the bridge in Waterfoot to Cushendun. Please confirm the service before your departure, see the route instructions for the telephone number.

THE WALK

Leave the car-park, turn right (NW) on to Main Road to cross the Glenariff river by the footbridge, and turn right again (NE). Walk on the pavement alongside the river, past **Nanny's Cave** carved into the red conglomerate on your left, to take the next lane left (N).

These twists and turns up the side of Crookanavick Hill formed the only coastal route north until the early nineteenth century. As you wind up the crest look through the hedge to your right (NE) at Red Bay Castle, an ancient defensive site, with a motte and bailey probably built in the thirteenth century under King John, crowned with the sandstone fragments of the MacDonnells' tower house built in 1561 during the early reign of

Elizabeth I of England, and eventually abandoned after the Cromwellian purge of Irish castles in the 1640s.

As the road starts to descend, turn left (W) at a lane junction.

As you walk up the lane, to your right, nestling between the shoreline and the small coastal plain formed by the junction of the Glens of Glenballyemon, Glenaan and Glencorp, is the village of Cushendall and the curiously shaped knoll of Tieveragh, site of a fairy fort which protects the fairy glen of Ballyemon.

At the crest of the road stop and gaze at the slopes of Lurigethan. Look carefully and you will see a vague but broad green zigzag route running to the top of the mountain from about half-way up. I assume this to be an old slipe (sledge, Walk 3) track. Following it will greatly ease your ascent.

Now at the crest of the road turn left (SW) and walk up a concrete track. After less than 150 m, fork right (WSW), and as the track turns left into a gate, do not follow it, but continue straight ahead (WSW) up an overgrown green lane. At the end, go through a gate and into pasture dotted with gorse and thistle. The summit of Lurigethan lies westward ahead of you.

This is the fabled birthplace of the hero Finn MacCool (Walks 1, 5, 9 and others) and his poet-warrior son, Ossian, and should seem daunting. But when Norah Henderson, a tourist here in the early 1930s, asked the farmer if he had ever climbed Lurigethan he modestly and quietly pointed out that he was up there every day tending the sheep. So take a breath and make a start.

Cut directly across (W) the pasture to find the lower portion of the slipe track. Join this to zigzag your way to the summit. Eventually the track breaks into threads. Follow the zigzag to the right (NW) towards a stile over the sheep fencing. Take a further zigzag, cross another fence and head W around and just below the summit. Stay with the track as it curves around the mountain, and take the left fork on to the summit of **Lurigethan**.

From the flat grassy cairn go ESE to join a sheep tread, cross the foundations of an old wall, and immediately turn SW to follow the sheep tread along the south-east edge of Lurigethan. For the next 5.6 km (3.5 miles) you follow treads and tracks on sometimes tussocky but frequently short sheep-cropped grass, running along the edge of the basalt escarpment above Glenariff. It is a fine upland walk.

Below you the fields of Glenariff appear arranged as if by accident but are tenderly manicured, a rich lush green and looking like a private garden set in wilderness, as the neat field hedges at the centre of the glen grow wild toward the edges and eventually give way to moorland slopes, steep escarpments and dry stone walls. Across the glen is the summit of Carn Neill and the dramatic escarpment of the Glenariff Mountains to the south and the wild moors beyond.

Above Kilmore (MR D 220235) it is necessary to find your way over two streams and their tributaries, and past the surrounding bogs, to continue along the edge of the escarpment. As you begin to approach the river, stay close to the edge and follow a sheep path as it skirts left around an area of bog, drops toward rough meadow and passes around and beneath a small outcrop. From here head towards the wall and fence that emerge on the opposite side of this shallow valley (WSW). To do this, cross a minor stream and an old collapsed wall to arrive at a wire fence; turn right and follow a wet route for a few metres between the fence and the bog towards a stile (crossing another intervening stream by way of a makeshift tin bridge found a few metres upstream). Turn left and cross the stile, and then cross the stream by boulders to gain and follow the wall and fence along the edge, and out of the valley.

After you pass beyond the knoll ahead you are presented with an engaging view (south-south-west) of the Glenariff Forest Park and of the Inver river flowing along the more southerly of the two ravines at the head of Glenariff.

So stay with the wall, and at a set of sheep pens aim right (WSW) and climb up and over the small rocky knoll to gain sight of a gate in a fence. Go through the gate and follow the track until the escarpment wall gains your height, and from the track, cross the pasture to return to the sheep tread by the wall. Stay with the wall as it descends to a gate in a pasture fence. Pass through the gate and follow the route of the wheel tracks which lead to the next gate. Cross the brook and go through another gate.

Divert here for a few moments; go left (E) through a gap in the wall, for a view up the valley toward the Mull of Kintyre. From here you can see the ladder farms characteristic of the glen, and the curious ruler-straight course of the Glenariff river contained with diagrammatic precision by flood defences constructed over generations. These were still unable to imprison the energy of the river in October 1990 when the banks burst, the river flooded the glen, precious farms were damaged and firefighters struggled to carry drowning sheep to safety. Of course, the flat-bottomed fertile nature of the glen is probably due directly to the alluvial plain deposited by a regularly flooding Glenariff river.

From the gate, carry straight on (S), continue along by the wall past old sheep pens, over a stream and along the fence (SW). When the wall turns left (S), do not follow it but stay with the sheep tread and continue SW alongside fragments of a stone wall until you reach a wire fence. Cross the fence at the wall by stones made into a stile. Pass the foundations of ruined buildings and head SSW to descend towards a stream. Cross the stream by large boulders and turn left (SE) on to the narrow path between the stream and the wall, and follow the deep sheep tread as it rises up the hillside and parallels the stream. Stay with the sheep tread as it curves gently right (SSE) and away from the stream, and upwards, across a grassy pasture (SSW), then dips into the source of yet another stream and heads towards another gate.

The glen narrows and the rugged face of the rocks of the escarpment opposite grows even more imposing. But as you cross the pasture, look to the humble plantation to your right (west); it appears to be set within the remains of a rath and offers a different kind of curiosity.

Follow the track through the gate (SW) toward the summit of Carncormick. Cross a number of small streams and boulders and head SSW to aim to the right of a small knoll and cabin. Stay with the track as it proceeds W and enters a cattle pasture. Now look for a tread that describes a long left-hand arc around the cabin and small plantation of coniferous trees, and follow this (SW). As the path begins to turn south toward the cabin, look for a gate in a fence on your right (W) in the corner of the pasture. Go through this and turn right (N) to walk past some sheep pens and join a track running SW to follow it to a gate.

Before going through the gate, pause for a moment to listen to the noisy little spring. Somehow air seems to be trapped in the waterflow under-ground and here it bubbles boisterously to the surface making strange wal-lowing noises.

This track will now carry you to the A43 road running up Glenariff from Waterfoot. Do not turn off the track, but continue descending the hillside past a number of farm buildings and gates, and a very neat farmyard – they may still rear geese here, a tra-dition of the glen. Finally follow a concrete drive as it zigzags first left and then right to reach the A43.

Taking care of the traffic, turn right (W) on to the road and walk uphill for 50 m, cross the road and fork left (SW) through trees on to a forest path. When the path reaches a stream, turn sharp left (SE) to descend to a gravel path and a wooden kiosk by the famous **Glenariff waterfalls**.

At the Glenariff river turn right for VARIATION A. Alternatively, turn left (VARIATION D joins here) and follow the well-made path with steps, handrails, bridges and shelters as it descends the ravine staying close by the river. At the park entrance by the Manor Lodge restaurant, turn right (SSW) (or left for VARIATION B), cross the bridge and follow the path. Pass the Ess-an-crough waterfall and at the top of the path meet a Bailey bridge on your left. Cross to the opposite bank of the River Inver and continue on up the right bank (SSW). The route returns to this point later, before making for the car-park. Therefore you may jump ahead, by turn-ing right, picking up these route instructions a little further on

and following the blue waymark triangles (1450 m) to the car-park and visitor centre.

Follow the path as it zigzags uphill between spruce, larch, beech, rowan, hawthorn and birch. As the footpath flattens out at a small shelf or plateau (course of the old railway) do not follow it, but turn sharp left and walk along a much less used portion.

This is the course of the old mineral railway. Built in 1873, by the Glenariff Iron Ore and Harbour Company, this was the first narrow gauge railway in Ireland. It linked the Cloghcor iron ore mines at the valley head with a purpose-built pier near Milltown, whence the ore was shipped to Britain. It closed with the mines in the 1880s.

This will take you through trees, over several small burns, and a fence. As you reach the edge of the forest, and the escarpment below Benbar, there are open views above the glen. Shortly reach an old metalled boreen which cuts the line of the railway and take a sharp left to descend into the glen. Follow this to a gate close to the River Inver. Go through the gate and turn immediately left (W), cross the stile and go over the Bailey bridge. Now follow the broad track which sweeps in broad zigzags out of the glen and to the visitor centre and car-park. Follow the blue triangle waymarks (1450 m). (Pick up here if you didn't cross the Bailey bridge.)

En route *pass a small log cabin in the valley on your right. This is a 1987 reproduction of the kind built by Ulstermen in the new frontiers of America and was made for a TV documentary.*

With the vistor centre now close in sight turn right on to a tarmac path which runs past the centre to the car-park. Cross the car-park to the information board (N). Now veer left to follow the Hermit's Walk (green waymarks) and the park entrance road. Rejoin from VARIATION A.

The derelict grey building hidden in the upper part of the ravine is no more than a modern archaeological artefact from the tourist industry – the first toilet block for those arriving by train from Ballymena on a second

Glenariff waterfall

mineral railway with a passenger service – and is located close to the original entrance.

Turn right and walk alongside the entrance road to the A43. Turn right again and cross over the road. Wait for the bus or a pre-arranged lift, by the red telephone kiosk.

THE COMMENTARIES

Nanny's Cave

Ann Murray was fifty when she arrived in Waterfoot in 1796; she was a frequent visitor to the first cave, made warm and dry by the work of its occupant, the blacksmith. Eventually Annie moved in next door, rent free, and supported herself spinning and knitting, and selling a drop of the 'native'. This seems to have annoyed the excise men. Piecing together a number of reports and local tales, it seems that for more than 170 years, right up until the 1960s, Nanny's Cave was the home of a succession of women who sold poteen. In the early eighteenth century there was quite a community in these caves. In addition to Ann and the blacksmith there was a fisherman, and a cave actually used as a schoolroom, probably during the Catholic persecution. It is said, it was here that Dr James MacDonnell, founder of the Belfast Medical School, received his early education.

To manufacture and sell spirits without a licence is of course illegal so one Nanny actually sold empty bottles; as a gift to the new-found friends who bought her bottles, she would fill them with her home-distilled poteen. Her kindness is reputed to have made her many friends. Other Nannys apparently sold water, and offered a glass of whisky free. It seems they all had discreet methods of avoiding the excise duty and annoying a succession of customs men. Ann was a hundred when she died during the famine in March 1847; she is buried in an ancient graveyard at Kilmore.

Lurigethan and the Promontory Fort

This summit mound is the remains of a prehistoric fortification called Dunclanamourna: the steep-sides and stiff climb show why it was well chosen for a promontory fort. The southern defensive dykes run from the eastern edge of the escarpment, past additional earthworks for the entrance, and then curve towards the north-west. The large area of enclosed land suggests the fort was self-sufficient, but it still remains difficult to date. Even an Iron Age settlement here would make it older than other promontory forts, and yet small cairns and the traces of hut circles push the date as far back as the Bronze Age. Others have ventured that it might be even older; evidence from the glen suggests that farmers may have arrived as much as 6000 years ago during the Neolithic, or New Stone Age. Lurigethan has a long history.

Across Glen Ballyemon, to the west-north-west is the rocky eastern face of Tievebullagh; at the foot of this rock buttress is the site of an axe factory, whose prehistoric products of porcellanite (a rock formed when the basalt lavas of the Giant's Causeway baked the chalk deposits) were exported across the British Isles and possibly beyond. Perhaps at that time the sea was still further up the glen. I wonder what those earlier people thought when they gazed out over this narrow channel at the exhilarating prospect of the Mull of Kintyre, the islands of Islay and Jura and the Dumfries and Galloway hills. Or if they travelled to the east-north-east to the tiny island of Sanda with its modern profile of an upturned spoon, or to Ailsa Craig that looks for all the world like a pudding. Or if generations of shepherds stood here in later times and watched the ships of war ebb and flow like tide into the bay: the Viking invaders, fleeing remnants of the Spanish Armada, ships of the MacDonnells and McQuillans, and the Second World War products of the Belfast shipyards. Perhaps the violent brush of men along the coast never penetrated to this promontory or the glen it guards.

Ladder Farms

You may have noticed that as you proceed up the glen the fields get smaller. I asked a local farmer, 'Why are the fields so small?' 'Because the farms are small,' he replied. And sure enough the ladder farms found higher in the glen are of only 10 or 12 acres. The name comes from the arrangement of the fields. They run in narrow strips from the slopes of the mountain into the glen,

Glenariff mountain

to give each farm a share of fertile ground and rough pasture, and in the days of common grazing on the tops a share of that too. And from above, this arrangement makes them appear like ladders.

I remember being taught to grow potatoes using lazy-beds. My father measured out the width of the bed to the length of the spade, and I spread the manure as he cut the sods from each side of the strip and folded them on to the top. Then my mother and sister made holes with a dibber and planted seed potatoes into this fertile sandwich. It must have been the same in this glen. Kelp (seaweed) would be used to fertilise the land, time was saved by not having to dig over the ground, and where the soil was shallow the depth was effectively doubled. Oats and barley were grown in the same way.

Glenariff Waterfalls Walk and Glenariff Forest Park

This is a captivating forest path, luxurious in vegetation with fine streams and splendid waterfalls. The river is a natural habitat for dippers and the woods the home of stoats and owls.

The path zigzags up and down like some crazy fairground ride, and I imagine that is something like the effect the planners wanted to create when they built it back in 1890 to attract tourists. Take it too fast and your head will spin. There is more than one spectacular drop (9 m / 30 ft and 7 m / 22 ft) into these fascinating gorges. Think hard about the way the rush of the water sought out the weaknesses in the rock and carved out these dramatic mini-canyons. Look for the strange tricks played by the sunlight as shafts peek through the trees illuminating sometimes the *great torrents of water, sometimes the clear trickling streams falling from the sides of the valley, and sometimes creating iridescent colours as it reflects from the water's bed. A special magic is created here by the canopy of trees, by the single shafts of sunlight that search their way through and by the great paint palette of colours; for as you descend into the valley the sunlight begins to triumph over this exotic natural baldachin.*

There is normally a small entrance fee for an adult in the forest park, and this money is used to maintain the wooden footpaths, bridges and handrails that allow you such spectacular views. It hardly seems credible, especially after heavy rain, that this raging torrent could have been so readily tamed into the railway-proportioned dyke you saw further down the valley. Which is exactly what the floods of 1990 showed.

VARIATIONS AND ALTERNATIVES

A: JUST LURIGETHAN: Follow the walk until the point, identified in the text, when you reach Glenariff Forest Park. Turn right and follow the path, known as the Hermit's Walk, up the left bank of Glenariff river, until it reaches a wooden bridge. Cross the river by the bridge and turn right on to the path to reach the park entrance road and rejoin the main route for the bus back to Waterfoot. (10 km/6 miles, ascent 420 m/1380 ft, high point 380 m/1248 ft, <3 hrs, Moderate, made Challenging only by the climb of Lurigethan.)

B: RAMBLE BACK TO WATERFOOT: A walk on very minor roads back to the car-park. Follow the route to a park exit by the Manor Lodge bar and restaurant. Turn left at a park entrance kiosk, and pass around the restaurant through a car-park to a metalled boreen. At a lane junction, fork right (NE). Now stay with this road (ignoring a fork to the left) until you reach the coast road at Milltown. Turn left (NW) to Waterfoot. (17 km/11 miles, ascent 385 m/1265 ft, high point 380 m/1248 ft, <6 hrs, Challenging.)

C: LURIGETHAN AND CROCKALOUGH: After you achieve the eastern edge of Lurigethan, aim right (SW) for the actual broad flat summit (385 m) and once gained continue along the broad flat ridge to the summit of Crockalough (402 m). Return the same way; or from here go NE descending the mountain toward Retreat Castle. From the castle turn left (SW) and follow the track down to the B14. At the road turn right (NE) and follow the road along the lower slopes of Lurigethan for 3.2 km (2 miles). Turn right (E) into a metalled boreen that will return you to 'The Old Road' and Red Bay. (11 km/7 miles, ascent 410 m/1345 ft, high point 402 m /1320 ft, >4 hrs, Challenging.)

D: GLENARIFF FOREST PARK: From the information board in the car-park follow the blue waymarked Hermit's Walk and descend by the Glenariff river to reach the path junction above the waterfalls shown in the route instructions for the walk as the start of VARIATION D. From here follow the route of the walk, until you return to the visitor centre. (Up to 7 km/4 miles, ascent: up to 150 m/490 ft, up to 3 hrs, Easy.)

E: OTHER WALKING: The Ulster and Moyle Ways both provide longer-distance routes for those properly equipped. The Glenariff Forest Park provides a number of waymarked trails, a visitor centre and café. All of this park walking is suitable for families, but there is a small charge. Finally, although it is plagued by numerous obstructions, once you have followed the walk to the old mineral railway, it is possible to follow this back to Milltown. However, there is no way you could describe this as a recognised route. You would need to take much care of fences and livestock, but the farmers I spoke to were happy for me to cross their land, just don't go in a gang. (19 km/12 miles. ascent 420 m/1380 ft, high point 380 m/1248 ft, >7 hrs, Strenuous/Difficult.)

Stepping Stones on the Northern Coast
GIANT'S CAUSEWAY AND THE ANTRIM SHORELINE

It was a report to the Royal Society in 1694 that first put the Giant's Causeway 'on the map', so to speak. Then in the early 1740s the engraving and publication of two drawings of the Causeway, by Mrs Susanna Drury of Dublin, caught the imagination of the world and the annual pilgrimage of scientists and tourists began.

Maps: OSNI 1:50 000 Sheet 5, Ballycastle. Maps of the National Trust section of the causeway coast are available from the visitor centre | *Distance: 7 km (4.5 miles)* | *Ascent: 75 m (247 ft)* | *High point: 80 m (262 ft)* | *Naismith time: >2 hours* | *Difficulty: Easy* | *Rescue services: 999* | *Local police Ballymoney: 0845 600 8000* | *Tourist information: 028 2076 2024* | *Miscellaneous: Ulsterbus Ballymena and Belfast: 028 2565 2214; National Trust Visitor Centre: 028 2073 1855*

ADVICE AND GRADING

There are no navigational difficulties on this walk; it is largely next to field fences and cliff tops, along old tramways and metalled lanes. The main route and all the variations are very easy walking. Some of the cliff path will become muddy when wet and footwear with some grip would be sensible, as there is always the possibility of danger when close to cliff edges. But the route is full of interest for all ages and tastes: archaeology, geography, geology, history and **natural history**; shoreline, seascape and distant landscape. Also, of course, it's simply a nice walk. Bearing in mind the possible hazard of cliffs, this should be a fun walk for children with lots to stimulate the imagination. And the length of the walk can be varied to suit.

GETTING THERE

It was getting to the place that inspired a famous quote from the English lexicographer Dr Samuel Johnson. When, late in the eighteenth century, his companion James Boswell enquired, 'Is not the causeway worth seeing?', Johnson replied, 'Aye, but not worth going to see!' Of course, travel today is much easier.

From Bushmills go N on the A2 for 1.7 km (1 mile). Turn left on to the B146 to follow the signs to the Giant's Causeway. After 800 m (0.5 mile) turn left (W) again to go down a hill. Stay on the metalled lane for 450 m (500 yd) to reach the Giant's Causeway and Bushmills railway terminus on your left at a minor junction (MR C 943437). Park here along the roadside up the hill.

THE WALK

Leave your car, ignore the minor lane and turn left (NE) on to the metalled lane and head around the left bend towards the National Trust Causeway Visitor Centre, to arrive at a T-junction. Turn right (NE) to pass **The Nook** on your left and at the second junction immediately ahead, turn left (ENE) to follow the lane (B146). After 300 m turn left through the second set of white gate pillars into the driveway of the **Causeway School**, now a museum. Let your curiosity propel you around the back of the building, through the small car-park, past the odd little garden beyond, to reach the front porch.

From the Causeway School Museum, go through the large Causeway Visitor Centre car-park (W) and to a set of steps and a representative map of the causeway coast on the right. Go up

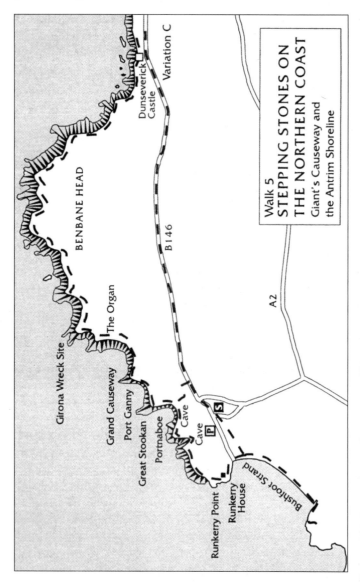

Walk 5
STEPPING STONES ON
THE NORTHERN COAST
Giant's Causeway and
the Antrim Shoreline

Variation C

Dunseverick
Castle

B 146

A2

BENBANE HEAD

Girona Wreck Site

The Organ

Grand Causeway

Port Ganny

Great Stookan

Portnaboe

Cave

Cave

P

S

Runkerry Point

Runkerry House

Bushfoot Strand

the steps and to the right (E) of the centre buildings. Follow the asphalt as it bends left around the centre and immediately turn right (N) to follow the cliff-top path by the fence. Alternatively go into the National Trust Visitor Centre. Emerge by the seaward doors and bear right (N) to reach the start of the clifftop path.

A detour into the centre will be well rewarded. Admission is free and there are some helpful wildlife displays of Portnaboe. And for a small charge there is a superb audio-visual presentation, explaining the formation of the causeway, fantasy and fact. The exhibition covers the story of the Lammas fare and dulse (a red seaweed dried and eaten as a snack), the history of the iron ore industry, the tramway, kelp, and the salmon fisheries and will give you a feel for the local living in past times.

Cross the road and continue on up the path to the first headland known as Weir's Snout, to look out NW over the Great Stookan, and NE for your first glimpse of the **Grand Causeway**. Then continue east along the cliff path and through the gate or over the stile, to arrive at Aird Snout, the headland above the Giant's Causeway. Now follow the gravel pad as it rounds the bay of Port Noffer (Port an aifir, the giant's inlet), and reaches the steps at the top of the Shepherd's Path. Descend into the bay by the steps, and at the path junction turn left (W) to walk back towards the causeway. Alternatively continue along the cliff path for VARIATIONS B and C.

*As you descend the steps and path to the bay look at the three basalt **dykes** running north-west from the shoreline, and the row of vertical 'pipes' of the 'organ' on the cliff face to your right as you turn back along the coast (NE).*

Explore the rockpools and boulders of the beach, by way of one of the minor paths, until you come across a large distinctive object, looking like a glacial erratic, but reputed to be the fossilised remains of the **Giant's Boot**. From the boot continue W, and follow the main shoreline path to reach the Giant's Gate, a gap in the causeway columns created by the clearing of the banks of basalt scree.

Giant's Causeway

If you arrive before 10 a.m. you may find yourself alone on the Grand Causeway. It is possible, even in August. Otherwise expect to enjoy the place amid an international band of tourists all eager to explore this phenomenon, transfixed by Nature's colour scheme, the yellow, grey and black of the lichens and the variegated reds and browns of minerals and rocks, or simply eager to have their photographs taken as a record of their visit; a tradition as old as photography. I have a photograph of my grand-father standing here perhaps eighty years ago.

Follow the asphalt road around the foot of the cliffs (SW) around Port Ganny (Port Gainmhe, sandy inlet), to reach the Great Stookan, and scramble up it if you wish, but take care of the drop to the sea. As you leave the Great Stookan, do not continue along the asphalt road but fork right (SW) to descend a small track towards a basalt shoreline, passing a small stone shelter on your left. Follow the narrow footpath, and keep right (W) at a junction around the bay of Portnaboe (Port na Bó, the cow's inlet).

On a warm day your senses may well be assaulted by the smell of kelp rotting on the shoreline in the sun. And close to the highwater line amid reeds, nettles and tall-growing grasses you may find small dry-stone walls. The two are well connected. This is a site for **May fleece***.*

Further around the bay, almost concealed by the rocky outcrop against which it is built, is a small fisherman's bothy, with corrugated iron supporting a turf roof. An old photograph shows nine drontheims (small boats) resting on the beach here and as I pass this bothy I wonder what tales – of piracy on the high seas, or mutiny on oak ships – may have been played out by centuries of fishermen's children.

Further still are the reconstructed degenerate remains of the Brenther Slip, a small port built from boulders off the beach, and a fragment of footpath made from the hexagonal pillars of the Causeway, looking like some kind of paving from a garden centre. And the basalt pinnacle of the Camel's Back looking for all the world like an ancient Roman wall, stripped of its ashlar veneer and about to topple over, but actually a **dyke***. Brenther, meaning 'steep harbour', is from Old Norse and tradition has it that Vikings sheltered here beneath their upturned longboat raised on columns from the causeway.*

From the Brenther Slip, retrace your steps along the footpath, and fork right at the Y-junction to go SE up the green cliff bank, out of the cove, and emerge at the tarmac drive at the NT contribution box. Turn right and go up the metalled lane to turn right again in front of the visitor centre. At the end of the buildings is an arch in classical style, which I assume to be the remains of the tram station. Do not go through this but keep to the right, take the steps made of the stuff of the Giant's Causeway and follow the cliff top path (W). Soon the path turns S to skirt above Portcoon (Port Cúng, narrow inlet). At a path junction divert right (N) to follow the path into the secluded bay.

Though the visitor centre may be teeming with tourists, this tiny cove is usually deserted, the only sounds, the crash of the waves on the beach of basalt boulders and the call of the gulls roosting on the crags. From here, if the tide allows, you may visit the **Portcoon Cave***.*

Return to the path and turn right (S) along the cliff top. Follow the path out of the bay and around the headland past Runkerry House (Rinn Cairthe, promontory of the pillar-stones) on your left to arrive at a salmon fishery.

Fishermen's nets are frequently left spread on the grass hereabouts drying in the sun, perhaps awaiting examination or repair.

From the fishery stay with the coastal path as it passes Blackrock and enters Bush Bay, to head S towards a small wooden bridge over a stream. Cross the stream and head left (E) along the path over the doon to reach a sandy track. Bear left again on to the track and within 100 m arrive at the site of an old tramway crossing. Turn left (NE) on to the route of the **Causeway Tram**, a pedestrian track, and follow this back to the car-park and the end of your walk.

THE COMMENTARIES

Natural History

Suffice it to say that there is more than enough here to content any natural historian. With more than seven types of habitat and variations created by wind and shelter, salt and spray, shade and soil type, the range of flora seems endless. There are badgers and foxes here and the Irish hare is almost common. The Royal Society for the Protection of Birds reports more than fifty resident species and thirty visitors. Noteworthy among these are the chough, buzzard and eider duck. If you are rarely by such a coast do enjoy the variety of seabirds and look out to the sea for sight of the great mass of the basking shark or the occasional playful grey seal.

The Nook

This pleasant building, now an excellent café, was built around 1850 as a school for the area, and was privately funded by Sir Francis Edmund MacNaghten of Dunderave. With the receipt of grant aid it became the first Causeway National School, and is reputed to have attracted pupils from neighbouring areas. By 1913 it had become too small for the number of

Antrim coast

pupils attending and a new school was needed.

The Causeway School Museum

Some love it; some hate it. Reminiscent of a New England church, this National School building, now a museum, was designed by Clough Williams-Ellis; you may know him for the Maud Cottages in Cushendun, Co. Antrim, or the village of Portmeirion in Wales. On the death of Lord MacNaghten of Runkerry in

1913, his children commissioned this new building which was completed in 1915, and although the school had no running water, it remained in service until 1962 and is now converted to a museum. Pop inside and find out what it meant to 'toe the line'.

Dykes

Easily recognised because of their dark colour and because they are so straight, these are frozen rivers, created as the basalt itself cooled and cracked creating fissures through which more hot molten lava searched. This lava too cooled, and weathered at a different rate leaving either channels or ridges of rock.

The Giant's Boot

According to a forensic scientist from North Carolina, consulted by the National Trust, the size of the footprint left by the petrified boot proves conclusively that Finn MacCool was 52 ft 6 inches tall. From this, using Naismith's rule with appropriate amendments for the conditions and the state of his footwear, I have determined that it would have taken him exactly twenty-two and a half minutes to walk to Scotland. Clearly MacCool was a walker looking for an unusual ramble just long enough to provide the right duration of cardiovascular exercise.

The Grand Causeway

These columns, strange to our eyes because of their mathematical precision, were formed by the even and progressive cooling of the liquid basalt extruded on to the landscape more than fifty million years ago. The concave and convex profile of their ends provides evidence of the process and the slight angle of the pillars of the causeway more evidence of the 'ponding' of the basalt as it cooled. Further east along the cliffs it is possible to see that there were once three levels of columns; the top is now mostly eroded away and the lower two are separated by earlier periods of erosion, which came between the extrusion of the basalt and are known as the inter-basaltic bed. Of course, if you have time for the research, you may prefer the Formorian (see Walk 7) explanation of events.

The May Fleece

From the 1700s to 1930s, the May fleece was gathered first for sodium and potassium for bleaching soap and glass production, and second for iodine for medicine and photography. These glistening fronds of the large brown seaweeds would also be used in lazy-beds to grow potates and other crops. Indeed, this 'kelp' was used to transform the landscape on Inis Oírr (Walk 12) whilst today the kelp fly larvae provide an abundant supply of food for some seabirds.

Portcoon Cave

Scramble around the foot of the cliffs on your right (east), past a prominent nose full of 'giant's eyes', 'dinosaur eggs' and other bizarre patterns, to scramble across large boulders to the mouth of the cavern, through the darkness to the main cave and its second shore. And watch the ocean hurl thundering breakers against this rock; now, as for a million years upon a million years, the energy of every wave seeking out the tiny fissures of weakness in the basalt and driving its way relentlessly forward.

Portcoon is 137 m (450 ft) long and to the west are two more caves, Runkerry and Rock Pigeon. Both are accessible only from the sea, and Runkerry is said to be more than 215 m (705 ft) long. Earlier visitors would be rowed by fishermen guides to view the mouths of the caves in drontheims, a traditional boat with bow and stern identical, and easily manoeuvred around these treacherous headlands. I wonder what tall tales were told then, what stories of smuggling, skulduggery or high adventure were invented to amuse and beguile.

The Causeway Tram

This narrow gague railway runs along the old route of the Causeway Tram line built from Portrush to Bushmills in 1881/83 and extended along this section to the causeway in 1887. The project was the dream of local engineer William Traille who saw it as a means of transforming the economy of the area. Regrettably he soon found that goods traffic didn't pay and the line stopped carrying freight in 1887. But the tourists loved it, and it quickly took over from the horse-drawn jaunting car and ran until 1949 when it in turn succumbed to competition from bus tours and the private motor car. An example of the 'toast rack' tram carriages can be seen in the causeway visitor centre. The line is now re-opened as the Giant's Causeway and Bushmills Railway, offering a 2 mile journey to visitors.

VARIATIONS AND ALTERNATIVES

A: SHORTER WALKING: Two short circular walks can be created by following the instructions for the walk, but dividing the route at

Giant's Causeway

the National Trust visitor centre. One walk follows the cliff top east, to include the Causeway and the Brenther Slip (3.5 km/2 miles, ascent 90 m/300 ft, >1 hr, Easy). Another goes west from the visitor centre, and includes Portcoon Cave and the salmon fishery (3 km/2 miles, ascent 70 m/230 ft, >1 hr, Easy).

B: HAMILTON'S SEAT: Follow the walk to the Shepherd's Path, and continue along the cliff top to the second set of steps at Hamilton's Seat. Turn left (SW) and descend by steps and path to reach the junction at the Shepherd's Path. Go right (W) toward

the shore to rejoin the walk (11 km/7 miles, ascent 90 m/300 ft, >2 hrs, Easy).

C: DUNSEVERICK CASTLE: From the visitor centre, follow the shoreline path past the **Grand Causeway** and the **Giant's Boot**, past the steps of the Shepherd's Path to the steps up the cliff to Hamilton's Seat. Stay with the National Trust cliff path, around Bengore Head (114 m/374 ft) until you reach Dunseverick Castle and the B146. Either return along the cliff top, or the B147, to the visitor centre (15 km/9 miles, ascent 100 m/330 ft, >3 hrs, Easy).

D: BUSHFOOT STRAND: From the car-park follow the route of the old tramway and path (SW) through the dunes to Port Ballintrae. Return along the beach of Bushfoot Strand. At the north end of the strand cross the stream by the small bridge, turn right and follow the path. Turn right on to a metalled lane that will return you to the car-park (4.5 km/3 miles, ascent 40 m/130 ft, 1.5 hrs, Easy).

E: OTHER WALKING: The cliff path continues eastwards from Dunseverick to the enchanting White Park Bay, and the North Antrim coast offers many opportunities for little explorations.

WALK 6 | *Sparkling Streams and Sperrin Skies*
SAWEL, DART AND THE GLENELLY VALLEY

Lying at the heart of Ulster, in the least populated part of Northern Ireland, are hills that touch the sky. A landscape made from fire and ice, of volcanic rocks crushed and folded skywards at immense pressure, scoured and ground by ice and concealed beneath a blanket of peat, with tranquil glens and steep-sided valleys, it is now protected as an Area of Outstanding Natural Beauty.

Map: OSNI 1:50 000 Sheet 13, The Sperrins | Distance: 18 km (11 miles) | Ascent: 594 m (1950 ft) | High point: 678 m (2224 ft) | Naismith time: 4.5 hours | Difficulty: Strenuous | Rescue services: 999 | Local police: Omagh: 0845 600 8000 | Tourist information: Strabane: 028 7188 3735; Omagh: 028 8224 7831 | Miscellaneous: Ulsterbus Omagh: 028 8224 2711; Sperrin Heritage Centre: 028 8164 8142

ADVICE AND GRADING

An introduction to the Sperrin hills, from the broad sweep of the rounded summits to the more intimate beauty of the delicate waterfalls of the secretive burns. A bit of a slog up Sawel, graded as Strenuous but with an Easy return. As always, route finding in the mist needs some care on the tops, and you may want to take your gaiters – parts of the route are apt to be a bit wet. The variations offer you short rambles, easy road walks and quick ascents, ranging from Easy on up. A fine overview of the Sperrin range can be had from the summit of Slieve Gallion in the east.

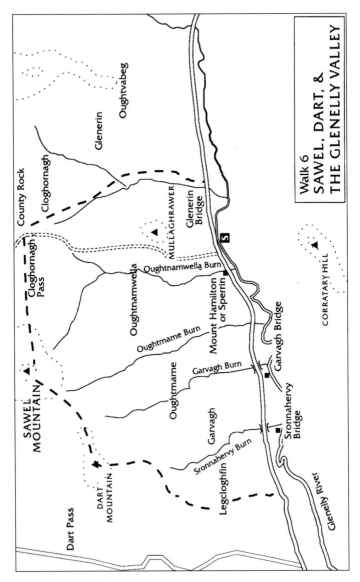

Walk 6
SAWEL, DART, &
THE GLENELLY VALLEY

Oughtvabeg

Glenerin

Oughtvabeg

County Rock

Cloghornagh

MULLAGHRAWER

Glenerin Bridge

Cloghornagh Pass

Oughtnamwella

Oughtnamwella Burn

Mount Hamilton or Sperrin

CORRATARY HILL

SAWEL MOUNTAIN

Oughtmame Burn

Oughtmame

Garvagh Burn

Garvagh Bridge

Garvagh

Sronnahervy Bridge

DART MOUNTAIN

Sronnahervy Burn

Legcloghfin

Glenelly River

Dart Pass

GETTING THERE

The starting point for this walk is at a small picnic site by the Glenelly river a little to the east of the hamlet of Sperrin on the B47, (MR H 637943). From Plumbridge in Co. Tyrone drive eastwards, through the subtly glaciated valley of Glenelly along the B47, about 13 km (8 miles) to the hamlet of Sperrin. The picnic site can be found 500 m (0.3 mile) further on from the staggered cross-roads in Sperrin on the right-hand (South) side of the road. There is a wide tarmac lay-by here where you may park your car. The scene by the river can be so tranquil that there is a danger you may never begin your walk.

THE WALK

Leave your car and set off E along the Glenelly Road (B47) over the rise toward Glenerin Bridge.

On your right (south), at the foot of Mullaghbane is Sawelabeg; partially covered by the trees of the plantation, the landscape is characterised by drumlins. This peculiar assembly of hillocks and knolls was formed by the deposition of debris as the ice retreated across the Sperrins some 15,000 years ago.

Cross the bridge and go through the second gate in the fence on your left (N) and follow the remains of a decayed bog road to the right (NE) of a small coniferous plantation.

As you pass over the Glenerin Bridge there is a fine view north up the Glenerin Burn. These steep-sided valleys, presumably cut by the burns that run through them, are an attractive feature of the area.

As the road evaporates into the bog, a little past the plantation, cross over the wall, but keep it close on your right (east) as you continue NNE. Shortly reach another old bog road and bear left (N). Follow this clear green lane along the lower slopes of Oughtvabeg, across the mouth of the upper valley of Glenerin to head NNW above the Binleanna Burn on the slopes of Cloghornagh and reach the road at the Cloghornagh Pass, sometimes called Sperrin or

Sawel Pass. This will take you through a series of gates, across a ford at the Glenerin Burn and past a recent farm track (NE) which services Glenerin.

*As you walk, the rounded summit of Sawel Mountain will appear ahead and to your left (north-west), whilst below you is the gently meandering Glenerin Burn. On your right, as you reach the burn, the fine grasses of the meadows of Glenerin are in stark contrast to the hardy purple moor grass thriving on the slopes of Meenard Mountain, whilst the silent summit ahead raises questions about the **names in the landscape.***

Emerge at the narrow tarmac road at the Cloghornagh Pass, to the west of the **County Rock**. Go straight over the road (NW) and begin ascending the long eastern spur of Sawel Mountain, first aiming toward the rocky outcrop and keeping the wire sheep fence on your right. Stay with the fence, which usually hugs the drier line, as it zigzags slightly but continues generally W up this long pull toward the broad round summit of Sawel. As you ascend please watch out for rusting and discarded sheep wire abandoned close to the fencing.

However difficult the climb might be in the wet, it is never so distressing as to prevent your attention wandering to the subtle range of plant life resident here. Liverwort and clubmoss contrast with the yellow flowers of the bog asphodel and delicate white feathery heads of the cotton grass. Crowberry, bilberry and clubmoss all grow here, though I confess I have not yet identified the rare cloudberry, typical of the bogs of other parts of Northern Europe, but found nowhere in the 'too warm' bogs of Ireland except in the mountain blanket bog of the Sperrins, hiding on the western slopes of Dart. Careful too that you do not tread upon the common frog, happy to croak its way through the day here, as you enjoy the views south over Oughtnamwella.

Pass through an old fence running south and continue to follow the boundary wire. As you near the summit cross the fence at a low point by the exposed face of a large boulder buried in the peat and walk NW to reach the summit cairn and triangulation pillar, the highest point of the **Sperrin Skyway**.

From the summit cairn of **Sawel Mountain** go W, and cross the fence by one of two stiles. In clear weather you may see Dart Mountain to the south-west of you on a bearing of 240°. It is best approached by descending into the col, bearing slightly left (S) to favour the southern aspect above Oughtmame and then bearing right (W) to ascend along the east-north-eastern spur of Dart to the summit, navigating your way around an area that may be the site of a small **bog-burst** at the south-western end of the col.

*You can meander at will as you descend toward the saddle, with pleasing views into Glenelly and over the rolling tops of the Sperrins to the west. If it is a wet and miserable day, then you may content yourself with the knowledge that these hills are rarely walked, and you may count the footmarks you can see pressed into the pools of peat at the col. That is if there are any footprints to be found. And as you cross the col you can see evidence of the **geological story** of the Sperrins.*

From the col you will quickly arrive at the summit of **Dart Mountain**. From the summit descend S along the crest of the southern spur.

If at some future time I am asked to close my eyes and conjure up a view of the Sperrins in my mind then it might possibly be the one now present on your right (west). The row of spurs running south from the western peaks and into the Glenelly is neither staggering, dramatic nor awe-inspiring. It has neither the rugged beauty of a granite crag nor the genteel prettiness of a rolling chalk upland. Perhaps it is the silent greetings they offer, or the subtle invitations they pose, that make them so memorable.

Descend a steep slope, stay S but begin to favour the western side of the spur. About 0.9 km (0.5 mile) from the summit (at MR H 603954) ahead of you (SSE) you will see the great convex slopes of Legcloghfin. Look to the west-south-west now to find an old bog road, running below you above the Oughtboy Burn. Turn WSW and descend the rough grassy slopes to the bog road, taking care to arrive at the road before it bends to navigate its way around a fast-flowing burn. Turn left (S) on to the old road and follow it now around Legcloghfin and back into Glenelly.

*There are a mixture of sheep here, Cheviots, Scottish Blackfaced and a whole range of cross-breeds. And older farming practices on the slopes you leave behind, have given rise to many customs, none less in the Sperrins than the **Easter house**. As you continue to descend towards the road you can begin to see the field pattern of the **modern farming landscape**, and as the Oughtboy valley opens up into Glenelly you may see the Catholic chapel of Cranagh which dates from 1815 and was originally designed without seats to hold a local congregation of 800 worshippers. It may be one of the few older buildings in the valley now in use following the improvements of the nineteenth century. And beyond enjoy the superb views of the long soft ridge from Mullaghbane in the east to Craignammady and Slievemore in the west.*

Arrive at the Glenelly road (B47), turn left and follow the road eastwards along the valley past the **Sperrin Heritage Centre** through the hamlet of **Sperrin** and back to your car. Alternatively for VARIATION A turn right.

Although this tarmac ribbon has all the appearance of a minor trunk road, it rarely seems to be busy. But neither is it a place to relax your senses; dippers are common amid these fast-flowing burns that flow under the road and the scents of the country are ever in the air. Locals know this as good peat country, and when times get hard, or the summer is cold, the distinctive aroma from the burning fuel blends with the pungent smells of the farmyard and the scents of the wildflowers in the hedgerows.

*And hanging above farm doorways, you may notice the occasional **Cross of St Brigid**.*

Once back at your car you may relax at the picnic tables or gaze at the trout in the river.

THE COMMENTARIES

Names in the Landscape

The officers and civil employees of the Ordnance Survey seem not to have been very diligent in their tasks in this part of the Sperrins. True it is a mountainous country and there tends to be less naming of things in such an area, but from comparisons with neighbouring districts and from

Sperrin village

the evidence of the handful of native Gaelic speakers who still lived here in the late 1950s, it is clear that there were many more names than those recorded on the maps. The peak between Sawel and Meenard has no name recorded, neither do the waterfalls on the Oughtmame Burn. And where the surveyors do seem to have bothered to enquire of a name from some member of the local population they have applied it to every kind of feature from a mountain to a stream. Then they added insult to injury by offering an English interpretation

that has rendered a gross corruption of the Gaelic original. So Ucht na Maola becomes Oughtnamwella and the meaning is all but lost; 'breast of the bare hilltops of the streams' says so much more than the guttural utterances for which those map makers are responsible.

The County Rock

What could be the secret of the name of this rock? There seems to be no mention of it in local archives, nor in the unpublished memoirs of the

Ordnance Survey. But its name and location are their own clues as the walk now follows the line of the old county boundary as it runs up Sawel and across to Dart. In 1584 the bastard son of Henry VIII, Sir John Perrot, was appointed Lord Deputy of Ireland; full of reforming zeal he immediately set about dividing Ulster into counties and generally attacking the Gaelic method of political succession (tánaiste), much to the distress of the Earl of Tyrone, Hugh O'Neill.

It is likely then that the name of this rock dates from that period, when county boundaries were being drawn, with Co. Tyrone to the south and Co. Coleraine (later to become Co. Londonderry) to the north of the rock.

Perrot retired from the office in 1588. As a result of the political intrigues of Elizabethan England and Ireland, by 1592 he was languishing in the Tower of London convicted of treason, where he died in September of the same year, whilst Hugh O'Neill went on to become a serious challenge to the stability of the reign of Elizabeth I of England. For as the Earl of Tyrone, he led what the English describe as an insurrection and what Irish historians call the Nine Years' War (1594–1603).

The Sperrin Skyway – the Roof of the World

If you made your climb to this broad expanse through cloud, you might be forgiven for thinking that the roof of the world was an unprepossessing place. But there are no jewels to imitate the splendour of the grasses on this summit when their tall stems hang heavy with the droplets of dew from the fine mist that caresses the mountain. It is true that there are times when, having walked to a hilltop with a reputation for incomparable views, it is distressing to be robbed of the reward. But there are times too when the gentle embrace of the lowering sky brings you tranquillity and solitude in such a place as this.

I never knew Joey Glover (Walk 7b), but when he named the route across these tops the Sperrin Skyway, it must have been with an intimate knowledge of the character of these hills: the contrast of the long-distance views on a fine autumn day and the familiarity of the mist, of the ice-blue peerless sky and the shafts of sunlight shot through billowing cloud, of dawn breaking over the rolling hills to the east and the sharp but subtle sunsets in the west. He must have thought himself on the roof of the world.

Sawel Mountain

The name 'Sabhal' is Gaelic for barn. The farmer whose sheep roam the Tyrone side of this mountain lives a little to the south in Glenelly, and he tells me that the best time of the year to get the best views from Sawel is October, after a good drop of rain has cleared the drizzle, the mist and the haze. 'Then,' he says with emphasis, 'with a good pair of binoculars you can see Scotland.' I don't doubt it, but as my first three visits to Sawel were blessed with a rather still mist, then I have to trust his word. However, you may see the granite peaks of the Mourne mountains to the south-east, and the basalt escarpment of north Antrim to the east-north-east (Knocklayd). Far below to the east-south-east you may glimpse the shores of Lough Neagh, and to the north the clear outline of the great sea inlet of Lough Foyle.

Bog-Burst

Tyrone is famous for its bogs with liquid cores. A reservoir below the surface of the bog under some conditions can burst out, issuing a great flood of semi-liquid matter. In The Way that I Went, natural historian Lloyd Praeger says that bog-bursts are not uncommon in Ireland and describes one burst in Kerry in 1896. Weakened by unwise turf cutting, the contents of the bog were precipitated 23 km (14 miles) down the valley. This is clearly not such a severe example, but I would guess that water pressure from higher up the slope may well have forced out this large pool of liquid peat from beneath the weak unsupported edge in the col.

The Geological Story

The Sperrin hills are composed mainly of schists. These are metamorphic rocks, and the layering that characterises them can be seen very clearly in the boulders lying in this col. The original volcanic rocks have been squeezed, pressed and folded into these hills, and the composition of the rocks which form the higher ground of Dart and Sawel suggests that temperatures of around 600° Centigrade and phenomenal pressures of several kilobars (1 kilobar equals 15,000 lb per square inch) were responsible for metamorphosing these rocks from the

Glenelly valley

parent material. But don't worry; the presence of cloudberry suggests that it has cooled now.

Dart Mountain

The rocky outcrop of Dart (Darta, the mountain of the yearling heifers) makes it unique in these hills but the view northwards is almost hypnotising and that alone would make it worth the walk. To the north-north-west is Slieve Snaght on Inishowen, to the north-west I think I have

made out the blue-white reflection of the upper reaches of Lough Swilly, and beyond, perhaps the distinctive profiles of Errigal and Muckish Mountain in Co. Donegal. To the south-east you can most definitely see the table-top escarpment of Cuilcagh, the border mountain for Connacht and Ulster.

Easter Houses

Before the 'modernisation' of agriculture in the valley, a key feature of the success of the Rundale system relied on freeing the winter pasture for the growing of summer crops; young people brought the cattle on to the slopes of the mountain where in spring they built booleys (Walks 10, 16 and others), summer houses which gave the summer pasture its name. Inevitably their younger siblings would copy them. And although the custom known as clúdóg or clúideog seems to have grown a little confused with the folk traditions of Easter eggs, young people would retire to a secluded spot and build themselves a fire to sit by, or a house in which to eat their Easter eggs. And still today, children at school play at building Easter houses from whatever objects or materials are available, and then share their Easter treats.

The Modern Farming Landscape

The glen of the stone fortress (Glenelly) is a relatively fertile place compared to the mountains if not to such places as the Golden Vale (Walk 16). The sands and gravels dumped by the retreating ice make for easier cultivation than the hard uncongenial soils of the schists of these hills. The valley was densely wooded by oak even until the early nineteenth century, and much of what you view now is a result of the 'improvement' of the Sperrins by the London companies who leased great estates here. In the 1820s, companies such as the Worshipful Fishmongers considered the landscape overpopulated, the Rundale system having reduced smallholdings to as little as half an acre, with a small cottage and a potato crop viewed as sufficient means to raise a family. Politically ambitious local landlords were frequently at fault; the greater the number of tenants they had, the greater the number of votes they could coerce at election time.

But by the 1880s tenant numbers had been reduced, by emigration and by famine, farms had been reassembled to reach maybe 30 acres, and new field enclosures and hawthorn hedges had been created, perhaps in an image of the rural England of two centuries earlier. Fields were drained and land reclaimed. Today it is possible to see the mountain recapturing its own, as moorland grasses reclaim the pastures. But people have been struggling to survive here for 3000 years and farmers don't give in so easily.

Here and there a pasture will be bull-dozed, turned by the plough and reseeded as fine grazing for a small dairy or beef herd.

The Sperrin Heritage Centre

An interesting 30-minute detour for an audio-visual presentation and a chance for a cup of tea and a snack. For a few pence you may hire a pan and seach for gold in the burn running from the hillside by the centre. Gold has been panned from these hills for centuries and there are ancient artefacts in the Ulster Museum in Belfast made from Sperrin gold. Barry McGuigan, a former boxing champion, was presented with a medallion of the stuff and at various times, geological surveys are made and rumours or proposals for a major gold mining operation emerge. But for now the Sperrins remain undisturbed.

The centre is an interesting building which appears to employ a modern style to imitate key features of the vernacular architecture of Ulster. As it nestles in a small cleft in the hillside it is not intrusive on to the general landscape.

The Cross of St Brigid

As you travel along the Glenelly road and through other parts of the Sperrin Mountains look to the gaily painted doorways of the white-washed farmhouses for the distinctive rush cross of St Brigid. It is there to ward off evil. St Brigid, who has strong associations with this area, is the protectress of the dairy worker and greatly venerated. All of the legends that surround her tell of her mercy and pity for the poor. Born at Faughart near Dundalk around 450AD, she took the veil in her youth, and founded the first Irish nunnery, at Kildare. She is a member of the Roman Martyrology, and the patron saint of Ireland after St Patrick. She died in 525AD.

Sperrin

It often seems that no part of this land has escaped its sometimes turbulent history, and I would guess that the alternative name for Sperrin, Mount Hamilton, reveals a connection with one of Cromwell's soldiers, Captain William Hamilton, a Scot from East Lothian, who was granted the Caledon estate of Sir Phelim

O'Neill (Walk 11) after the battle of Benburb in 1646.

The Ordnance Survey memoirs of the eighteenth century report that Sperrin had a corn mill with a breast water wheel 12 ft in diameter and 2 ft broad. Today, it boasts a pub.

VARIATIONS AND ALTERNATIVES

A: CORRAMORE AND CORRATARY: A variation of the main route with very quiet lanes that offer you superb views of Dart and Sawel from the opposite bank of Glenelly. Emerge from the farm track and turn right. After 500 m (0.3 mile) turn left (S). Descend the boreen, cross the river and reach a T-junction. Turn left (E) and follow the road back to the Sperrin crossroad. Turn right (E) and return to your car. (22 km/14 miles, ascent 720 m/2360 ft, high point 678 m/2224 ft, 5.5 hrs, Strenuous.)

B: SHORT ROUTES TO DART AND SAWEL: For Sawel follow the route instructions of the main walk from Cloghorna (Sawel) Pass and either return the same way or continue on to Dart. Ascend Dart from the cattle grid at Dart Pass (MR H 589970), following the boundary fence to the summit. Descend the same way. (From 3 km/2 miles, ascent from 180 m/590 ft, high point 619 m/2031 ft or 678 m/2224 ft, from <1.5 hrs, Easy to Moderate.)

C: GLENELLY VALLEY: Quiet roads. From Sperrin follow the B47 Glenelly Road westwards for about 4.5 km (2.75 miles). Turn left and follow VARIATION A back to Sperrin. (12 km/7.5 miles, ascent 110 m/360 ft, >2.5 hrs, Easy.)

D: GLENERIN BRIDGE AND COUNTY ROCK: Follow the opening route directions of the main walk from the Glenerin Bridge on the B47 to County Rock or as far as desired. Return the same way or by the road. (Max. 8 km/5 miles, ascent max. 200 m/655 ft, >2 hrs, Easy to Moderate.)

E: OTHER WALKING: The Sperrin Skyway and the Ulster Way are both well-known walks, the Ulster Way offering some easy walking. There is a pleasant walk to Lough Lark from Sperrin; the Burn Walk from Gortin is only 3.2 km (2 miles) long and there is other easy walking to be had in the area, as well as the Gortin Glen Forest Park and neigbouring peaks Mullaghcarn and Slieveard.

| *Mountain of Snows and the Poisoned Glen*
SLIEVE SNAGHT AND THE DERRYVEAGH
MOUNTAINS

In the somewhat remote north-west of Ireland, at the heart of Donegal, rest the Derryveagh Mountains. This is a place for memory and imagination. A place to reach out and touch the wilderness, a place of incomparable beauty and countless possibilities for solitude. And it is to a place such as this that everyone should come at least once in their lives.

Toward the southern end of this rugged ridge of ice-ground granite rests the Poisoned Glen, a deep glaciated valley running from the north-east, south-west spine of the range, and offering sometimes imperceptible, but always intriguing, contrasts with the mountain of Snaght to its south.

Map: OSi 1:50 000 Discovery Series Sheet 1, Donegal (NW) (part) | Distance: 13 km (8 miles) | Ascent: 2500 ft (750 m) | High point: 2240 ft (683 m) | Naismith time: 4 hours | Difficulty: Strenuous/Difficult | Mountain rescue service: 999 | Garda station: Milford: 074 915 3114 | Tourist information: Letterkenny: 074 912 1160 | Miscellaneous: Glenveagh National Park 074 913 7090; Dunlewey Lakeside Centre: 074 953 1699

ADVICE AND GRADING

There is great variety here, provided by the boggy routes alongside the Owenabhainn and Devlin river (Dubh Linn, black pools), a little scrambling both up and down, loughside strolling, rock-hopping in the Devlin river gorge and good views provided by the granite ridge and the summit of Snaght. But this is a 'tough auld walk' as the Irish say and, although only just falling within the Difficult grade, it is definitely the realm of the seasoned hill walker. However, there are a number of alternatives explained at the end.

A superb overview of most of the walk can be had from the summit of Errigal (An Earagail). Alternatively, as you pass east-wards beyond Dunlewey (Dún Lúiche) from the direction of Dunglow (An Clochán Liath), there is a large vehicle lay-by on the right-hand side of the road, as it bends from the SSW to the NNE around Errigal (MR C 931194). From here you gain a good view of the Poisoned Glen, the granite ridge running to Slieve Snaght (Sliabh Sneachta or Snechta) and the Devlin river valley and gorge.

GETTING THERE

The starting point for this walk, the townland of **Dunlewey**, rests in a wide glen on the sandy shores of a lough and the southern slopes of Errigal, at the very heart of the Gaeltacht. From whichever direction you arrive, you are treated to exceptionally fine views of the granite slabs of the Sléibhte Dhoire Bheatha (mountains of the birch wood, Derryveagh Mountains) and the shattered scree slopes of the imposing elongated cone of Errigal.

From Letterkenny (Leitir Ceanainn) take the R250 and R251 to the entrance of the Glenveagh National Park Visitor Centre at the north-eastern tip of Lough Veagh (Beagh). Stay on the R251 as it heads WNW and then SW around the Derryveagh Mountains. After a further 14 km (9 miles) the road takes you around the southern slopes of Errigal. Take a sharp left hairpin turn, down a small boreen with a tourist signpost to the Poisoned Glen. Descend past the **ruined church** on your right, around a tight right bend to a left bend before a granite bridge, which inciden-tally leads to the gates of Dunlewey House. Park your car off the

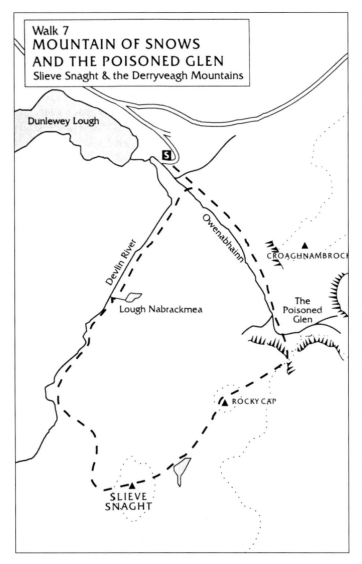

Walk 7
MOUNTAIN OF SNOWS
AND THE POISONED GLEN
Slieve Snaght & the Derryveagh Mountains

Dunlewey Lough

S

Owenabhainn

Devlin River

Lough Nabrackmea

CROAGHNAMBROC

The
Poisoned
Glen

ROCKY CAP

SLIEVE
SNAGHT

road on the spare ground, at the bend just before the bridge (MR C 929191).

THE WALK

Leave your car and walk back up the bohereen (ESE). At the hairpin bend leave the metalled road to carry straight on, and follow a decaying **causeway**. The Owenabhainn flows in the valley below you on your right (SW). It means River of the Poisoned Glen, but is marked as the Cronaniy Burn (Cró na Neimh, the hut of poison) by the cartographers responsible for the half-inch OS map. The causeway heads SE along the north-eastern slopes of the glen. It crosses the Owenwee (Bhuí abhainn, yellow river, a tributary of the Owenabhainn) by a small granite bridge, forks left, and a sometimes vague path follows it, as it variously appears and disappears into the bog, finally to reach another stream.

*As you might expect, this being a glen, and this being Donegal, your route through this valley is likely to be wet. But there will be much to entertain you. Look for the common frog, the newt and the heron. All have their habitat here or close by, and the solo walker will have opportunities to arrive on them undisturbed. And as you pass through the drier portions look for a difference in the colour of the flowers, and the shape of the leaves of the ling. Not the striking difference of the bell heather and the cross-leaved heath, but the subtle variation of **Mackay's heath** (Erica mackaiana).*

At the stream turn right (W). Follow this burn, first on its right bank then on its left, as it zigzags to reach the Owenabhainn. Now turn left and stay on the right bank of the Owenabhainn (stream to your right) to follow the general direction (SE) as it takes you into the heart of the **Poisoned Glen** toward a seemingly impassable wall of rock. But look carefully. As you walk up the glen, directly ahead of you (SSE) in the granite wall is a distinctive cleft; a 'V' shape in the profile of the ridge. This is your objective. Finally, at the head of the glen arrive at a rowan and a holly growing from opposite banks of the burn.

Only the stoniest of souls would fail to recognise these lovers as they reach toward each other, their branches entwined in a loving embrace. It is, of course, Diarmaid and Grainne, free from the wrath of Finn MacCool and the pursuit of the Fianna, their immortal spirits together and at peace at last, at the heart of this tranquil glen.

Pass these 'sweethearts' and cross the burn to enter the **Glenveagh National Park** unannounced. Head SSE and ascend the granite wall into the cleft. This is a short stiff climb with a little pleasant scrambling as you near the crest, but does not require experience of the Himalayas, friends, cleats, rope or harness. The vertical appearance as you approach from the glen is merely an illusion. Soon emerge through a small wet gulley to the crest, and a view of one small and two larger tarns below you (SSE).

Ahead of you (SSE) is the north-west face of Moylenanav in the Glendowan Mountains (Sléibhte Ghléann Domhain). The steep-sided Gweebara Glen hidden from view, cradles the Barra and Owenveigh rivers and conceals the NE-SW line of the Gweebara geological fault-plane, which I guess is a tear fault and probably part of a family related to the Great Glen fault in Scotland.

The shores of Lough Slievesnacht and the summit of the mountain now lie, out of view, to your right (SW) toward the end of the granite ridge. But your next objective lies a little closer on an approximate bearing of 238° and entails a climb of 150 m/500 ft or so: the open summit of Rocky Cap. There are two routes. You may choose to contour up and around the eastern and southern slopes of the ridge toward the summit, and so pass along the south-eastern shores of a number of small tarns, hidden amid the vertical-sided saddles formed between the faces of these giant tors. Or you may prefer a more exciting route, to meander up and down and in and out, along the crest of the ridge. For this, first go to an unnamed summit at a bearing of approximately 245°, where from the small piles of stones you may gain your first glimpse of Snaght (SW) since you entered the glen, and then on to Rocky Cap (I could find no other name), the final summit in the ridge before Snaght. If you choose this second airy route take care of the deep granite escarpments that lie at right angles across your path, you will need to navigate around them.

I love this mountainscape. The denuded granite offers evidence of glaciation in whatever direction you choose to look, and I assume that the exposed aspect and poor nutrition from the earth are responsible for the lack of peat, except in the most sheltered gullies and slopes. You would wonder that anything could survive here, but tracks and droppings are the tell-tale signs of the summer grazing of deer. And one of the two largest herds of red deer in Ireland is resident within a 42 km (26 mile), nine-wire deer fence a little to the north-east; the other of course is in Killarney. Neither is it difficult to understand that these inspiring heights were once the haunt of the golden eagle, or that peregrines and merlins still soar ever skyward here.

Once you attain the summit of Rocky Cap with its pile of stones, do not go straight to Slieve Snaght as there is a very deep defile. Rather head generally SW until Lough Slievesnacht comes into view, then drop (SSE) into a peat lined valley to head straight for the shores of the lough (SSW).

The shore is adorned with places where you may perch, remove your shoes and dangle your feet into the water; unless, of course, it's winter. Local fishermen tell me that Lough Slievesnacht offers good brown trout. But these fish are reputed to be very canny and difficult to catch. All of the loughs hereabouts were stocked by the Electricity Board. Some say 'over-stocked', and it is probably the fry from these loughs that attract the heron to fish in the streams in these hills.

From the shoreline head WSW towards the obvious wide summit of Snaght. As you reach the summit the slope begins to level out and the top of the mountain is revealed as a series of rounded hags, groughs, peat pools and small tarns. And to the west, the substantial cairn of **Slieve Snaght**.

Mount Errigal

The aim now is to reach the right bank of the Devlin river safely! This is best done by following a snake-like route that will twist you down the mountain and above the wetter portions of the valley below. From the summit descend generally W/WSW down the steep slope of slabs, turf and boulders, towards a shallow gulley running NW–SE around the lower part of the mountain. As you descend you may see the Devlin river running north-east from Lough Agganive (sandy lake). But don't let the view distract you from your descent. And take care where you place your feet, there seem to be countless foot-sized swallow holes, frequently hidden by long grasses. A twisted ankle or a broken leg would be most inconvenient here.

At the gulley turn right (N) and as it reaches the granite slabs around the lower slopes of Snaght, ahead of you (NNW) you will see the confluence of the Devlin river and its tributary running from your left (west). Aim for this by continuing generally N around the foot of Snaght to describe a large arc on the higher ground above the wet basin on your left (west), eventually walking WNW to join the Devlin river on its right bank.

Notice the waterfall on your left (south) as you reach the river. Do not cross the burn but turn right to head N. There now follows some mildly heavy going generally alongside the river (N, later veering NE), until you are eventually drawn by the attractive profile of **Errigal**.

As the river begins to cut a beautiful wooded gorge you have the choice to remain above, still following the now straight course of the river, or to walk the banks and rock-hop along the river bed. There are a number of spots where you may climb in and out of the gorge and so (rainfall allowing) you may choose a mixture of both.

*This is an appealing gorge, supporting pioneer scrub and woodland of birch and oak, and as you walk along the tops, you will inevitably come across fragments of earlier but similar trees – **bog wood**. The exploitation of this and the lichens that decorate the granite boulders are examples of the way the folk here eked out a living from this inhospitable land.*

As the gorge ends and you descend, stay with the right bank of the river. As it turns left (NW), leave the river and take a line NE to cross the open bog towards the small granite bridge you will recall from earlier in the day. Reach the Owenabhainn, cross this by the stones, and carry on to reach the causeway that crosses the bridge. Turn left (NW) and return along causeway and bohereen, to your car.

THE COMMENTARIES

Dunlewey

Could it be that the small raised features on the floor at the heart of the glen might be the remains of the fort of the giant sun god Lú, from which Dún Lúchie (Dunlewey) gains its name? For the scarred face of the granite sides of the glen reputedly result from a horrendous battle between Lú and his unwilling grandfather Balor (Bilor), the mightiest and the most evil of the Formorian tribe (builders of the Giant's Causeway,

Walk 5). Balor, the giant god of darkness with one eye in his forehead, was virtually indestructible, but for a vulnerability in his baleful, second eye fixed in the back of his head. It is said that it took more than four men just to lift his great eyelid, and that his gaze turned all enemies to dust. But Balor was a giant god living in fear, for it was foretold that he would be destroyed by his own grandson. So afraid was he of this ancient prophecy, that he imprisoned his only daughter Aoife on the island of Tory, so that she might not be impregnated by a man. But Balor's enemy McAneely smuggled himself on to the island and into the company of Aoife as a handmaiden, whereupon he seduced her and all her servants. And in the way of these things Aoife gave birth to Lú and two other sons. And all of the servants had sons. Balor killed McAneely and tossed the babies into the sea, but Lú escaped by the cunning of Aoife, and by his own magical powers. Found on the seashore by his blacksmith uncle, he was taught the ways of fighting and became the hero of his father's tribe the Danaans, ancient enemies of the Formorians. Eventually, after many adventures, Lú sought justice for the murder of his father McAneely. A terrible battle raged between him and Balor. But Lú was not to be defeated and drove his magical burning spear deep into the baleful eye of Balor. Whereupon vile fluid erupted from that noxious and malignant place and, as you may see, cleft a rock the size of a man, and poisoned the glen.

The Ruined Church

Every feature of the landscape has a story to tell, this church no less than any other. In the late 1850s, Mr John Adair, the landlord of the Derryveagh estate (now the national park), introduced sheep farming on to these uplands. By April 1861, this was to result in Adair being responsible for a series of evictions that were seen to cause such terrible hardship that even the local police would not be party to carrying them through. Police from Sligo and further away had to be brought in to throw the tenants out into a cold April, destroy their belongings and their homes and sentence them to emigration or the workhouse.

However, the success of the sheep farming in Derryveagh so impressed Mrs Russell, the wife of the landlord of the Dunlewey estate, and resident at Dunlewey House, that she decided to implement a similar scheme. Having acquired the sheep and put them to graze on these hills to the south, she brought over Scottish shepherds from the same small village from which she herself had come. Now the church was originally built in 1845 to help foster the Protestant religion, and Mrs Russell saw this as a way of injecting new life into the plan. The shepherds were Protestant and Mrs Russell hoped that they would marry local Catholic girls, who would thereby convert, and the Protestant religion would prosper. But within two or three months, the grass on the hills had turned brown, the sheep starved and most of the shepherds went back home. Those that remained married the Catholic girls as expected but, influenced perhaps by their wives, or by a desire to fit in with their new neighbours, they adopted the Catholic religion. The quiet empty churchyard offers testimony to the small congregations that must have gathered there; perhaps only the landowners' families and professional acquaintances. And so it must have continued until 1935 when the last service was held.

Over the years the Dunlewey estate had a number of landlords, including William Augustine Ross, a Belfast mill owner who built the prominent Catholic church, reputedly of French style, that can be seen further down the glen. In 1943 Henry McIlhenny bought the estate for his sister, Mrs Winterstein, but for various reasons she never became resident in house or estate. In 1952 the estate was sold on and I believe it was the new owners who had the roof removed in 1956, though I cannot be certain. It was rumoured that the building had become dangerous

and needed these works to make it safe, but a photograph by W. A. Poucher from the early 1950s shows it replete with attractive blue slate roof. It is more likely that this was a means to reduce the estate's running costs. Removing the roof and the interior removed any liability for the local community tax called 'rates'.

The blend of white marble and granite from which the church is built reflects the contrasting rocks of Snaght (granite) and Errigal (quartzite), and the church still poses a striking appearance in the glen.

Various proposals have been floated for its future from heritage to field study centre, and I notice it has featured in at least one video by the musician Enya whose family live nearby. Personally I'd like to see it remain as it is – decaying slowly and adding to the air of mystery in the glen.

Causeway

I can only guess at the age and purpose of this causeway. Certainly the route that runs off to the left after the granite bridge gave access to a small quarry, and I am told that the route running off to the right may have been intended to give access to a manse, or rectory, built with Mr Russell's money, south across the river, where some remains lie amid the trees. James Bor, the only permanent curate, served from 1853 to 1872. But I'd like to believe that the route is much older, and wonder for how long people have been walking into this glen. A crannog in Lough Dunlewey is thought to be more than 3500 years old; although a water regulation scheme raised the water level in the lough by almost 6 m (20 ft) in the 1950s, you can still see the tip of the crannog off the southern loughshore. An entire community must have lived there. Perhaps they were the fabled Nemidians; perhaps they hunted in this glen.

Later, farmers would have moved to the more fertile land of the coastal plain around Gweedore, as life became safe there. As elsewhere in Ireland, the young people would have brought cattle into the glen for summer grazing, freeing the winter pasture for summer crops: hence a route into the glen and a possible causeway, now partially covered by lough and tarmac and bog. The young people would have needed shelter, and those early booleys would have been built from turf (bothógs, bog houses), perhaps like modern-day grouse butts, or the homes of the Sami people who live close to the Arctic Circle; only later would they have collected granite boulders and built them from stone. Both were common ways to build homes in Gweedore even into the twentieth century, and the faint remains of these techniques may still be detected in the glen.

Mackay's Heath (Erica Mackaiana)

Looking similar to the cross-leaved heath (Erica tetralix), this interesting variant has a brighter, stronger purple-pink bloom, and apparently flowers later, usually July and August. The leaves can be seen to point outwards much more than tetralix, and there seem to be a lot more of them. However, it is difficult to tell if it is truly Mackay's heath. I guess it is likely that the plants here are actually a hybrid of the two, but there is a difference and it is very clearly seen when the two are side by side. Still, botanists have reported the presence of Mackay's heath hereabouts, and the only other places it is known to grow are the west of Ireland (Walk 11) and Oviedo in Spain.

The Poisoned Glen

The Poisoned Glen

Was it a plant reputed to poison the cattle and sheep, a glen so beautiful that it demanded to be described as heavenly, or the home of one of the tribes of Ireland? The Gaelic for neimhbhe *(poisoned),* neamha *(heavenly) and* Neimei *(Nemidians) would have sounded very similar to the first English map-makers, and a lost fragment of nineteenth-century heritage becomes a twentieth-century enigma.*

Spurges are sometimes suggested as the culprits of the Poisoned Glen; both petty spurge (Euphorbia peplus) and wood spurge (E. amygdaloides) contain a poisonous and caustic milky white juice in the stems and leaves, which is known to make cattle or horses very ill, and even kill them. You might expect to find it with nettles, but I didn't see any.

Claiming the glen as the home of the Nemidians certainly has its romantic attraction, although there is no real historical evidence. But there is a similarity in the spelling of the name of the glen and of the name for heaven written in a Catholic catechism of 1705, now in the charge of Franciscan monks in Belgium.

Perhaps how it sounds is more important than what it means and maybe we should best be satisfied with the musical chime of the Gaelic name as it peals from the tongue of a resident of Dunlewey. Go ask one!

Glenveagh National Park

The lion's share of the 10,000 hectares (23,887 acres) of the park was purchased by the state in 1975 from the millionaire curator of the Philadelphia Museum of Art, Mr Henry McIlhenny. Subsequently, in 1981, Mr McIlhenny donated the castle and gardens at the heart of the Glenveagh.

It is the deep steep-sided glen that harbours the lough and castle that gives the park its name. It was this estate that Mr John Adair from Co. Laois created in 1857–59, by buying and amalgamating several smaller holdings. He set sheep to graze immediately, evicted the tenants in 1861, built his castle in 1870 and died in 1885. Even by the standard of English landlords in Ireland (Walk 10), Adair's reputation is infamous. Not so his wife, who lived until 1921 and is remembered rather more fondly.

Arthur Kingsley Porter had no time to establish any reputation. He bought the estate in 1929, and then disappeared in mysterious circumstances on Inishbofin in 1933, leaving Henry McIlhenny to buy the estate in 1937. McIlhenny, whose ancestors came from this part of Donegal, is remembered for the attention he gave to the estate and for his support of the local tweed and knitwear industries; he took friends, often American visitors, to visit local weavers such as Manus Ferry who lived close to Dunlewey Lough, and encouraged commercial links with the United States. Today the estate seems to be administered around the delicate balance of maintaining the wilderness, providing access, and managing tourism and the revenue it brings. Apart, perhaps, from the castle, the gardens and the evictions, the landscape is viewed as the heritage and it is this that the park seeks to protect.

Slieve Snaght

This mountain is old. People like to say, older even than the Alps, and once higher than the Himalayas. The original sediments were laid down in the sea-bed 700 million years ago. 200 million years later movement in the earth's crust brought two great masses together and forced a folding of these rocks. 100 million years after that a massive balloon of molten granite (a pluton) formed below the surface of the earth. And all the forms of erosion known to Nature have probably done the rest, especially the ice of 15,000 or more years ago.

At 2240 ft (683 m) Snaght is the highest complete peak in the national park, the second highest in Donegal, and though it is not as exhilarating as Errigal the views are well earned. The neighbouring peaks, the islands of Aran and Tory, and the coastal features of Donegal are easily identified, but take the time to look ENE for Lough Swilly (Louch Súilí), another of the great Irish sea inlets.

Errigal

The highest peak in Donegal at 2466 ft (752 m), at the southern end of the distinctive quartzite range. The scree slopes that deny a foothold to pioneering vegetation are the product of the intense cold of the last Ice Age.

Bog Wood, Lichens and Tweed

A trip to the local wood yard or DIY superstore will satisfy the timber requirements of most people in the Western world, and our need for fabric dyes, fabric and clothes can be satisfied even more easily. So it rarely occurs to us to think of the difficulties of earlier generations.

When, early in the twentieth century, Manus Ferry from Dunlewey turned to weaving as a way of earning a living he needed to build his own weaving frame, which he built from pine and oak won from the bog – the remains of once great forests. Two stumps were recently dated at almost 4000 years old, and probably represent the last stages of the woods that covered the area. Derryveagh means a forest of oak and birch.

Occasionally, oak and pine stumps would be found by accident but more frequently, those in need would search the bog by divining. It seems there *were different ways of achieving success. One, presumably used by those without any other divining talent, was to search the bog early in the morning, in the belief that areas without morning dew concealed bog wood. Alternatively, they might use divining rods or other witnesses. And the size of the find would be divined, to check if it was large enough, before excavating it from the bog.*

Manus's brother would shepherd sheep for wool, and probably gather the plants and lichens growing in this glen, which were used even until the middle of the twentieth century as organic dyes for the wool. Their sister would spin and manage their business, while Manus made himself and his family famous in local tweed-weaving competitions. The site of their endeavour, their old home, with its weaving shed and bog wood weaving frame, now forms the home of the Dunlewey Lakeside Centre.

VARIATIONS AND ALTERNATIVES

A: SNAGHT: The aim of the walk is to provide you with a day in the wilderness. And providing you avoid the steeper granite slabs of the mountainsides, you can really wander at will, using the route to the ridge through the Poisoned Glen, and/or the route along the Devlin river, as your routes of access and return. However, if your primary aim is to climb Slieve Snaght, then shorter routes approach from the south-south-east. Do note, there is need for careful scrambling, or perhaps scrabbling, and this route shoud be avoided in the wet. From the minor road north of Lough Barra (MR B 933136) follow the right bank of the most northerly of the two streams (the Scardangal Burn). Stay close by the stream until you have ascended the granite slabs, then go NNW and upwards towards the summit. From the summit descend SW into the col and turn left (SSE) to reach another stream (the Shruhanerolee river), cross to the right bank, ease your way down the crag and descend (SE) with the river, back to the road. (5 km/3 miles, ascent 1760 ft/536 m, high point 2240 ft/683 m, <2 hrs, Challenging.)

B: ERRIGAL: Errigal offers a short, easy, though steep climb, via boggy tread, waymark stakes, cairns and a scree path, to ascend the mountain by its eastern spur. Whilst you will need good footwear for bog and scree, people do wear trainers in summer, and I have met families with children of five, six and seven years of age, who, properly equipped, used to walking and given the time, were able to climb Errigal on a calm sunny day.

From Dunlewey follow the R251 for 1.6 km (1 mile) to reach a car-park. Follow the path past the waymark stake and head straight (E) for the summit. As you reach the lower slopes, turn right (NE) and contour around the mountain until you reach a line of stakes heading 'straight up' (NW). Follow these to reach a shelf and the foot of the scree. Now follow the path which rises up the ridge to the two summit peaks. Pass a memorial cairn to Joey Glover (Walk 6) on the way and return by the same route. This can be quite exhilarating, with a very rewarding summit view for such a short walk, but avoid weekends if you want solitude. (4 km/2.5 miles, ascent 1935 ft/590 m, high point 2466 ft/752 m, >2 hrs, Challenging, but only just, Moderate when dry.)

C: ALTAN LOUGH: There is a pleasant trackway walk to the shores of Altan Lough from the R251 Gweedore/Letterkenny road. The track runs N from the road at map reference B 954205. Park your car off the road and follow the obvious track down to the lough. Return the same way. (Up to 5 km/3 miles, ascent 140 ft/43 m, >1 hrs, Easy.)

D: SOME SHORT RAMBLES: Both the beginning and the end stages of the walk can form pleasant short rambles, perhaps for a summer afternoon or evening. From the ruined church in Dunlewey you could choose to walk alongside the right bank of the Owenabhainn as far into the glen as you wished, or similarly alongside the Devlin river perhaps as far as Lough Nabrackmea (fat trout lake) or even Lough Maam. (Up to 6 km/4 miles, ascent up to 50 ft/15 m, up to 1.5 hrs, Easy.)

E: OTHER WALKING: Easy and pleasant family walking can be had on constructed pads and paths nearby in the Glenveagh National Park and by the shores of Lough Dunlewey, which you can reach through the Dunlewey Lakeside Centre. Both of these centres make a small charge but provide interesting and differing approaches to heritage.

| *Holy Mountain of St Aodh Mhac Briaena*

SLIABH LIAG (SLIEVE LEAGUE),
CO. DONEGAL

In the early mists of Ireland's past, her tribes built tombs and other cairns on high places. Then the Celtic peoples arrived and fired beacons at the change of every season. And so it was to a land with a cult of high places that Christianity came, a new religion that needed to build itself on to the old in order to overcome suspicion and opposition. We therefore frequently find an oratory, a hermitage or a holy well at the summit of a prominent hill. Such sites of special religious significance were later used for the secret taking of Mass, until the beginning of Catholic relief in 1829, and then for turas in celebration of the saints.

Perhaps that's why Ireland produced four great mountains of pilgrimage: Slieve Donard (Walk 3) in the Mountains of Mourne, Croagh Patrick overlooking Clew Bay in Co. Mayo (Walk 10d), Mount Brandon on the Dingle Peninsula (Walk 13d) and Slieve League on this long finger of land that points westward into the Atlantic Ocean.

Map: OSi 1:50 000 Discovery Series Sheet 10, Donegal (part) | Distance: 13 km (8 miles) | Ascent: 2300 ft (700 m) | High point: 1972 ft (601 m) | Naismith time: 4 hours | Difficulty: Moderate/Challenging | Rescue services: 999 | Garda station: Glenties: 074 955 1108 | Boat trip information: Letterkenny: 074 912 1160

ADVICE AND GRADING

Graded on the Challenging side of Moderate, this walk presents little difficulty; however, you must observe sensible precautions

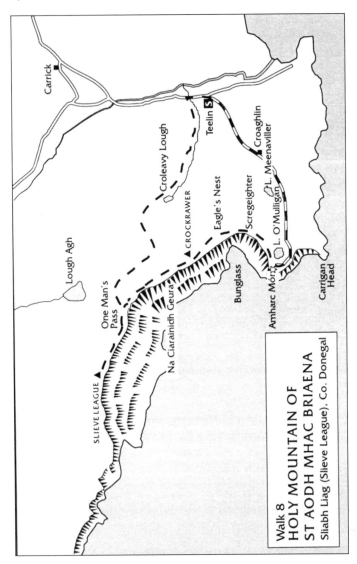

Walk 8

HOLY MOUNTAIN OF
ST AODH MHAC BRIAENA

Sliabh Liag (Slieve League), Co. Donegal

when walking above escarpments and cliffs, and in locations susceptible to mist or sea fret. Route finding is easy and the famed One Man's Pass would have carried Hannibal with his entire army including elephants. The narrow (400 mm) rib of rock at the head of Na Ciarainidh Geura can be safely avoided by taking the landward path.

GETTING THERE

Take the R263 from Donegal town, W to the hamlet of Carrick (An Charraig). Then turn left toward Teelin and follow the road with the Glen river on your left. Within 3 km (1.8 miles), arrive at the Cul a Duin pub on your left. Park your car off the road here (MR G 585767).

THE WALK

Leave your car and continue S along the tarmac boreen and almost immediately reach the junction in Teelin and turn right (SW) by the Irish Language College. Follow this now for perhaps 1.5 km as it rises gently past a left turn at a twist in the road through tiny Croaghlin and makes a short steep climb before arriving at a gate.

On your left behind the Irish College is yet another Mass rock, used by the local priest and population in the days of Catholic persecution before 1829. And before twisting up the hill, in the townland which I believe is called Umerawurrneen, the road passes a site recorded by the OS in 1900 as Uaghneenderg. Now destroyed by the construction of a path, it appears to have been a cairn with a grave made from quite large flags. As you walk further, the rock they must have used outcrops all around you and it may be this feature which gave the mountain its name, Sliabh Liag, mountain of the flagstones, although some say the name recalls the colour of the peak, grey mountain.

Pass through the gate by Lough Meenaviller and along the track WSW. Ignore the turn left to Carrigan Head and follow the road through a series of bends, heading generally N, to arrive at and cross a rough car-park(NNW) to join the footpath above the cliff at **Amharc Mór** to gaze below at the beautiful bight called Bunglass.

At the cliff edge turn sharp right (NE) and follow the path as it climbs the first hill, Scregeighter (1021 ft/311 m) and turns N to seek its way above the **Eagle's Nest**. Although there is no difficulty, it can be a little steep in places, depending on the route you choose. In windy conditions you should avoid the edges of the cliff.

As well as the obvious draw of the sea cliffs, the climb will also give you a glimpse or two of Lough O'Mulligan to your right (south-east) and, as you go higher, hopeful souls fishing off the end of Teelin pier. And higher still, back on Carrigan Head you will see the remains of a signalling tower from the 1790s. There are others at Malin Beg and at Glen Head. Dating back to the time of Napoleon they line the whole west coast (see Walk 1 on Martello towers and Walk 15).

From the Eagle's Nest, descend slightly before climbing again to Crockrawer. The path is becoming badly eroded in parts and threads occasionally and it doesn't take long to leave the tourists behind. The way now grows narrow along Na Ciarainidh Geura to meet with a narrow rib of rock now known as the eastern One Man's Pass. Some people skip along this rib, others are terrified by it. I make no judgement. If you don't like the look of it, there is a landward path, or you can sit with your legs inland and 'inch' your way along.

You soon regain more comfortable going and reach the first broad summit with its fragmented limestone moonscape, a number of cairns and a curious tiny oratory at its centre. Everything has its purpose; the Pilgrims' Path joins the mountain here and you will need to return to this spot shortly after your visit to the summit proper.

I originally thought the small monument might be the shroud for a well, as a number are reported on this mountain, but they are north-north-east of here. Folklore also has it that a small community of Carmelite monks were resident on the summit at some time. I thought this might be the spot. Slieve League is said to bear a resemblance to Mount Carmel, which is why the monks chose to come here.

From the tiny oratory continue along the cliff across the broad grassy saddle, traditionally, perhaps erroneously, called One Man's Pass, to the Ordnance Survey pillar at the summit of Slieve League.

This pillar never quite appears to be the absolute summit, I tend to favour a mound off to the north-west, not that it matters. But I'm also curious about this site, which looks as if it might have been a megalithic cairn, although there are no references in the various reputable sources. The views, on the other hand, speak for themselves and I'm told you can see Croagh Patrick, which somehow seems fitting.

On your return follow the path to the landward side along the lip of the corrie which cradles Lough Agh, perhaps returning to the cliff edge for one final view back towards Bunglass.

The corrie around Lough Agh has a reputation amongst botanists for holding a great variety of alpine plants, whilst budding geologists are bound to notice the extraordinarily clear folding within these shales; the angle of dip must be 45° or more. Some spectacular forces must have tilted this land to create this mountain. You may also spot on the southern back wall of the corrie the site of **St Hugh MacBrick's Church.**

Return to the tiny oratory and turn left, away from the sea, to begin to seek the other cairns which offer guidance for the Pilgrims' Path, which lies in the valley ENE ahead of you. So go NE from the oratory to descend into the denuded saddle of the eastern spur of Slieve League. The small remaining islands of peat hint at its past cloak of sphagnum moss and other turf plants.

At a pair of cairns, one built on an outcrop of limestone, turn right (SE) to descend along the **Pilgrims' Path**. Do not descend

View from eastern One Man's Pass

with a small burn but stay with the path as it hugs the side of the mountain heading directly S of the cairns and then twists its way left and right, heading generally SE to pass Croleavy Lough and reach a modern tubular steel gate 1.5 km or so down the mountain.

As you descend, there are views back to Teelin, and on to Muckross Head, St John's Point and across Donegal Bay to Benbulbin (Walk 9) and the Dartry Hills.

Go through the gate and as the road descends enter a more pastoral landscape, full of interest from hay stooks to limekilns. Emerge at a T-junction and turn right (S) to follow the signs to Teelin pier, Bunglass and the cliffs, and walk the short distance back to your car.

Perhaps you will have time to visit the Cul a Duin for light refreshment with twentieth-century heritage. The bar has character and the toilets have unusual decoration!

THE COMMENTARIES

Amharc Mór

It means simply 'great view', but what an understatement. Certainly you can see into the distance and more immediately north-west across to Malin Beg, the signalling tower and the lighthouse on Rathlin O'Byrne island. But the greatest view has to be of the sea and cliffs, the incredible collision of colours, sounds, shapes and movement. From the silver shades of the wheeling gulls and still beaches, to the rushing pigments of the brittle rock and the endless thrusting of the waves. From fragmented shales and leeching minerals and metals, the endless variation of grasses, sedges, mosses and lichens, to the bright sea foam and the brilliant hue of the pebbles at the foot of the mountain which give rise to the name Bunglass (green bottom).

And none of this has been lost on the generations of fishermen who christened each feature in the rock with a Gaelic name, like An Seol Mór, the big sail. The two pinnacles below are known as the Giant's Desk and Chair, whilst the long slope of green and red bracken is known as Foree, and once at least, sheep were set to graze on it. Is it any wonder that, like so many beautiful places we visit in this book, this has been the setting for a TV drama – this time for the BBC and perhaps well chosen for the film Murder in Eden.

Eagle's Nest

When eagles flew in Ireland, they built a nest here; in 1867 Kinfella recalls a tale from one Nanny O'Byrne of Malinbeg, then eighty years of age, whose great grandmother was actually carried off by an eagle when she was only a small child. The mother and others chased after the bird, who dropped the child on the cliff edge at Carrigan Head and flew off toward Malin Beg. Apparently very badly lacerated, the girl nevertheless survived, but still carried the scars when she died at almost a hundred years of age.

Some time later, one Andrew McIntyre found himself and his family suffering the worst of privation during a period of famine in 1817. Andrew lived in Croughlin and one day, passing above the Eagle's Nest, he saw the carcass of a lamb in the eyrie, and the chance to feed his family. Quickly he stole the lamb from the fledgelings and then made repeated visits as needed. Of course others were not so lucky and people in the locality began to die. That's when Andrew first discovered human limbs in the nest; after several such finds, he secured the eagles and burned the nest.

St Hugh Macbrick's Church

Naomh Aodh Mhac Briaena (St Hugh MacBrick) lived for a while on this hilltop in the early sixth century, during which time he became famous for his sanctity and for curing those with ailments of the head. It is believed he had both an oratory and a hermitage. But disguised by its own collapsed rubble, it's impossible to tell the outline of this dry stone building. To the south-west are the collapsed remains of a beehive hut, perhaps the saint's hermitage, whilst down toward Lough Agh is a pillar stone inscribed with a cross. Also hereabouts the old half-inch OS map shows a number of wells. You can't help but notice the cairns; the Archaeological Survey for Donegal reports that there are twenty-six in all, possibly the penitential stations

for the turas, strung out along the edges of the ridge. Although these now seem long forgotten, it's still thought that three of the cairns may be the remains of hut sites.

The Pilgrims' Path

This is a well-constructed path. Cairns guide the early descent and, except for a stream near the top, a bridge keeps the route quite dry. However, I could find nothing as to its origin, except from the library at Letterkenny. The Illustrated Handbook to South Western Donegal of 1872 tells the would-be tourist that the ascent of Slieve League is achieved in easy stages from the road at Teelin to the top of the mountain, by means of the winding pathway constructed especially for that purpose by the MP for Donegal, one Thomas Conolly. More than that I cannot say and it seems to me that Thomas Conolly's pathway could be either this well built road, or perhaps the track from Teelin to Amharc Mór. A description of the view at the time suggests that this could be Mr Conolly's path; perhaps the Handbook exaggerates and the path ran to Amharc Mór and not to the summit. And then

between 1829 and 1862 the people of Carrick had no church, just a Mass House. To build their church they carried the blocks by hand every Sunday on their way to Mass until the job was done. Such dedication and faith is more than capable of constructing a pilgrims' path in celebration of St Hugh in the release of worship that followed 1829.

VARIATIONS AND ALTERNATIVES

A: MALIN BEG: Start at Bunglass, end at Malin Beg. Follow VARIATION B and the walk to the summit of Slieve League then descend WNW into the col and onwards to the summit of Leahan (1418 ft/432 m). Then descend WSW to reach the road at Malin Beg above the tiny dazzling 'Silver Strand' (or stick to the easier cliff-top route). (10 km/6 miles, ascent 1900 ft/580 m, high point 1972 ft/601 m, <3 hrs, Moderate/Challenging.)

B: A SHORT WALK: Drive on past the Rusty Mackerel and in your car follow the route of the walk to the car-park at Bunglass and Amharc Mór. Park here and continue to follow the route as far as you wish. Return the same way. Some favour the easier Pilgrims' Path as an up-and-down route, but interesting as it is, it does not compare with the spectacular walk above Bunglass, although driving to the start of the Path does make it shorter. (Up to 10 km/6 miles, ascent 1300 ft/395 m, high point 1972 ft/601 m, <3 hrs, Easy to Challenging.)

C: OTHER WALKING: Malin Beg and Malin More both provide opportunities for ambling. At the Beg you can walk to the ruin of the 1790s signalling tower and gaze out at the island of Rathlin O'Byrne. There are more opportunities in Glencolumbkille (ask at the folk village), and Slieve Tooey on the north of the peninsula provides similar delights to Slieve League, though without the drama of the cliffs.

Pilgrims' Path

| *'Now They Ride the Wintry Dawn where Ben Bulben sets the Scene'*
BENBULBIN AND THE KING'S MOUNTAIN

For anyone who has read the poetry of William Butler Yeats (see also Walk 1), the history of St Colmcille, or the story of Diarmaid and Grainne, Benbulbin needs no introduction. This giant limestone plateau rests prominent in the landscape, the folklore and the literature of Ireland.

Map: OSi 1:50 000 Discovery Series Sheet 16, Sligo and others | Distance: 8.5 km (5 miles) | Ascent: 330 m (1080 ft) | High point: Benbulbin 526 m (1726 ft) | Naismith time: >2.5 hours | Difficulty: Challenging | Mountain rescue service: 999 | Garda station: Sligo: 071 915 7000 | Tourist information: Sligo: 071 916 1201

ADVICE AND GRADING

Benbulbin is a mountain to enjoy at all seasons. It can be a delight in winter when the sky is clear and groughs of the plateau become frozen rivers of liquid peat. Spring brings the exotic plants found sheltering in the limestone gullies, and summer finds ramblers seeking the same, a place to enjoy a picnic with a grandstand view of Yeats Country. In autumn your attention may turn to the trail of the fox, the call of the curlew or the whittering flight of the snipe and the woodcock.

The walk borders on the Moderate side of Challenging, with a warning that there is a steep descent on the return and you might

want to carry a walking-stick. But this is not a problem; VARIA-
TION A leads you down the way you went up, and provides no difficulty. Other variations and alternatives provide walking graded
from Easy to Strenuous, and plenty of variety.

GETTING THERE

The walk begins in a most tranquil spot, at the centre of a colour-
ful red bog, seemingly populated only by the occasional curlew
or the lone turf cutter. From Sligo drive north along the N15
Bundoran road for 16km (10 miles). As you drive north the
powerful profiles of Cope's Mountain, King's Mountain and
Benbulbin stand like sentries on guard above the verdant coastal
plain. Pass the road to the grave of W. B. Yeats, turn right on to a
lane signposted to Ballaghantrillick and after 2.5 km (1.5 miles),
just before Ardnaglass Bridge, turn right on to a boreen. After
another 2.5 km cross Luke's Bridge and fork right to follow the
the asphalt bog road alongside a major tributary of the Grange
river through its wide deep clough (for less than 1 km), to reach
a flat concrete bridge over the stream (MR G 703467). Park either
side of the bridge, taking care not to block the track for the
vehicles of the turf cutters.

THE WALK

Set off generally SSE along the stony track; ignore the right fork
and head toward the stream and waterfall that descend from the
plateau to the left (east) of a prominent buttress and unnamed
summit.

*As you cross this huge basin you may notice the different habits for
harvesting the turf. The plastic bag seems to have created a revolution in
peat transport and storage and here they add bright splashes of colour to
the bog. In vigorous contrast the small cairns of turves, especially those
thatched and roped, recall an older world with different skills. Living in a*

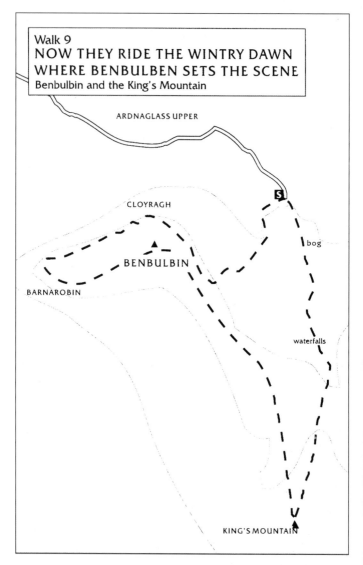

Walk 9
NOW THEY RIDE THE WINTRY DAWN
WHERE BENBULBEN SETS THE SCENE
Benbulbin and the King's Mountain

ARDNAGLASS UPPER

CLOYRAGH

BENBULBIN

BARNAROBIN

S

bog

waterfalls

KING'S MOUNTAIN

privileged society I find it difficult to be critical of others' treatment of the world, but I am aware that whilst the thatch of the traditional turf cairns will decay and return to nourish the earth fairly rapidly, the plastic bags will not. Of course it's also true to say that these bags will be used time and again by the turf cutters, a genuinely effective recycling, more so perhaps than the packaging which accompanies the food and goods that many of us buy and which then has to be buried somewhere in a landscape such as this.

When the track ends, follow the bog road around the left (east) of the higher ground, as it turns towards the SW and again reaches the banks of the stream. When the 'road' finally peters out in this fast-disappearing bog, making use of dry ground and sheep tracks head S to join the stream and take a route up the hillside alongside it.

This is a fine spot in winter. The bog walking is made easy by the frozen peat; rivulets of rainwater are cast still in their cascade down the green sward, whilst giant icicles falling over the limestone edges appear as though a still frame photograph had captured the water and rendered it motionless. The sphagnum, frozen crisp by the night air, offers a soft but firm footfall. Even in winter the water steps daintily down the mountainside, falling in a most ordered way, like a formation team of sky divers.

On the right bank are reminders that this is limestone country, for another strong stream tumbling down this hillside has a pair of swallow holes and vauclusian springs, each just a few metres apart, which demonstrate the effect most beautifully. Twice the stream disappears and twice it reappears as if miraculously, reminding us why in legend the sudden appearance of water rushing from the ground could have seemed so mysterious, and perhaps god-given. And as you proceed further it turns out that these are just a prelude to the major event where the stream disappears for some 50 m or more.

Follow the stream to its source in a wide gulley near the top of the plateau. Emerge from the gulley heading SSW and so favouring the right (west). Your next objective is the summit of the King's Mountain (Finn MacCool's Table) which lies on a bearing of 196°, SSW.

*As you rise on to the plateau, you will encounter more than one series of pits of varying sizes from about 1.5 m to 4 m across, perhaps relics of the **barytes** exploitation. On your left (east) you may spot the TV mast marking the summit of Truskmore, just inside Sligo's border with Leitrim and, at 647 m (2123 ft), the highest point in the county.*

Trust in your compass and continue for a short distance across the plateau until the summit of King's Mountain comes into view ahead of you and the promise of spectacular vistas begins to hold true. Your traverse takes you over a mound of high ground and into your first clough (a tributary of the upper reaches of King's Gulley).

Slievemore, immediately on your left, is the highest point on this part of the plateau at 466 m (1529 ft).

As you rise out of the gulley pick up one of a number of conspicuous sheep tracks running in the direction of King's Mountain. However, the ling is quite short and it is no matter if you miss them. Traverse another area of high ground with its summit on your right (west at 459 m) which is crossed by sheep paths tending to run NE–SW at a tangent to your own course, but you can make good use of them if you choose. Finally reach another clough at the foot of King's Mountain, which also runs east into King's Gulley. Cross this towards the eastern end of the mountain to take the gentler, though still a little stiff, slope to the top. Arrive at the small flat-topped summit of **Finn MacCool's Table**.

Your next objective, at a bearing of 315° NW, is the beginning of the escarpment which forms the prepossessing western nose of Benbulbin above Barnarobin. This is achieved in stages by seeking the route along the higher ground, along the saddle between Benbulbin and Cartronwilliamoge and via the triangulation pillar on Benbulbin's summit. This takes you first N, NW then WSW.

Begin by descending from the Table, the way that you came. There is a gulley to the north offering a quick descent but this is already badly eroded and should best be left alone. Now head

NNW toward the summit of Cartronwilliamoge. This will keep you on the higher ground, there are plenty of dry groughs to aid your passage, and quite early, you will gain a view of the white paint on the concrete pillar on the summit of Benbulbin. Veer NW (left) around the foot of the high ground of Cartronwilliamoge, cross a low fence taking care not to damage the wire and soon reach the saddle.

Gain a striking view of the summit of Benwiskin to the north-east and a bird's-eye view of the turf cutting before your attention is drawn progressively north toward the distinctive spit of Killogue and **Mullaghmore harbour***.*

From the saddle head NE along the crest keeping above the broad bowl on your left (south-west) and maintaining views to your left and right as long as possible, making use of the convenient sheep paths, with the changing views of Benwiskin on your right and the revealing seascape and Slieve Gamph on the left.

At a wide grough, by a wooden stake now weathered silver, the top of the white OS triangulation pillar comes into view. Cross the grough and head for the pillar across the soft carpet of ling and sphagnum moss. Reach the pillar.

In strong winds this is not a place to rest, but on a fine day look to the north-west: 7 km (4.5 miles) from the coast, you may see the island of **Inishmurray** *and closer to hand the coastal features of Streedagh Point, Back Strand and the Conors and Dernish islands.*

There are many recorded cases of ships from the Spanish Armada coming to grief on rocks along the north and west coasts of Ireland, including the Gerona that you may have encountered on Walk 5. But perhaps the best-documented account of survivors is of those whose three ships were wrecked here off Streedagh Point.

From the pillar, strike out (left) across the open mountain top, SW, perhaps aiming toward the coastal fringe to the right (west) of Knocknarae. Cross wet tussocky open mountain until you encounter the grassier fringes of rough pasture rising up the slopes of the mountain or the cap above the escarpment. Turn

Benbulbin's northern cliff

right to follow sheep paths that lead around the south-western edge and reach the western promontory – known as **Leabaidh Dhiarmaid**.

This place was once known as a spot for local poteen makers, but I find it hard to believe they brought all their tackle up here, unless of course they were barytes miners already working on the mountain. In sharp contrast below is the churchyard at Drumcliff, and the grave of Ireland's great poet William Butler Yeats. Yeats loved Sligo, and in one of his last poems wrote:

> *Under bare Ben Bulben's head*
> *In Drumcliff churchyard Yeats is laid…*
> *On limestone quarried near the spot*
> *By his command these words are cut:*
>> Cast a cold eye
>> On life, on death.
>> Horseman, pass by!

From this nose, turn NE and amble in, out and around the steep ravines scoring the vertical face of the escarpment. Eventually reach the north-eastern face of the escarpment with views down toward your starting point. Turn right (SE) and follow the top of the escarpment above this huge basin.

This appears to be an impossible way to return to your car and the start, unless you think I intend you to paraglide down. However, continue along the edge until the escarpment gives way to a steep mountain slope and the buttress of Cartronwilliamoge is in full view and a less steep shelf appears to be running northwards down the mountainside a little below you. Follow the escarpment to the higher beginnings of the shelf, and from here plan a left, right, left zigzag down the slope. The last zag should be a line N through Benwiskin and your car. Alternatively remain on the ridge and follow VARIATION A.

Reach the foot of the hill and saunter your way back to the start by making a short traverse across the cut bog to reach a gravel bog road and turn left (NW). Walk along the left bank of the stream, ford the stream and at a junction turn right (NE).

Finally, look back and savour the memory.

THE COMMENTARIES

Barytes

It has been known for perhaps two centuries that the heights between Gleniff and Benbulbin are rich in the mineral barytes, used to adulterate more expensive substances in a variety of manufacturing processes.

I assume these pits to be early open cast workings and exploration, to expose and trace the barytes lode running through the limestone of the plateau. Apparently, though there is plenty to go at, the mineral is of a generally low grade, badly stained with iron and intermixed with quartz and other impurities. Interestingly, reports dating to 1870 talk of 'a novel means of transit for minerals in the County of Sligo'. This was a very early aerial ropeway with a station on the mountain and *one in the valley. The weight of the mineral in the suspended tubs drove the machine. There is no record of its exact location and there appear to be no traces remaining today; however, it does explain the lack of slipe tracks from the mountain top. Monocable ropeways came later, but I believe a similar device was used to transport galena (lead ore) from the mines of Van Diemen's land in the Glenealo valley to the Miners' Road in Glendalough (Walk 20).*

Finn MacCool's Table.

The views from this mountain are truly breathtaking making it a place to sit with your map and learn to name the landscape: from the spurs of Cope's Mountain in the south-east to the inlet of Drumcliff Bay and Sligo harbour in the south-west; the river Garvoge, the hill of Knocknarae with Queen Maeve's cairn, Lough Gill with its romantic Isle of Inisfree made famous by Yeat's poem (Walk 1) and the distant mystery of the profiles of the Slieve Gamph.

Mullaghmore Harbour

It was Lord Palmerston (1784–1865), British Prime Minister and landowner in Ireland, who built the Mullaghmore harbour. His family mansion, Classie Bawn, can still be seen on the west of the peninsula inland from Roskeeragh point, and Palmerston apparently owned the land between Cliffony and Mullaghmore. Unlike John Adair at Derryveagh in Donegal (Walk 7) or Captain Boycott in Achill (Walk 10), Palmerston is reputed to have been a sympathetic landlord, doing away with agents, dealing directly with tenants, improving the properties and helping to reclaim areas of dune by planting bent. He must have spent a small fortune on the harbour, though I'm really not sure why; later it was used for barytes export.

Inishmurray

Significant because of its isolation, this tiny island still contains the remains of an early monastic settlement begun in the sixth century. Even though the monks left in 1100 AD, some secular islanders remained, and in 1802 the islanders claimed that their lands had descended from father to son for 700 years. In 1880 the census showed a population of 102, but this suffered the usual twentieth-century fate of island communities and was below 50 in November 1948 when the last islander finally left.

Leabaidh Dhiarmaid

I am told that at least some locals at the foot of the mountain used to call this Diarmaid's Bed. After Diarmaid eloped with Finn's betrothed Grainne, Finn chased them over every mountain and through all the glens in Ireland; there is many a dolmen known as Grainne's Bed and high place known as Finn's Seat (Seefin). But Finn and Diarmaid had been loyal friends, and many times Finn allowed Diarmaid and Grainne to escape. On one occasion, Finn even took advice from Diarmaid on the best move in a board game he was playing at the foot of the tree in which Diarmaid was hiding. Eventually the two were thought reconciled, and to celebrate they came hunting wild boar on this very mountain top.

Then in an accident Diarmaid was injured and lay dying. Now Finn had many qualities, among them the gift of healing, but he needed water. Having nothing in which to carry the precious fluid, he took it in his cupped hands, perhaps from the very source you passed earlier in your walk. But each time he knelt beside Diarmaid to offer the healing drink, the image of his betrayal with Grainne filled his thoughts and he opened his hands and let the water trickle through. Three times Finn went to get the life-saving liquor, three times he knelt beside Diarmaid, and three times he could not bring himself to pass the water to Diarmaid's lips, but opened out his cupped hands and let the precious fluid soak into the mountain and his most loyal friend die.

VARIATIONS AND ALTERNATIVES

A: A LESS STEEP DESCENT: If you would rather follow a less steep descent, simply continue SE across the saddle and rise over the unnamed summit (MR G 701455) to descend ESE into the gulley which brought you on to the plateau. Turn left (N) and descend the way you came back to your car. (10 km/6 miles, ascent 350 m/1150 ft, high point Benbulbin 526 m/1726 ft, <3 hrs, Challenging.)

B: KING S GULLEY: A less steep route up and down is provided by the very prominent King's Gulley, which leads you right to the heart of the plateau. Follow the track from MR G 704426 well into the gulley and continue straight ahead when the track goes right (east). As you emerge on to the plateau, cut SW to climb the King's Mountain and join the walk. On your return cut SE into the upper reaches of the gulley and return to your start. (13 km/8 miles, ascent 470 m/1540 ft, high point Benbulbin 526 m/1726 ft, >3.5 hrs, Strenuous)

C: A BIT OF A HILL: KNOCKNAREA: Go to the car-park at MR G 638337 and in summer follow the hordes NW up the clear path. (OS Sheet 25, 4 km/2.5 miles, ascent: 210 m/690 ft, high point Knocknarea 327 m/1073 ft, <1.5 hrs, Moderate.)

D: A WOODLAND STROLL: The Hazelwood Sculpture Trail on the shores of Lough Gill, a waymarked trail by Half Moon Bay. Head SE from Sligo on the R286 for 5 km (3 miles) and turn right to Hazelwood House and Lough Gill. Car-park at MR G 722345 (<1.5 hrs, Easy.)

E: OTHER WALKING: There is wonderful walking in the counties of Sligo and Leitrim, in the hills and lowlands, by lough, lake, river and sea.

Waterfall on King's Mountain

| *Island of Eagles*
CROAGHAUN, ACHILL

Once the home of sea eagles, Achill (Eagle Island) remains one of the jewels of Co. Mayo. It is made of the same stuff as the Sperrin Mountains (Walk 6), and evidence of the faulted and folded quartzites and schists abounds on this walk. Unlike the Sperrins, but perhaps like the Comeraghs (Walk 17), the western hills of Achill may have escaped the attention of the last ice sheet, leaving local ice to carve out the corries to the north and east of Croaghaun (see Walk 17).

Maps: Map and Guide Achill Island, Bob Kingston, 1988.
OSi 1:50 000 Discovery Series Sheet 30, Mayo | Distance: 13 km (8 miles) | Ascent: 912 m (3000 ft) | High point: Croaghaun 2192 ft (668 m) | Naismith time: >4 hours | Difficulty: Challenging/Strenuous | Rescue services: 999 | Garda station: Achill Sound: 098 45108, Westport (24 hr): 098 25555 | Tourist information: Westport: 098 25711

ADVICE AND GRADING

With sea cliffs, steep climbs and steep descents, but graded on the Challenging side of Strenuous, an average fit walker will find it straightforward. But do tell people where you are going. Mayo is the least populated of all the Irish counties, and this walk is especially quiet. At the end of one December day, in encroaching darkness, after exploring the northern corries of Croaghaun, something possessed me to go back toward Ben More. I found a woman, stranded and alone. She had been there all day and, had

I not come along, would likely have remained there until the shepherd found her the following morning. Do leave word. But don't let that put you off; with Easy, Moderate and Challenging variations, you should find something to suit.

GETTING THERE

There is a most delightful drive to the start of this walk, taking you along the fringe of coast and mountain. From Westport take the N59 around the east and north of Clew Bay to Mallaranny (Mulrany). Continue straight on at a junction as the road becomes the R319 and passes around the north of the Curraun Peninsula to reach the Michael Davitt Bridge and cross on to Achill Island. Stay with the road as it passes around mountains, through woods and across bog, forming the spine of the 'Atlantic Drive' scenic route, across the island to Dooagh (Dú Acha). The peak of Slievemore rises before you and draws you gently away from the fascination of the ranges you now leave behind, tempting you into thinking about the walk to come. As you round the heights of Minaun on your left, Croaghaun dominates your view, rising over Dooagh as though to protect it from the ravages of the Atlantic gales that plunder the strand at Keel. Pass through the village (Dooagh) and continue along the coast road for about 2.5 km (1.5 miles) until you reach the distinctive promontory past Rusheen Cove with its attendant islands of Carrickmore and Carrickmore South. Here on the right is the start of a drive which I believe leads to Carrymore Lodge. Park here on the wide lay-by on the right hand side of the road, 20 km (12 miles) out of Achill Sound by a stream which pitches its way into a roadside gutter (MR F 580044).

THE WALK

Begin your walk heading W up the tarmacked bohereen, perhaps picking the softer way along the seaward verges. Pass a lane on

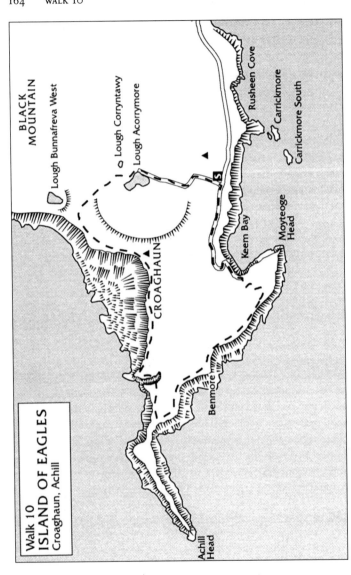

Walk 10
ISLAND OF EAGLES
Croaghaun, Achill

BLACK MOUNTAIN

Lough Bunnafreva West

Lough Corryntawy

Lough Acorrymore

Lough Corryntawy

Rusheen Cove

Carrickmore

Carrickmore South

Keem Bay

Moyteoge Head

CROAGHAUN

Benmore

Achill Head

your right signposted to Lough Accorymore, which will offer you pleasant strolling on your return.

The tiny **Dysaghy Rocks** *due south of you now may be visible only by the disturbance they create in the waves, and the island you may see beyond is probably Bills Rocks, which tells you that is not much of an island at all. But as you walk along the road you will gain good views of Moyteoge Head where you will soon be walking. Once young men would sit upon the slopes there, searching the seas for the salmon shoals that would swim around the head. Once spotted, they would shout or wave flags at their kinsmen in their curraghs in the bay, but all rather surreptitiously so as not to alert the crewmen of competing boats!*

Continue along the road accompanied by the orchestra of the ocean and of the streams that spill down the mountain and are caught by the gutter at the side of the lane. At a road junction by a small car-park, turn left (E) to follow the road to the white strand and a car-park.

I am told there was an amethyst quarry on the slopes of the mountain (Croaghaun) above you, close by the way you've just come, and a local man showed me the fragments of the semiprecious stone he had collected there. And now redundant industry of a different kind appears on your left, with two beach cabins which I assume remain from the **Achill basking shark fisheries***.*

Your next objective is the remains of the look-out post ahead of you on Moyteogue Head. To get there, take the path to the left of the stream at the back of the car-park. Head up the slope ahead, swinging L to reach the ruins of the look-out station and signalling tower.

The look-out cabin is, I guess a relic from the 1940s, but the bits of wall remaining of the tower say nothing of its origin. At first I thought it might be one of the chain of signalling towers, but it is probably a Marconi signal tower. The remains certainly look the right age. Whatever, it's a sad sight now. Interestingly, to the east are the heights of Minaun, today's centre of telecommunications.

Now go NW along the visible path which undulates close to the sharp crested ridge, and runs along the short sheep-cropped sward, sometimes following ditches, drains, dykes and walls. But take care in inclement weather. The absence of trees on Achill should tell you something about the strength of the winds from the Atlantic. Soon reach the first cliff peak called Ben More (big peak), and continue on to the summit of the small knoll to the NW.

As you traverse this ridge, below you on the right (northeast), you will see ample evidence of a deserted village. The fields show all the signs of cultivation, probably from before the famine or the time that Captain Boycott was in gaol. On the opposite bank of the stream are the ruins of the old coastguard station of Keem, and above that in a smaller triangular enclosure are the remains of a house and outbuildings rented by the infamous Captain Boycott. But more of him later. Turning to look back you may glimpse a more noble sight, the summit of Mweelrea, one of Ireland's finest mountains.

From the final knoll you can win reasonably good views of the cliffs. Only marginally better views can be obtained by scrambling along the rocks and grassy slopes of Achill Head. Personally I found it did more for my adrenalin levels than I expected! Then as you move on from the knoll you will have good views south east into the valley, to the remains of an old **booleying village**.

From the knoll descend ENE over the rough wet lea almost to sea level. Cross the stream a little inland using the fords offered by boulders and used by sheep. Then pick up a sheep track heading NW, to join a distinct drain. Follow this now, first NE and then SE, as it turns to follow the lip of a deep gulley that cuts into the flank of the mountain. This steep but progressive route will take you around the head of the gulley. Where the drain ends a shallow stream bed begins and can be seen running generally W from the brow of the mountain. Follow it and make the steep climb past the outcropping tors.

Croagh Patrick

This now takes you to a short boggy shelf and then on to the summit of a short horn, offering fine views of the cliffs. Now above some rather dramatic slabs, follow this appealing ridge as it progresses generally E to arrive at the peculiar tower of stones which serves as a summit cairn.

It's common to interpret Croaghaun as meaning round hill. But it can also mean piled hill and, looking around at the contours piled up against the cliffs, I rather think it's the latter. There's nothing to spoil the view here, not even a sight of the look-out post that a local tells me the Irish government apparently installed here in 1940. So on a clear day take a deep breath and go 'Wow!' but don't tell too many people or someone will want to build a cable car up here.

From the summit, your next objective is the lip of a corrie now hidden from view to the NE and sheltering Lough Bunnafreva West. Descend from the summit and follow the cliff edge, noting Lough Acorrymore deep in its own corrie below you on your right (east). Stay with the cliff edge until it becomes necessary to pass to the right of a deep trench that runs parallel to the cliff.

Interesting for itself, I wonder how it was formed. Is it the result of a collapsed water course or some other kind of slumping?

Finally reach the lip of the corrie harbouring the enigmatic lozenge-shaped Lough Bunnafreva West. Turn right and head SE, undulating downwards towards the lip of the much larger corrie now home to Lough Acorrymore (large corrie – would you believe!). Reach the lip and bear left and follow the lip of the corrie SE along its northern shoulder. Pass a number of gulleys on your right until you reach the very last which is quite distinctive, running north-north-east from the centre of the north-east shore of Lough Acorrymore. Step your way down this gulley (SSW) which quickly becomes a ridge of silt, thus reducing the gradient at the jaw of the corrie. Nevertheless it is very steep and needs some care, and you may prefer the alternative below. Before reaching the foot of the ridge pick up a definite sheep path running at right angles to your descent, follow it right (W) and allow it to arc you leftwards around a small boulder field on to the ridge of moraine running parallel with the shore of the lough. Follow this ridge between the two loughs, which remains wet for all its profile and location. Soon reach a large triangular-shaped rock looking like a prototype hump-backed bridge and begin to veer SE toward the dam wall.

A less hazardous route: Stay on the gentler slopes of the shoulder and head ESE above Lough Corryntawy, until level with the ridge of moraine running across the mouth of the corrie. Then turn progressively SSW and head to the east of the small lough and over the moraine ridge toward the dam wall.

Cross this dam to the sounds of the gently lapping lough waters and the tunes played by the overflow that rains down the concrete wall to the brook below. Now follow the road generally S toward the coast road.

*On the hillside below on your left are the rooftops of **Corrymore House**, once the home of the infamous **Captain Boycott**. But such things seem light years away as redwings fly before you and you gaze into Clew Bay, with a sky perhaps the hue of orange blossom as the sun sets over the Atlantic, hidden now by Croaghaun. While on Achill the Cliffs of Minaun strike a dramatic pose in the evening sun, guarding the holy well blessed by St Finnian when he returned from Lindisfarne almost 800 years ago.*

Arrive at the coast road and turn left (E) to return to your car.

THE COMMENTARIES

Dysaghy Rocks and the Achill Curragh

I am told that within living memory a local writer took out an Achill curragh, together with friends, to go to Clare Island which sits south-south-east of you in the mouth of *Clew Bay. Now the Achill curragh, which is somewhat wider than an Aran or a Galway curragh, has a reputation for great manoeuvrability. It can be rowed almost with seeming impunity in and out of rocky gulleys and coves. The lightweight boat sits like a cork on the water, and this is*

Moyteogue Head

its only real weakness, since a wave
that drops directly over it may
quickly capsize it. But to the story:
apparently the swell on the sea was
so great on this day that the curragh
was lifted up and down many fath-
oms. And, alas, as they neared the
Dysaghy Rocks hidden by the height
of the swell, the thinly constructed
curragh was dropped directly on to
the top of the rocks crashing it to
pieces and injuring its occupants. It
seems that only the writer escaped
severe injury, and he was able to

swim successfully into Keem Bay
where he reached the strand safe but
exhausted.

Achill Basking Shark Fisheries

Certorlinus maximus, *not a Roman
guidebook writer, but the
scientific name for the basking shark,
as you may know from Walk 5 and a
visit to the Giant's Causeway Visitor
Centre. On Achill they called it the
sunfish. For almost forty years after
the Second World War, Keem Strand*

was the home of the fishery and processing plant where hundreds of these giant fish were landed by men in their frail curraghs. But although it may be 9–12 m long, like me it's a vegetarian, and uses its huge jaws to filter the plankton and krill from the seawater. Its massive body is rich in oils, which put it in high demand throughout Ireland, Britain and the rest of Europe during the 1950s and 60s; this may have led to over-fishing and the decline in its population. However, the giant hulking bodies can still be seen basking off the western and northern coastlines.

Booleying Village

The name comes from the Gaelic for milk, buaile, and the practice of booleying is mentioned in several walks, including 6 and 16. The primary home was at the foot of Slievemore and the hamlet now at Dooagh was a booleying site: in fact, almost all of the settlements in the west of Achill began as booleying villages, homes for the younger members of the family whilst they grazed the livestock on summer pasture, milked them and made butter and cheese. Here there are nine distinct foundations of huts and an enclosure, perhaps still undisturbed because of their remote location.

The Corrymore House and Captain Boycott

I hope that I am not held responsible for all the sins of my countrymen. Charles Cunningham Boycott was born on 12 March 1832 at a time when at least some of my ancestors were deeply committed to challenging the ways of the ruling class. Boycott arrived in Achill in 1854. The landlord in Achill, Murray McGregor, became a close friend and by 1856 Boycott was able to lease 7000 acres of land around Lough Accorymore. The ensuing reputation Boycott developed as a land agent is well known and the tenants' strategy, fostered by the Land League, of treating him as persona non grata has entered the language as 'boycotting'. He moved to Claremorris in 1880 and eventually died in England, in 1897. Boycott was involved in various dishonest dealings during his time on Achill, convicted of assault, suing and being sued, and surrounded by stories of bad debts: he truly was an infamous man. But amidst all of this, Boycott managed to build Corrymore House in 1870, move from Keem Strand and live there for ten years.

One final small irony is the name of the bridge over Achill Sound, which you crossed to get here. Widened to a road bridge in 1947, it was originally built just as a footbridge and in 1886 was opened by Co. Mayo's most famous son, founder of the Land League, Michael Davitt. Naturally they called it the Michael Davitt Bridge.

VARIATIONS AND ALTERNATIVES

A: A SHORT WALK: Park in one of the car-parks in Keem Bay. The route runs anti-clockwise. From the remains of the coast road scramble up on to the old meadow as the walk does, then divert and take one of the sheep treads running ENE up the valley. As you near the col veer left and aim toward the cliff edge. Reach the path on the cliff edge, turn left (SE) and follow this to the ruins of the look-out post. From there descend N to the low wall, cross this and continue down to your starting point. (3.5 km/2 miles, ascent 750 ft/230 m, high point approaching Benmore 700 ft/214 m, >1.5 hrs, Easy.)

B: QUICK ASCENT: Personally I don't think the reward is worth the effort, but you may climb Croaghaun directly from Keem Bay. Follow the obvious track and stream valley running NE to N from Keem Bay to the summit. But don't be fooled; what you perceive from the bay is a false summit, the actual top is several hundred feet higher. Return the same way or follow the walk. (3 km/2 miles, ascent 2100 ft/640 m, high point Croaghaun 2192 ft/668 m, >2 hrs, Moderate/Challenging and Strenuous if you make the rest of the walk.)

C: AN EASY VIEW: Drive to the TV mast on Minaun and make the short ramble to the summit. (Easy)

D: KEEL STRAND: An afternoon or evening dawdle, when the sun illuminates the bay, easy walking with no climbing, but offering an interesting window of life on Achill. From the village of Keel go SE along the strand past the monument to Manus Sweeny, to reach the road at Dookinella. Turn left (N) and follow this to the main road. Turn left again (W), then walk alongside the road until you are able to follow the shores of Lough Keel and at the western shore veer left (SW) back to the road at Keel. (7 km/4.5 miles, <1.5 hrs, Easy.)

E: OTHER WALKING: Try the green lane to Gubalenaun More, the cape just east of Dooagh; the more adventurous walking of the Nefin Beg range, or the challenging traditional pilgrim route to the summit of Croagh Patrick.

| *A Taste of Connemara*

DERRYCLARE, BENCORR AND BENCORR BEG

What makes this country so wild? There are higher mountains, hills as remote and landscapes that can appear just as bleak. But even St Patrick never set foot here. Legend has it that he climbed to the place known as St Patrick's Bed in the windy pass of Maumean (the pass of the birds), took one look at the Twelve Bens, murmured something to the effect that no Christian soul could live there, blessed the mountains and turned back, leaving it to another less popular crusading Christian to go trudging through the wet Inagh valley in 1652. Cromwell launched his campaign against the Confederation of Kilkenny from Galway and must have taken his troops, half starved and afflicted by disease, along the foot of these mountains to defeat the army of Phelim O'Neill at Cleggan.

Maps: OSi 1:50 000 Discovery Series Sheet 37, Mayo, Galway: Folding Landscapes 1:50 000 sheet | Distance: 11 km (7 miles) | Ascent: 871 m (2860 ft) | High point: Bencorr 712 m (2336 ft) | Naismith time: >3.5 hours | Difficulty: Strenuous | Mountain rescue service: 999 | Garda station: Recess: 095 34603; Clifden (24 hours): 091 22500 | Tourist information: Galway: 091 563081; Westport: 098 25711 | Miscellaneous: Connemara National Park: 095 41054; Folding Landscapes: 095 35886

ADVICE AND GRADING

This has to be some of the wildest walking in the book, comparing with Walk 7, in Donegal. In a landscape such as this

Bencorr

there comes a point where superlatives are meaningless and simple description is sufficient to fire the imagination, once a taste of the country has been taken. So this is a walk for those who want to get into the hills, a modest introduction, no more. Nevertheless it is graded as a Strenuous walk, and intended for the experienced walker. Its difficulty should not be underestimated in bad weather. The alternatives and variations offer different and easier rambling.

GETTING THERE

From Clifden head E on the N59. Does your heart rise as you drive along the road with its views up the valley of the Owenglin river into the heart of the Twelve Bens, or do you gaze south to

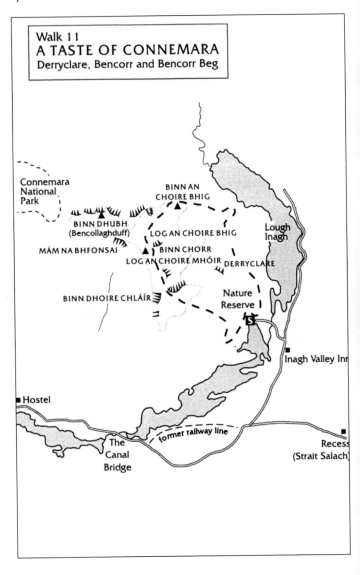

Walk 11
A TASTE OF CONNEMARA
Derryclare, Bencorr and Bencorr Beg

Connemara
National
Park

BINN AN
CHOIRE BHIG

BINN DHUBH
(Bencollaghduff)

LOG AN CHOIRE BHIG

Lough
Inagh

MÁM NA BHFONSAI

BINN CHORR

LOG AN CHOIRE MHÓIR   DERRYCLARE

BINN DHOIRE CHLÁIR

Nature
Reserve

S

Inagh Valley Inn

Hostel

former railway line

Recess
(Strait Salach)

The
Canal
Bridge

the lone profile of Errisbeg? Until you pass the An Óige hostel, resting at the foot of Ben Lettery and advance on towards the Glencoaghan river, the summits of Derryclare and Bencorr draw your view toward the Bens.

Cross the Canal Bridge traversing the narrow strait which adjoins the two loughs of Ballynahinch and Derryclare, with the sugar loaf profile of Cashel (itself easily climbed) on your right (south). Then, by the shores of Glendallagh Lough, turn left (N) on to the R344 to Letterfrack. This deep wide valley Gleann Eidhneach (Gleninagh, Glen Inagh, the ivied glen), with its open vistas and sublime views of the Twelve Bens (left/east) and the Maumturks (right/west) forces a remarkable contrast between these similar ranges.

Less than 2.2 km (1.3 miles) after the junction, pass the Inagh Valley Inn, now closed, on your left. Go for another 0.5 km (0.3 mile), reaching a narrow strip of forestry on your left which shields a gated entrance to a forestry track (opposite a neat bungalow concealed behind some trees on your right). Park here outside the gate. The gate can be locked without warning.

THE WALK

Follow the forestry track towards Lough Inagh fishery and cross the bridges over the narrow strait which divides Lough Derryclare (left/south) from Lough Inagh (right/north). Continue along the track, passing tracks to the right, and through an area of young plantation to a truning place by a stream, just before a mature plantation. Walk upstream to the junction with another stream.

Cross the stream by the confluence and take the path running NW roughly alongside the tributary. Let this stream and the gulley it has eroded guide you now over the lower slopes of Derryclare to the foot of the angular quartzite slabs. Keep the gulley on your right (northeast) and as you rise note that it has four major tributaries. Pick a route along the higher ground between the most southern (left) pair of tributaries. Soon reach a

Derryclare and pines

small shelf and head NW to reach several small rocky knolls rising to the summit of Derryclare.

Derryclare, or to give it its full Irish title, Binn Dhoire an Chláir means 'peak of the wood of the plain or plan'. Tim Robinson, a well-regarded local writer, suggests it might have been a way across the river and as such the peak has taken its name from the most local, natural or man-made feature. Which leads me to a view to the south and east of the route of the

former **Galway to Clifden railway**, which is now disappearing into the land that surrounds it.

I don't need to tell you that the views are rewarding, or more than justify the effort of the relatively minor ascent. Certainly it's easy to understand St Patrick's perspective: on a dark day it would be difficult to determine which was the most inhospitable – the blanket bog with its underlying schists and gneiss or the uncongenial quartzite slabs of the twelve Bens.

Bencorr now lies to the north-north-west across an alternately rocky and boggy saddle. There is a path for most of the route along the ridge although you must take care not to follow this too religiously as in mist it may lead you astray. I would suggest that you always thumb your way along the map, as paths can be notoriously difficult to find if you need them.

From the summit go generally NNW along the narrow summit spur/ridge, over a narrow boggy saddle, a small peak and attendant cairn to descend into the peaty col between Gleann Chóchan to your left (south-east) and the glen of Derryclare to your right (east-north-east). Pass what looks like the remains of a bothy, perhaps once a booleying hut, but more likely a religious retreat I guess. Finally reach a large pile of sharp and rocky fragments which serves as the **summit of Bencorr** and which is barely distinguishable from its cairn.

Take the steep path descending down the jagged rocks (320°) a little north of NW, which runs roughly north-north-west along a narrow ridge. This is where you must exercise caution in mist, both to avoid crossing too far west toward Bencollaghduff or confronting the impossible slopes of Carrot Ridge.

300 m from the summit of Bencorr, the popular Twelve Bens route goes left (east) around a minor peak and descends sharply from the ridge to go east toward Mám na bhFonsaí. Do not go that way. At this point (MR L 081520) you must stay on the ridge, going first N then NE along Binn an tSaighdiúra.

Binn an tSaighdiúra is an apt description, meaning the peak of the shoulder. It is said that a sapper fell to his death here. He must have been one of the team camped on the mountain and manning the beacon on Binn an Choire Mhóir in Derryclare during the first Ordnance Survey around 1833.

To the north of the end of this long peak is the famed, and possibly frightening, Carrot Ridge, well known to mountaineers as the longest rock climb in Ireland. As usual the name is a mistranslation. Although the shade of the rock does look like beta carotene, the stuff that gives the yellow-

orange colour to carrots, the name Meacan Buí really means 'yellowish lump'. I guess it's easy to see where the confusion occurred.

Again do not go that way, but descend NE into the saddle, before your final ascent to the **summit of Bencorr Beg**. Care must now be taken with your descent. The peak has a long east-running spur with southern slopes that are far more precipitous than a map might suggest and your safe route must pass between two substantial escarpments that might surprise the unwary.

From the summit stones descend E. Cross the more gentle slopes of a large shelf, edged on the north and south by steep escarpments, and begin to look for your way of passage through the dense plantation. A little south of E you may see a shale heap blighting the line of evergreen trees; this is the terminus of a forestry track and your objective (MR L 832532). Continue your descent of Bencorr Beg, getting wetter all the time, taking care not to slip on this waterlogged sponge.

Walk or swim across the open bog toward the forestry track. Cross the streams and fence and rise up on to the track. Begin the easier walking by heading generally SE through the **Derryclare Wood**. Follow the track as it undulates toward east and west but continues ever S past the long narrow rib from Bencorr, around the bold eastern spur of Derryclare and the appealing, diminutive peak of Eochair.

Eochair: they say that once you have climbed this charming little height then all of the Twelve Bens are open to you ... Let your legs get into an easy rhythm now and allow your body to relax after the rigours of these peaks. Take the time to look for the wildlife and at the flora that surround you.

Ignore all routes to the left and right until after 3 km (1.75 miles) of woodland walking you reach a forestry track junction. There turn left (SW) and follow the track back to your car.

On your left as you return, visible through the conifers, is the OPW **nature reserve**. *Now your walk is complete, turn left when you exit the wood and enjoy the drive along the Inagh valley to Kylemore and the office of the* **Connemara National Park**.

Bens and Maumturks from Loch Derryclare

THE COMMENTARIES

The Galway to Clifden Railway

Running along the southern shores of Derryclare Lough you may see faint traces of the old Galway to Clifden railway, now barely discernible in the landscape. Protracted periods of struggle and argument followed the first proposal to build the railway, around 1870, until construction began in late 1892; it opened on New Year's Day in 1895. 1935 saw the start of twenty-five years' further wrangling, followed by the decision to close the line, mainly because it was in bad need of repair and had proved to be uneconomic: the company claimed to be subsidising it heavily. An innocuous existence was punctured only by its use one night by the Black and Tans who travelled to Clifden to raze the town with fire!

The Summit of Bencorr

*Binn an Choire Mhóir, the peak of the big corrie, is also known as Binn Corr, the conical peak; the name Bencorr is found on the early OS map and was the primary triangulation point of the Ordnance Survey of 1833. Land on the horizons embraces the Aran Islands, the coast of Clare, Galway city, Achill Island and the summit of Mweelrae. Strangely enough, it is not possible to see all Twelve Bens at once from any single point on the ground, which I suppose is part of the charm and the mystery they offer. It is, however, possible to look north-west to the eastern fringes of the **Connemara National Park**.*

The Connemara National Park

I think if ever I won the National Lottery my first actions would be to buy two parcels of land, the

Mountains of Mourne to donate to the British National Trust, and those eight of the Twelve Bens not yet part of Connemara National Park. The 2000 or so hectares (5000 acres) presently in the possession of the park were acquired over ten years or so and include only four of the Twelve Bens.

The park centre is reached from Letterfrack, and offers excellent facilities as well as information on a variety of walking routes in and round the park. Other information includes an interpretation of the landscape and a discussion on the move to re-establish an Irish red deer herd within the park boundary.

Summit of Bencorr Beg

The charm of Binn an Choire Bhig, the peak of the small corrie, is in the views it gives of the way you have come as well as the blanket bog landscape below. I believe it was botanist David Bellamy who described the immense variety of bog landscape and composition here as 'terrain-bogling'. And amidst this is a recently discovered alignment of six small boulders, probably of Bronze Age date, sited on the crest of a moraine directly to the north of

you on the far bank of the river in Glen Eidhneach. Tim Robinson made the discovery during the course of the fieldwork for the Folding Landscapes map of the area. In addition a group of stones near the track to the north-east may also be remains of an ancient structure.

Derryclare Wood

The wood is, of course, the property of Coillte Teoranta, the state forestry service, and should be respected accordingly. The dominant tree seems to be Sitka spruce, but I am notorious among my rambling friends for sometimes getting these things totally wrong; certainly there is a sprinkling of birch. And here and there you will see heather, gorse, furze and a variety of wildflowers that seem able to survive, if not establish themselves, in this environment.

This surprising habitat may harbour a variety of voles and other munchies suitable for the fox and the badger, as well as an astounding variety of bird life. Keep your eyes peeled.

Nature Reserve

The OPW handbook describes this as

'an excellent example of native semi-natural woodland of the hyper-oceanic type.' So there! It is a blend of wet woodland, moorland, pond and lake shore, together with all the wildlife you might expect. There is no public access.

The reserve is a reminder of times past when even as late as Cromwell's march in the seventeenth century, life hereabouts was very different. The hills then were partly wooded and the slopes were roamed by red deer. Black eagles would feed by harrowing the herds and forcing individuals to fall over the steep escarpments to their deaths. Seals might be seen in Ballynahinsh Lake, chasing after salmon, and men would hunt wolves for fur. Perhaps then there was cause for St Patrick's caution.

VARIATIONS AND ALTERNATIVES

A: THE TWELVE BENS: Well, six of them anyway. A straightforward horseshoe walk, begining either at the An Óige hostel (MR L 777482) or from the quarry (MR L 800485). Follow the track, or cut across moor to ascend to the summit of Derryclare. Then follow the ridge in a horseshoe to reach Benlettery. Descend to the hostel or quarry. (14 km/8.5 miles, ascent 1727 m/5665 ft, high point Bencorr 712 m/2336 ft, 5/6 hrs, Difficult.)

B: THE CONNEMARA NATIONAL PARKS: Two signposted nature trails begin from the park visitor centre at Letterfrack. The easier route passes through Ellis Wood, whilst the more challenging route, the Sruffaunboy Trail, will take you to meet the Connemara ponies. There are other routes, notably up Diamond Hill. However, there are erosion problems and you should enquire at the park centre for current preferred routes.

Data for these routes obviously varies. Diamond Hill (Binn Ghuáire) is the highest point other than the Bens, at 445 m/1460 ft, offering an ascent of 385 m/1260 ft. Journey times are up to 90 minutes, with difficulties ranging from Easy, through Moderate to Challenging.

C: A WALK WITH A VIEW: Tim Robinson, of *Folding Landscapes* fame, wrote about the view from Errisbeg in a chapter of *Book of the Irish Countryside* (ed. Frank Mitchell). Beware of bathing in the pools at the summit of the mountain; legend has it that they turn your hair white, perhaps in contrast to the black crags of gabbro of the hill itself. There are a number of ways up from the south, but the most popular runs to the summit from the west, from the north-running green lane off the R341 at MR L 684398. (2 km/1 mile, ascent 870 ft/265 m, high point Errisbeg 987 ft/301 m, <1 hr, Moderate.)

D: AN EVENING STROLL: The coastline is littered with pleasant places to stroll, along strand and pier. If you're encamped in Clifden try strolling out west along the coast road, above the Owenglin river.

E: OTHER WALKING: Connemara can make you serious about walking. If it has, you could seek further advice at the Connemara National Park Visitor Centre and in particular from the staff at the library in Clifden. – Tell them I sent you!

| *Remoteness and Hardship*
ON INIS OÍRR (AN ARAN ISLAND)

Inis Oírr, east island, smallest of the three Oileán Árann (Aran islands) lies off the coasts of Galway and Clare on the rim of a harsh Atlantic sea, whose implacability is only occasionally tempered by her generosity. Though their history is hidden in the sea frets of this western coast, their low limestone profiles are littered with the remains of their past and prehistory, which have occasionally been the subject of story-telling or study; they have offered home and hope to every writer and anthropologist who has visited them since W. B. Yeats first suggested to J. M. Synge, in Paris, that these islands would be the cure for his writer's block. And so they were. Like pulling the cork out of a bottle, the Everyman adventure.

Maps: OSi Discovery Series 1:25 000 Sheet 51 – Clare, Galway, Oileán Árann, Aran Islands. *T.D.Robinson,* Oileán Árann.
Forbairt Oileán Áirainn Teo produce the Inis Oírr Way leaflet which has a very usable map | Distance: 11 km (7 miles) | Ascent: 500 ft (150 m) | High point: By Cathair na mBan 212 ft (65 m) | Naismith time <3 hours | Difficulty: Easy | Rescue services: 999 | Garda: Kilronan: 099 61102; Galway (24 hours): 091 538000 | Tourist information: Inis Mór: 099 61263; Galway: 091 537700 | Miscellaneous: Aer Árann: 091 593034, www.aerarann.ie; Boat sevices: from Doolin: 065 707 4455; from Galway and Rossveal (west coast of Co. Galway): Island Ferries: 091 568903

ADVICE AND GRADING

The best advice is 'Enjoy it!' Long summer days encourage you to

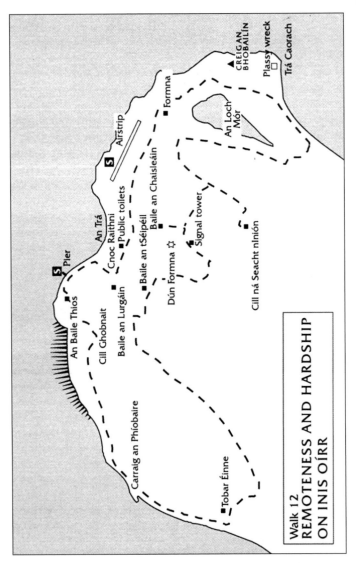

Walk 12
REMOTENESS AND HARDSHIP ON INIS OÍRR

linger, to chat to everyone you meet, and to enjoy the hospitality of the islanders of an evening. But there are no guarantees. I've known it fog-bound in spring, storm-bound in autumn, and yet have enjoyed a day-long ramble in beautiful sun in December. If the weather is dry, it is possible to walk in trainers, but some of the stonier tracks and parts of the shore can be a little uncomfortable underfoot. But all of the going is Easy and the main route is waymarked by the COSPOIR symbol of a walking person with pack, painted yellow on a black background, usually on a post.

The variations provide you with shorter or alternative routes on the island and suggestions for walks on the mainland, or the other Aran islands.

GETTING THERE

Getting there is half the fun, and turns this easy ramble into an adventure. Whether you go by the Britten – Norman Islander or Piper Aztec aeroplanes of Aer Árann, the *Happy Hooker* boat from Doolin, Co. Clare, or one of the ferries from Galway or Rossaveal, you will have to abandon your car. You don't need it and it shouldn't be a hardship. There are carparking facilities at Doolin, Rossaveal and Connemara airport (Inverin), and the operators run a bus pick-up service from Galway, if you are flying from Connemara or sailing from Rossaveal. The island has a range of accommodation from hostels to hotels; the Galway tourist office will be pleased to assist you, if you wish to stay more than a day.

THE WALK

Disembark from the ferry, walk along the pier and turn left (SE) on to the shore road to follow this towards the broad white sweep of An Trá (the strand). If you arrived at the airstrip look through the text to joint the walk at that point, marked AIRSTRIP.

Cottage on Inis Oírr

Doesn't that sound grand. But a few years ago, the island had no pier at all and travellers had to struggle ashore from the only small boats able to beach on the strand ahead of you. For the curious, there is now an information board, displaying a map of the island, on your right, and beyond that, the litter of curragh, fuel drums and pieces of fishing paraphernalia. The fragile wooden-framed, tar-coated canvas boats are, of course, the narrow Galway currachs, whilst the wider ones were originally popular around Achill (Walk 10). These days they also come in marine ply and fibreglass, and have abandoned oars for the outboard motor.

Go around the right bend, pass the slipway and strand on your left, to follow the road inland past the co-op building on your right. Take the left fork and directly ahead is **Cnoc Raithni**. (Forking right and continuing straight ahead will bring you to the commercial centre of the island, the general store and post office.) Go past the mound and turn left (ESE); pass the modern toilet block on your left and a rather desolate municipal park on your right.

The evidence that 3500 years ago the local inhabitants built a cashel with a wall more than 3 m deep (Cnoc Raithni) suggests that drifting sand has been a problem for humans as long as they have been here. Which is why you will see earth-moving machines here, out of scale with their surroundings, and why these dunes have been seeded with what I guess is bent and marram grass, now a traditional method for stabilising sand dunes, and used here to help create a base for a park and a campsite.

Ignore the road running inland to the distinctive rift valley of An Gleann below O'Brien's Castle and keep left (E) to reach a minor crossroads. Fork right of the main road to follow an old track which dissolves as you cross the dunes. Keep going and head (SE) towards the grave markers and headstones; enter the island's cemetery by gate or stile to view the ruins in the sand-surrounded hollow of **Teampull Chaomháin**. Return to the cemetery gate, turn right (NNE) and descend to the asphalt road, turn right again (ESE) and follow the road past the airstrip on your left.

AIRSTRIP: If you arrived by Aer Árann leave the airstrip and turn left to join the walk on the asphalt boreen.

As you reach the end of the Aer Árann runway on your left, continue straight ahead by the yellow symbol of the walking figure and pass a lane on your right which leads to the village of Formna. Your route, however, continues onwards to reach the distinctive stone walls and the island's field-system proper.

On your right An Loch Mór may look especially beautiful set in the tiny rift valley, with the natural limestone crags and the hand-built limestone walls, shining silver in the sun and rain that frequent Áran. The material used to fill the gaps in the walls may be recognised as various pieces of rusting salvage from the wreck of the Plassy *or empty oil drums and pig wire. Here and there, though, are gaps that have been bricked closed with limestone rocks by the traditional Aran method, between pillars of quoins; a technique developed because there was no wood for gates. All is accompanied by the occasional clanking of a zinc-coated steel gate, to remind us that the people of Áran are well able to take even the apparently most simple benefit from the modern age.*

At a junction of neat green lanes continue straight on to head S around the eastern side of the island; or if you have the time turn right (SW) and amble between the stone walls to the slipway at the shore of **An Loch Mór**.

As you rise up the bohereen, on your left you may spot a rock cairn (Creig an Bhobailín, cap of the crag) which I assume to be a fishermen's waymark. As you reach the crest you may see the twin masts of the wreck of the Plassy *and beyond them the Cliffs of Moher, supporting O'Brien's Tower and the ruins of the Moher Tower (VARIATION D). It's thought likely that the first inhabitants came from the area of Clare. Inis Oírr in particular had strong links with the county, as the name O'Brien will suggest, and there are stories of suspicions from the residents of the other islands because of Inis Oírr's proximity to the coast road. But following the invasion of the O'Flahertys in the sixteenth century, the island began to develop stronger connections with Galway.*

You also begin to see how difficult it is to farm this landscape of large Burren-like slabs of limestone. Try putting a spade in that. What fields you will see on this walk have been produced by the islanders over generations, out of sandwiches of sand and kelp gathered laboriously at the shoreline and used to transform this country with hours of back-breaking labour.

To explore the wreck of the *Plassy* at Trá Caorach turn left (E) when the wall on your left (east) ends and the lane reaches the shore by a number of kelp walls.

You may see that this spot is visited by a variety of seabirds. I particularly enjoyed watching a flock of turnstones dart their way along the shoreline and glide like one great wing over the breaking waves, while the hooded crows were cracking open shells for dinner, well camouflaged amid the grey boulders of the beach.

Now follow the causeway E alongside the wall toward the **Plassy Wreck**, respecting the danger that it represents. Curiosity satisfied, retrace your steps W from the *Plassy* and turn left back on to the coastal lane to pass a series of low kelp walls and what may be the remains of a kelp kiln.

At the first junction turn right to follow the route inland at a yellow waymark arrow. Ignore tracks off to the left and right. Follow the lane as it twists right, left, right into and out of the upper reaches of the rift valley that nurses An Loch Mór. Soon enter the village of Formna and turn left (W).

As you rise toward Formna look out over your right shoulder to a point 750 m south-east of the Plassy *to see the waves crashing over the Carraig na Finnise reef on which the* Plassy *foundered. Up the rise on your left (east) is the mystical cave known as An Uamhain (the cave). A piper went into the cave, playing his pipe so that all above the earth could trace his progress through the cave. The last they heard of him on Inis Oírr was at Carraig an Phíobaire, the piper's rock, on the west coast, which you may pass later in your walk. The piper eventually emerged unscathed from the* aran *(land) on Inis Meáin.*

The name Formna is a pre-Celtic word believed to be derived from the name of the tribe that originally occupied the island and mentioned in a number of other walks: the Fir Bolg. The site is an ideal location for a promontory fort as this bluff rises almost like the prow of a ship above the northern shoreline. Anywhere else, such as Lurigethan in Walk 4 or the Baily in Walk 1, you might look for a foss running east–west giving the final defensive line to the upturned U-plan of the fort. But not here, not unless the early inhabitants were able to cut out great slabs of limestone or somehow increase the dimensions of the grykes. I don't imagine there would have been much in the way of wood for pales either, so I would expect to see a dry stone construction. But if anything ever existed here it's likely the stone would have been stolen for new buildings for later communities.

Today, the the tourist material still describes Formna as an old-style Aran village and you may see small cabins and cottages with roped thatch. Regrettably, attractive though it is, some of the modern thatch is more reminiscent of the English shires than the west of Ireland; the slate I assume to be imported, perhaps as ballast.

O'Brien's Castle

Follow the walled road gently downhill (SSW), perhaps past goats or other livestock, to reach the second lane on your right. You will want to take this lane, but not yet. Your route now takes a spur to visit the ruins of the Cill ná Seacht nIníon, but will return to this spot shortly.

Continue to follow the 'New Road' (SSW) and as the light-house comes into view directly ahead reach two metal gates facing each other on opposite sides of the lane; turn right (W) here and take the stile to the left of the gate. Go along the right edge of three fields, and through the gaps or over the stile of three walls. In the fourth field turn left and cross it to reach a small gate hidden in the wall on your left, and the remains of the **Cill ná**

Seacht nIníon. Look and linger, before you retrace your steps along the 'New Road'. Then take the first left (NW) down the green lane that you paused at earlier in your walk past the island power station on your right.

The electricity 'grid' was built in 1977 and, whilst the transmission wires and poles may not be a delight to the eye, the introduction of electricity was well appreciated by the residents now able to buy and use the consumer goods that the rest of us so readily take for granted.

At a lane junction turn left and rise left and right up the hill toward the highest point on Inis Oírr at 65 m, by the site of Cahar na mBan (over the wall to your left/south-west) and a T-junction.

Cahar na mBan, city of the women, is described by Tim Robinson on his Aran map as 'completely ruinous and looks more like a hilltop cairn'. Nothing is known of this site or of its name, and I couldn't find a similar dedication anywhere on Áran.

At the junction turn left (WSW). Alternatively you may detour to visit Dún Formna, by turning right (N) and making a short descent of the hill to reach a stile in the wall on your left. Rise up the side of the mound bearing left between a pair of stone and cement pillars to reach the centre of **Dún Formna** and peer about the ruins of **O'Brien's Castle**. Retrace your steps up the hill to the road junction, and past the modern communications tower of Telecom Eireann.

Carry straight on SW past the ruins of the signalling tower, presumably built in 1804/5 by the British along with all the others along the west coast of Ireland begun in the 1790s, and the original National School house, to turn right and follow the yellow waymarks through a forest of limestone walls across the upper reaches of An Gleann.

The island is well supplied with fresh water, if you'll forgive the awful pun, and on your left now it bubbles to the surface through a fissure in the limestone. Though, as islanders will tell you, this isn't always so and there have been times of severe drought. Perhaps you will notice that the animal water troughs dotted in the fields usually have a large concrete catchment, to substitute for the poor surface collection qualities of the porous limestone.

As you enter Baile an tSéipéil (Chapel Village) join a stonier track and turn right (NNE); at the next T-junction turn left (NW) towards the church of St Caomhán, built as the nineteenth century turned into the twentieth.

The field walls have an amber tan from the algae but I am curious about the obviously different styles of construction as I wander about the island. The differences in field fences and house walls I can understand, and the differences created by boulders from shoreline and field. But the rest I put down to different habits, the styles of different builders with different family traditions and techniques, perhaps the differing customs of Clare and Galway. I don't know – maybe you could ask?

Pass a small monument (*mná na héireann*) and a water pump on your right to reach the church, and turn left (W) to follow a long right bend around a field on your right which sometimes harbours a donkey. Reach a rope-thatched byre at a T-junction and turn left (W) again. Then at a fork in the lane turn left (SW), whilst the shorter VARIATION A goes right (N).

As the lane progresses towards the southern part of the island, for the first time you really begin to get a feel for the wilder nature of these islands and notice how the grey herds are forced to graze in the cracks and grykes between the limestone slabs. There are times when grazing can be so poor that livestock will be tethered in the lanes to let them eat the vegetation growing there. 'Herds' is a generous term: these meagre fields support only a few animals. But it seems they have always been here, at least as long as man. Archaeological exploration of shell-sites and middens reveals that men have long kept animals and used them for food on this island.

And as you go further south along this track some simple lessons are learned. From here over the fields, over the stone walls and slabs to the lonely limestone byre in the west, the sharp Atlantic breeze blowing about your face and prattling around your clothing teaches you that this can be a different place to the warm image generated by the hospitality of the people of the island's five villages.

After 1.5 km turn right to descend WNW towards the coast. Follow the lane right (NE) and then turn immediately left (NW) again towards the west coast. Then within 300 m on your right reach a gap in the wall capped by two mudstone boulders, attractive rustic finials placed either side of the gap. Go through the gap to reach **Tobar Éinne**.

Don't worry, this is not the Hampton Court maze, and you should be able to navigate your way back to the start from this apparently isolated spot. So return to the lane, and turn right to continue walking toward the sea (W), reach the limestone shoreline track and turn right (N).

Now you are here, don't miss the chance to climb to the crest of the shingle. The small increase in height will give you a chance to look back at the limestone slabs inland, gain a different view of the rock fields or watch the Atlantic waves drumming along the beach and the strange acid-eroded formations of the limestone slabs at the shoreline. There is a vague but distinct pathway that will take you straight ahead on to the beach.

Go generally N/NE now, along the track, for a kilometre or so, passing the Piper's Rock (Carraig an Phíobaire) on your left, and fork right (ENE) at a Y-junction to walk beneath a limestone escarpment low, but long and conspicuous, on your right.

Once much more of the island looked like this, until the islanders over the centuries gathered countless tons of seaweed and sand and laid them in sandwich-like layers in order to create the fields you have seen today.

It is also this same seaweed, this 'tangle' or laminaria, that has occasionally given the islanders some cash income. During the 1930s, when the dried strands were burnt in kilns to form kelp, the government helped finance the building of the kelp walls and kilns and the rectangular enclosures you may see close by the coastline. The 'resin' was used for a variety of medical and other products, especially iodine, until modern methods allowed the production of a cheap synthetic replacement and the demand declined. In 1993, islanders were still able to earn about £130 a tonne for the dried weed, and some found it worth gathering.

As you follow the track now you can see the mainland of Galway, the hill of Errisbeg, the Twelve Bens of Connemara and the Maumturk mountains. The cairn on the left, built on the tip of a large stone, I take to be another fishermen's waymark. The shape of the escarpment now on your right, I believe, gives the local name to the village ahead which in English means 'the shin', and which on the map is called Baile an Lurgáin.

At the next T-junction the Inis Oírr Way goes left (NE) but you should turn right (S), then 40 m on the right is a gate in the wall. Go through this to the ruins of **Cill Ghobnait**. From the ruins return to the lane and turn left (NE) to descend towards An Baile Thios (West Village) to pass between the wells, water pump, freshwater mere and cultivated fields of vegetables.

At yet another lane junction turn right (ENE), twist left and right with the lane and take the next left (NE) passing the heritage house on your right, to twist right and left through the buildings to reach the shore road, with the sea ahead of you. Turn right (SE) toward the pier.

Alternatively, if you have the time, turn right at the lane junction, twist left and right with the lane, pass the heritage shop on your left and turn right to go to Baile an Lurgáin to visit the fleshpots of the island, the hotel, pub and shop.

Here you may wait for your return ferry to Galway or Doolin. Those flying by Aer Árann may wish to make their way to the pier, or Cnoc Raithní and then continue following the Walk instructions from the beginning to visit Cnoc Raithní and Teampull Chaomháin before returning to wait at the airstrip, where a nice cup of tea or a cold drink is often available.

THE COMMENTARIES

Cnoc Raithni

The hill of ferns, this modest tumulus, is one of the most significant sites in Aran as it confirms human occupation, at least on Inis Oírr, during the Bronze Age, 1500 BC. Were these the legendary Fir Bolg? This tiny hill (cnoc) was discovered after a period of heavy gales in 1885 when a few tons of sand must have been blown away, to reveal a dry stone wall encircling a low mound. Excavation found pottery urns containing cremated bones, and other decorated urns. The wall, which has foundations more than 3 m deep, was repaired in 1896.

Teampull Chaomháin

The information board will tell you that Caomhán (Cavan) was the patron saint of Inis Oírr. Argument rages as to whether he was also brother to the great St Kevin (Walk 20), but it is not without interest that the ground plan of the church is so similar to that of Trinity Church at Glendalough and may originate from the tenth century. The burial place of the saint is now protected within a stone cabin to the ENE. It it well known that many Christian buildings are on older significant sites (Walk 8), such as beacon points, burial cairns, passage graves and so on. This one was built on a midden (rubbish tip).

An Loch Mór

The big lake. This placid freshwater lough might have been a harbour but for the procrastination of official-dom and the establishment of the Aer Árann service and airstrip. More than one hundred years ago, islanders were pleading for a safe haven for their boats; the depth of the lough, measured then at more than 28 m (90 ft), and its proximity to the seashore, less than 90 m (300 ft), made An Loch Mór a favoured site and in 1893 even the Congested Districts Board urged consideration of the proposal. But it seems the repeated broken promises for its con-struction were just a sop to keep the islanders quiet. Of course it does mean that you are not now looking at an array of rusting hulks or ruined dockside furniture.

Plassy Wreck

After striking Carraig na Finnise, the reef you may see offshore (south-east), the Plassy was thrown aground in March 1960. Subsequent storm tides have driven her to this spot.

Following the furore between the islanders and Irish officials, over the rights of salvage and the unwritten Law of Wrack, you might have expected no trace of the Plassy, only stories of twilight nights and the duping of officialdom, or the raping of the landscape by some visiting salvage crew. As it is, apart from the odd fragments you may see put to good use around the island, the hulk remains here as a silent memorial, a reminder of the dangers of An Sunda ó Dheas (south sound) and of the readiness and bravery of those who live by the sea. For it was islanders who rescued the crew and helped prevent any loss of life. They say the cargo of Scotch whisky never was found.

Cill Ná Seacht nInión

The church of the seven daughters. The name remains a mystery to all, but the fiction writer in me can imagine a million stories on the ori-gin of the place and the name. Although there is now little remain-ing but foundations, the walls are noticeably different. Built as double walls with a rubble infill, they are much more articulate in their con-struction with dressed limestone blocks than the surrounding field walls.

If this and other buildings on the island were built by monks, I am curious to know what they used to form the basis for the thatching, there being virtually no trees on the island to form rafters and no turf sods to form a base for the rye-straw. And I wonder if they perhaps made wattles, woven from the 'salles' or willow rods that can be seen growing in the damp hollows and tiny rift valleys of the island.

There is now no trace of the fort that once surrounded the ruin, and that may have drawn the monks to build here (see Walk 8), but the view across the sound to the Cliffs of Moher and South Clare must be as striking as ever, if no longer strategically important.

Dún Formna and O'Brien's Castle

Both the view from the wall of Dún Formna and that from the strand and the pier tell us why this modest hill may have dominated the history of the island. The castle sits at the centre of a much older, oval fort with walls almost 3 m thick, which may be as much as 1500 years old.

There is some argument about the age of the castle. The O'Brien lands also included Clare and historians have used building programmes there to date the three-storey castle to the turn of the fifteenth century, late fourteenth century; others say it was begun a hundred years later, probably in the early sixteenth century. Either way, in 1585 they were ousted pretty brutally by the O'Flahertys from Galway. Oral history has it that until that time the island was almost entirely settled by Clare folk, but that during the twenty years after the rout the picture changed so much that most islanders are now descended from the Galway invaders.

Finally, like so many other castles, this one took a battering from Cromwell's troops during the 1650s. The last inhabitants I read of were a family of choughs, though even they seem to have departed now.

Tobar Éinne

Enda's well. Perhaps chosen by St Enda, now the patron saint of Inis Oírr, as the most remote freshwater source on the island; it is said that he lived nearby in a dry stone clochán, similar to those found on Walk 13, and the site is now venerated by islanders and pilgrims. On a balmy summer's day the water still tastes fresh and cool on a rambler's lips.

Cill Ghobnait

Named after St Gobnat, a holy woman originating from Co. Cork and a patroness of bees, who escaped from Clare as a refugee and gave her name to this small eighth- or ninth-century church. The three stone tombs covered with slabs of lime-stone I take to be the graves of a bishop and his priests, who folklore declares are buried here, whilst inside the church is an engraving with a stone cross above the altar.

By the oratory door are a number of ballauns (Walk 19) and opposite the ruin of a corbelled clochán. If you half close your eyes and let the wild scents and sounds fill your head, you might drift back a thousand years and hear monastic voices on the wind.

VARIATIONS AND ALTERNATIVES

A: TAKING THE SHORT CUT: The final part of the walk can be shortened considerably by missing out the trip to the holy well Tobar Éinne. Follow the instructions in the text. (8 km/5 miles, ascent 450 ft/140 m, high point by Cathair na mBan 212 ft/65 m, <2 hrs, Easy.)

B: HISTORICAL HIGHLIGHTS: Follow the walk and turn right (SW) as indicated in the text to climb the hill to the village of Formna. Stay on the lane through the village to regain the walk and follow this to the Baile an tSéipéil, omitting Cill ná Seacht nInión. Turn right to enter Baile an Lurgáin, commercial centre of the island, and finish your walk. You should find your way back to the pier or the airstrip without much difficulty. (4 km/2.5 miles, ascent: 300 ft/90 m, high point by Cathair na mBan 212 ft/65 m, 1 hr, Easy.)

C: HOPPING ALONG THE LITTORAL: If you plan to spend any time on Inis Oírr you should know that it is possible to walk around

Galway hooker and curragh

the southern shore along the littoral and to return to the villages along any one of the lanes running N. Use the routes at the start and finish of the walk to reach or leave the eastern and western shorelines, and follow the littoral around the rest of the island. (10 km/6 miles, ascent 130 ft/40 m, >2.5 hrs, Easy.)

D: THE CLIFFS OF MOHER: In case you only have time to visit the mainland. From the visitor centre (go in and crush a penny piece) car-park (MR R 042920) forgo O'Brien's Tower and head SW along the cliff tops to the ruins of the ubiquitous Napoleonic signalling tower at the Hag's Head (Moher Tower). Return the same way or go ESE to reach a track, turn left (N) and return to the car park along green lane and asphalt. Or consult Walk 11 in Co. Galway. (*Maps*: OSi Discovery Series 1:50 000 Sheet 51, TírEolas *The Burren – O'Brien Country.* 10 km/6 miles, 2 hrs, Easy.)

E: OTHER WALKING: There are a number of COSPOIR long-distance routes nearby, suitable for adapting to day walking. These include the Aran Way, with a walk on Inis Mór (34 km/21 miles) and a walk on Inis Meain (8 km/5 miles), and the Burren Way (45 km/28 miles). Other walking of strikingly different character can be found in south Clare, the Burren and Galway city, where there is a 'Tourist Trail of Old Galway'.

| *Next Parish, America*

MOUNT EAGLE ON THE DINGLE
PENINSULA

Dingle is a peninsula of powerful contrasts, of rolling wolds with
green fields, whin hedges, golden strands and rugged rocks, flat
coastal lowlands, blanket bog and angular craggy peaks. Once the
home of Brendan the Navigator, the monk who set sail for
America in a small leather craft, and of Tom Crean, born in
Annascaul in 1877 and a much-neglected Antarctic explorer, it is
the site of Garfinny Bridge (MR Q 475020), an unmortared stone
arch bridge, which may be one of the oldest bridges in Ireland
and Britain.

Today the peninsula draws people from around the globe, not
least to view the many artefacts of ages past that clutter the countryside, and perhaps to see Fungi, the dolphin that has made its
home in Dingle Bay.

---

*Map: OSi 1:50 000 Discovery Series Sheet 70, Kerry | Distance:
18 km (11 miles) | Ascent: 800 m (2625 ft) | High point:
Mount Eagle 515 m (1692 ft) | Naismith time: <5 hours | Difficulty:
Strenuous | Rescue service: 999 | Garda: Dingle:
066 915 1522 | Tourist information: Killarney: 064 31633*

ADVICE AND GRADING

This route offers an excellent blend of green lane, moorland and
pasture. Perhaps more of 'countryside' walking than can be had
elsewhere in Ireland. It is graded Strenuous through an even combination of distance, ascent and the feel of ground underfoot, but
it really shouldn't cause any difficulty for the average rambler.

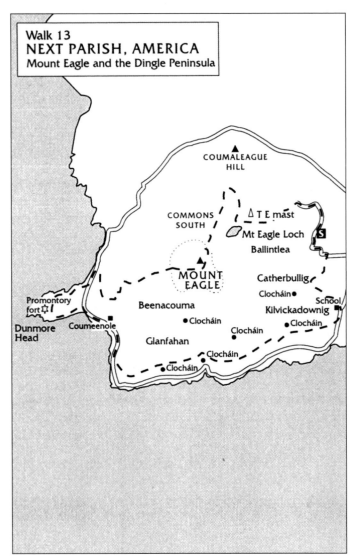

Walk 13
NEXT PARISH, AMERICA
Mount Eagle and the Dingle Peninsula

COUMALEAGUE
HILL

COMMONS
SOUTH

△ T E mast

Mt Eagle Loch

Ballintlea

MOUNT
EAGLE

Catherbullig

Clocháin●

Beenacouma

Kilvickadownig

School

Promontory
fort ☆⌘

● Clocháin

● Clocháin

Dunmore
Head

Coumeenole

● Clocháin

Glanfahan

● Clocháin

● Clocháin

Although I should warn you that it does get wet in autumn and winter, especially after periods of heavy rain – pack your gaiters, just in case! The variations provide for other walks rated Easy through to Strenuous, from evening strolls, to the opportunity to explore all of Mount Eagle.

GETTING THERE

Drive W from Ventry (MR Q 385005) along the Slea Head Drive (R559) for about 1.6 km (1 mile) to reach the heart of a small community of homes, with a church at a crossroads. Turn right to follow the signs to the An Óige hostel at Dunquin and Eagle Lake (Mount Eagle Lough); after 400 m (0.25 mile) turn left (following the signs to Eagle Lake) and after 1.25 km (0.75 mile) reach a T-junction and turn left. Reach a small clearing by the side of the lane, at the site of a vigorous stream and a boreen on your right (west): one running from Mount Eagle Lough, the other running towards it! Park your car off the road here.

THE WALK

Leave your car and walk due S along the lane, following the blue waymarks that show the route of the Pilgrim's Way, and pass an interesting byre on your right.

Inside you may look up to the roof to see the way that turf sods are used: laid over wooden laths to provide a base for the thatch. Where turf was scarce, as on Inis Oírr (Walk 12), the thatchers would probably do without, or use heather instead.

At a T-junction turn left (E) to follow the blue waymark arrows. Turning right offers you the quick ascent of Mount Eagle explained in VARIATION A. Stay with the lane as it twists right (S), left (E) and right (S) and follow the Pilgrim's Way waymark to continue straight on, past a left (east) turn and up a slightly rising road toward the tiny community at Caherbullig. Turn left (SSE) opposite a barn into a green path. Ford a stream and continue along the muddy way, between substantial dry stone walls, with their Aran gaps, covered in bramble.

At a path junction turn left (E) with the blue waymarks to pass through a modern tubular steel gate a little beyond the junction. Follow this old green pathway, sheltered but poorly drained, to reach another junction and turn right (S).

Reach another track and turn left (E) to follow the way around a right and left bend to reach the asphalt of the Slea Head Drive and turn right (S) into the heart of the townland of Kilvickadownig. Pass the School House, from 1928, on your right (west) and at a group of houses pick up a yellow COSPOIR waymark for the Dingle Way and turn right (SW) into a green lane between a bungalow and a cottage and through a modern steel gate.

As you make your way along this next stretch you may catch glimpses of the barbed and broken crags of the Skelligs. These three precipitous rocks lie about 12 km (7.5 miles) off Bolus Head. The largest, Skellig Michael, was once the home of monks, and their beehive clocháns remain; today it serves as the home of a number of species of breeding seabirds such as the Manx shearwater, storm petrel and puffin. Little Skellig is a reserve of the Irish Wildlife Conservation and is home to kittiwakes, guillemots and one of Europe's largest colonies of gannets.

Follow this pleasant, genuinely green lane, past a series of giant boulders to climb gently WSW, with fine views south toward the Iveragh Peninsula. Pass through a gap in the fence and over the stile in the wall. Continue on W across the field, to another wall and cross by the COSPOIR waymark to stay with the green lane and descend gently. At an asphalt lane junction by a small settlement follow the waymark straight on WSW.

Below you now, on the left, although generally out of sight, is the promontory fort of Dunbeg (Dún Beag). A substantial relic, Iron Age in design, it's thought to have offered shelter when the local population was under threat from some enemy. The fort can be reached by turning left off the route at this last junction, walking down to the coast road and turning right. Return the same way or remain on the coast road to regain the Dingle Way via the track on the left bank of the stream in Glanfahan.

At the next junction notice the shed belonging to the cottage; part of its walls are the remains of Teampull Beag, an early Christian church with a cross slab.

Reach a small white cottage and turn right (NW) to rise up the track. Pass a well on your left and a curious-looking isolated silt stack, topped with ling, on your right. Go beyond a gate to reach a second modern gate which leads on to open mountain by a Dingle Way waymark. Go through the gate and turn left (WSW) to follow the wall through the townland and the **City of Fahan**.

I wonder if the landward lean on the wall here has been created by centuries of sheep leaning against it for shelter?

As the path undulates gently around the slopes of Mount Eagle, reach the crest of the south-south-east spur; directly ahead westwards are the long hulks of the Blaskets. Descend into Glanfahan with fields planted with giant stone cairns. The wall turns right (N) before curving back left (W) to descend toward the stream. Well before reaching the stream look out for a Dingle Way waymark, directing you left (S) over the wall to descend through the field SW toward a gap in the far wall, and then turn left to head S across the field aiming for the point on the horizon where the river meets the sea, and reach a field gate. Go through the gate (closing it after you) and turn right (WSW). Rejoin the route here if you diverted to Dunbeg. Cross the River Glanfahan by the concrete bridge to head along the track uphill.

I'd like to tell you that these cairns are evidence of a pre-Celtic civilisation, in fact conclusive evidence of the occupation of this part of Ireland by the ancient tribe of the Fir Bolg, about whom there are many stories. But as you can see from the boulder-shattered slopes of the mountainside, the only way these green fields were created was by painstakingly collecting every fragment of conglomerate and mudstone and creating these cairns.

Three Sisters, Blaskets

Think about it as you watch the water bubbling enthusiastically down the Glanfahan river.

After a short climb fork left in front of (south) an old cottage, passing another of the curious cairns to descend across a rough clearing, past the cottage (WSW) to reach a path that passes between two walls. Rejoin the Dingle Way coming down from the right (north). Follow this green path as it undulates alongside the wall on your left.

Follow the route along the wall and up a rise which is the south-west-running spur of Mount Eagle called Beenacouma and which runs on to the sea to form Slea Head. Reach the crest of the spur (above Slea Head) and get the full view of Dunmore Head to the

north-west and the great whale hump of Great Blasket Island with its summit of Croaghmore to the west and the much smaller Beginish to the right (north-east) and Inishtooskert beyond.

Reach the wall running along the crest of the spur. Turn right (NE) for VARIATION B. Cross the wall by the Dingle Way sign and continue generally N to descend the steep grassy slopes towards the small golden strand at Coumeenole. Aim for the gate at the foot of the field by the Slea Head Drive coast road. Go through the gate and turn right (N). Enter the district of Dúnchoin and at a car-park on your left (west) pass a small Bord Fáilte plaque that commemorates **The Blaskets** and an information board for the Slea Head Drive.

Tarmac is never my favourite material for a ramble, but this can be a quiet road, busy only with village activity. That and the engaging contradictions of the landscape draw your eye away from the grey twentieth-century pad. To your right the rise to the summit of Eagle holds flourishing green fields in sharp relief to its rock-shattered brow, whilst the spirited activity of the sea at the shoreline serves only to reinforce the wilderness and wild aspect of the Blaskets. And soon you forget about the road.

Follow the tarmac N and NW through the community of Coumeenole until you reach the sign for Trá Choum euí Neóil. (If the road is busy with summer traffic, you might be able to take the green lane and cliff path and cross the fields above the cliff.) Turn left (SW) to follow the line of the asphalt boreen past the car-park and through the picnic area and at the hairpin bend going left (south-east) fork right, generally WNW, to follow a path upwards by the fence on your right. Cross a substantial wall by a stile at a gap in the fence and follow the low earth wall and fosse W around the peninsula.

After walking about 300 m from the boreen you are around the mid-portion of a plateau in the fosse and wall and directly south of the summit. Turn right (N) and climb the tussocky slopes. After a few metres spot the single-storey look-out post on the summit of Dunmore Head (Dún Mór, the big fort).

Welcome to the most westerly cape in Ireland, site of an ancient promontory fort and the ruin of a Second World War/coastguard look-out post. You may also have noticed the signalling tower above Dingle at the beginning of the walk, a relic from the Napoleonic generation of military defences. But this tiny building with its diminutive chimney gives a superb view of the Blasket islands and the surrounding coasts.

From the look-out post walk ENE toward the **Ogham stone**, from where you can see part of the route ahead, as it zigzags up the nose of the western spur of Mount Eagle.

From this point you may return the way you came, back to the road. Alternatively you descend ENE down the hill to fenced pasture and then aim NNE to reach an old cliff-top path. Follow the seaward edge of the fields until you reach a ravine running inland. Here turn right (ESE) alongside the ravine, rise to reach the road (R559) and turn left (N).

N.B. It is important to remember that this is not a right of way. If you see a farmer, seek permission to cross and take care not to damage fences and gates or disturb livestock.

Follow the road and quickly reach a left bend. On your right is the start of a farm track set in a deep cutting. Turn right into the track and follow it as it zigzags up the nose of the spur. At the end of the track rise to the fence in the corner and strike out SE up the mountain slope. Reach the crest of the spur by a short dry stone structure that looks as if it might have been an old turf stack, and turn left (NE) to follow a curving line along the crest of this widening spur, toward the summit of Eagle. For easier walking follow the line of the drain until you reach an area of isolated hags and evidence of recent turf cutting. Pass beyond this to drier slopes and views of the ridge of Beenacouma running in from the south-west; and of Brandon ahead and left, to the north-east. Reach a line of stakes identifying the path from Beenacouma and follow them E along the slight rise to the concrete triangulation post at the **summit of Mount Eagle** and sit down and have a drink and a sandwich!

From the trig. pillar head NNE toward the summit of Brandon. This takes you on a steep grassy descent along the narrow ridge of a north-running spur. (Take care not to descend too far to the east, which will lead you into the large steep-sided corrie which nurses the smaller Mount Eagle Lough.) Then at around the 450 m contour line look out for an area of exposed mudstone that marks the terminus of a bog road. Join this mudstone track and follow it as it swings around a hairpin bend and heads NNE along the ridge of the spur to provide an easy descent of the mountain. Keep right at a junction.

The track rises over the final small knoll of the spur and then heads due N toward Coumaleague Hill. At a distinct track junction fork right on to a little-used section of the original road, which now swings east and south to give a gentle descent of the mountain. You might find easier walking on the drier margins.

Once past the few islands of peat that remain to show the depth of the turf, the descent of the bog road becomes a feast of views with the whole southern coastline of Dingle, its precious jewels ornamenting the peninsula; and to the north the field patterns above Dunquin and the landscape that bid farewell to St Brendan.

Soon spot the TV mast and the hamlet of Kildurrihy, followed by the loughshore and reach a fine view of the sculptured face of the corrie. Turn left (E) with the road, but by all means dally by the loughshore if you wish. Follow the track through the gate and past the TV mast. Now remove your trainers from your sack, take off your boots and jog your way back to your car. OK! Just follow the compressed ribbon of road running between lines of fuchsia on to the hamlet of Kildurrihy below you. At a junction turn right and pass a waymark that confirms you have rejoined Pilgrim's Way. Cross a small concrete bridge and on the asphalt boreen pass the large stone between the farm buildings. Continue between a variety of buildings and a byre thatched with net, ropes, pegs and weighted with rocks. Then at a lane junction turn right (S) and follow the boreen back to your car.

THE COMMENTARIES

The City of Fahan

As you ramble into Glanfahan and rise up and over the spur ahead, toward Coumeenole, you pass through the townland of Fahan, populated with a remarkable number of well-preserved beehive huts or clocháns (clocháin), which led to its modern description as a 'city'. Some huts and ruins are visible from your route, and some (Cathair Connor and Cathair na Máiríneach for which there is a small charge) are best visited from the coast road; especially if you are on your way to rejoin the walk after visiting Dunbeg.

Wild monbretia

At least one local historian has ventured to say that before the days of the Normans the people inhabiting these huts were the serfs of the O'Falvey family who controlled the productive agriculture around Ventry; Steve MacDonogh (see VARIATION A) reports a number of other explanations, including the most recent from the historian Peter Harbison. He has suggested that the huts might have formed accommodation for those on pilgrimage along the Saint's Road to Mount Brandon, *arriving on the peninsula by sea from the south, and for similar pilgrimages to the Skelligs or other parts west. A fascinating idea. A sort of ancient ecologically friendly motorway service station and stopover.*

The Blasket Islands

I can describe the Blaskets as the most westerly group of islands off the Irish coast, comprising seven sizeable islands and isolated rocks spread in a line west by south over 4 km (2.5 miles) of the Atlantic, but none of this tells you of the attraction, or of the hardships endured by those who lived there, or of the certain sadness that remains from the passing of a way of life.

Who knows when man first set foot there? Antiquities from the early Christians include oratories, crosses and beehive cells on Inis Mhicileáin and Inis Tuaisceart and church ruins on the Great Blasket. Records show that in 1839 the islands supported thirteen families, surviving mainly on fishing and some farming. But by 1953/54, mainly because of a number of bad fishing seasons, the community moved to new homes on the mainland. It seems life had both

its hardships and its rewards, as David Quinn records in his poem 'Lucht an Oileán', Pity the Islanders:

> *...for they lived before the age of trivia*
> *and never made it to the age of anxiety, and did not suffer ennui because*
> *there was turf to be cut; for they did not rush into the future...*

and access is by boat from the pier at Dunquin.

The Ogham Stone

Starting from the bottom and reading upwards the inscription on the north-western script line reads: ERC MAQI MAQI-ERCIAS (MU) DOVINI(A). Professor Macalister, 'sometime Professor of Celtic Archaeology at University College Dublin' (as his 1945 publication describes him), says that this stone was found lying prostrate when discovered by three Cork antiquaries in 1838, and then re-erected the following year by a local priest. Which is why they now call it 'the Priest's Stone' and why Father John Casey is still remembered irrespective of the quality of his pastoral vocation. Even in 1945 it was apparently still legible, but possibly amended, for 1500 years ago, as today, differences between men led to subterfuge and it is possible that the message has an ambiguous meaning offered in order to throw potential destroyers off the scent. He thought it might commemorate the owner of the promontory fort. Unfortunately he doesn't actually tell us what it means. And though the Ogham has been retranslated into Early Irish in the Latin alphabet, it bears as much resemblance to modern Irish as does any early language to its twentieth-century descendants. The closest we can get is an early nineteenth-century suggestion that this was a place of ritual and a sanctuary of the goddess Duibhne.

The Irish Archaeological Survey reports that the earliest recorded form of the Irish language is provided by the inscriptions on Ogham stones. Ogham is an alphabetic cipher based on the Roman alphabet with each letter represented by a group of from one to five parallel lines carved to either side of a corner, or across a stem line. This stem line is usually provided by the face of one of the sharp edges. The inscription, following the instruc-

tions for deciphering, could mean:
ERC THE SON OF THE SON OF ERCIAS DESCENDANT OF DOVINIAS. *Dovinias is Duben, second-century founding ancestor of the tribe who gave their name to the present day barony Corca Duibne (I think! It all gets very complicated trying to understand the way that names change in Irish).*

There are 350 Ogham stones in Ireland and about 58 come from this area south and west of Mount Brandon. Whilst there are examples from the fourth and seventh centuries, most tend to be from the fifth or sixth century. Their relationship with the early Christian Church is not clear. Some stones are defaced, perhaps to remove their pagan origins, and some bear crosses or are found at sites with strong ecclesiastical connections. Some may have been gravestones, or boundary markers, or even associated with pilgrimage.

Summit of Mount Eagle

Your respite here may be accompanied by the Aeolian refrain created by the breeze across the waymarking metal tubular poles. These masquerade as organ pipes and fill the air with exotic melodies as you survey

Mount Brandon summit

the horizon from Ventry harbour and Dingle Bay away to Iveragh and across the broad Atlantic; then to Croaghmarhin and beyond to the coastal peaks of the Three Sisters and back to the peak of Brandon.

Finally, you may know of the MGM film Ryan's Daughter. It was on the western slopes of Croaghmarhin that they built their village, Kirarry. Don't strain to look too hard; they dismantled it when they'd finished filming, I'm pleased to say, and now the only relics are in Dunquin.

VARIATIONS AND ALTERNATIVES

A: A QUICK ASCENT: Follow the walk for about 250 m to the first junction and turn right (W). Follow the old bog route as it makes its way up the south shoulder of the corrie of Mount Eagle Lough on to the rounded slopes of the south-east spur of Eagle. Head generally W around the lip of the corrie to the summit. Follow the walk directions from there to return you to your car. (8 km/5 miles, ascent 470 m/1540 ft, high point Mount Eagle 515 m/1692 ft, <2.5 hrs, Challenging.) For additional reading: *The Dingle Peninsula,* Steve MacDonogh, Brandon, 1993.

B: ENDLESS VARIATION: Five separate routes to the summit of Eagle make for endless (well, almost) variation. In addition to the ascent and the descent covered in the walk and the ascent covered in VARIATION A, are VARIATION B1 which leaves the walk at Slea Head and heads N up the nose of Beenacouma and along the ridge to the summit (13 km/8 miles, ascent: 640 m/2100 ft, high point Mount Eagle 515 m/1692 ft, >3.5 hrs, Challenging) and VARIATION B2, which on the descent leaves the bog road above Mount Eagle Lough and heads W across Commons North and forks left twice to descend to the R559 at Dunquin. You could easily devise four different walks up Eagle and not retrace your steps. All would be under 5 hours and have a difficulty between Moderate and Challenging.

C: A SHORT WALK: DUNMORE HEAD: From the car-park at Dunmore Head (MR Q 312982) follow the route of the walk to the summit of Dunmore Head, wander at will and return roughly the same way; or walk around the perimeter of the cape. (2 km/1.25 miles, ascent 60 m/200 ft, high point Dunmore Head 96 m/315 ft, <1 hr, Easy.)

D: THE CHALLENGE OF BRANDON: My favourite Irish mountain. There are a variety of ways up or along. If you're feeling lazy you could make the 20 km (12 miles) (return) walk along the ridge from the car-park on Connor Hill (Connair Pass), but the more traditional ascent is along the Saint's Road (named the Pilgrim's Path in error on the OS 1:50 000 map; the Pilgrim's Path is further south over Mullaghveal). From Ballybrack (MR Q 424092) go NE to the summit and remains of Brendan's Oratory. Return the same way. (10 km/6 miles, ascent 960 m/3150 ft, high point Brandon Mountain 952 m/3123 ft, 3.5 hrs, but allow 5 hrs, Challenging/Strenuous.)

E: OTHER WALKING: Dingle offers about as wide a variety of walking as you can get in Ireland, from the wild peaks of Brandon to the almost pastoral experience that is so rare elsewhere in the country, and all with a wide range of interest certain to draw your attention. For example, The Three Sisters provide a memorable cliff walk, reached by following the bog road from Smerwick.

At least part of my introduction to walking in the Dingle Peninsula came from the booklets of Maurice Sheehy, a Ventry man. These are readily available in local shops and in the Dingle public library.

| *A Lakeland Ramble*

MUCKROSS AND THE KILLARNEY NATIONAL PARK

It was the ancient yew trees of the abbey that first brought me to Muckross and were the means by which I discovered the romance and drama of this popular lakeland. But I suspect it was a very different array of jewels that attracted those that came before us. Maybe it was the small deposits of copper and tin that first brought the Bronze Age dwellers to Muckross; whatever, the history of the people since then makes for a 'right riveting read', as one newspaper once proclaimed of its contents. But in this case, at least some of the evidence has lingered, for your perusal.

Maps: OSi 1:50 000 Discovery Series Sheet 78, Kerry. There is also a usable map in the OPW publication, A Visitor's Guide to Killarney National Park, 1993 | Distance: 14 km (9 miles) | Ascent: 520 m (1700 ft) | High point: Slopes of Torc Mountain 420 m (1380 ft) | Naismith time: >3.5 hours | Difficulty: Challenging | Mountain rescue service: 999 | Garda: Killarney: 064 31222 | Tourist information: Killarney: 064 31663 | Miscellaneous: Killarney National Park and Muckross House: 064 31440

ADVICE AND RATING

There's no excuse for staying in bed in Killarney; there is plenty of good walking to be had, and plenty of guidebooks offer routes across the mountains – hardly surprising, since to describe everything of interest on this walk would fill several volumes.

Loch Leane from Muckross Park

Early starters will have the friary (abbey) and the walk around Muckross to themselves, as will almost anyone walking in winter, when the trees are bare and the lough levels are high; it is quite different in the summer when the route is much more intimate and the landscape far more velveted.

For the most part the way follows a narrow asphalt ribbon that runs over island and causeway through woods, between loughs, over sandstone and limestone, past ancient yew and traditional oak: a neat blend of country park, lakeland walking and hill. And whilst the ascent of the slopes of Torc is steep in parts, with one or two large boulders *en route,* it is not unduly difficult and VARIATION A allows you to avoid the mountain altogether

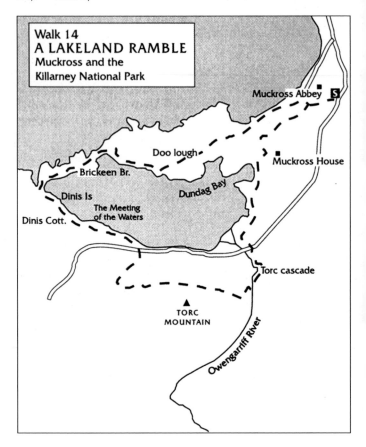

whilst still capturing the intimacy of the lakes. Finally I should say that there is such a fascinating array of trees, shrubs and plants in the Muckross gardens you might want to take a field guide. The place is also flooded with birds.

Other variations provide for a variety of different adventures, on Torc and Carrauntuohill.

GETTING THERE

From Killarney town centre take the N71 south, signposted to Kenmare and to Muckross House and gardens. After a little more than 4 km (2.5 miles) enter the Killarney National Park, then after a further 1.8 km (1 mile) at a right bend amid buildings reach the Muckross Hotel on your left and a sign pointing right (West) to Muckross Friary. Immediately opposite on the right-hand side of the road is a small car-park. Stop here (MR V 978873).

THE WALK

Leave your car and go WNW through the iron gate to take the asphalt drive and follow the sign and the drive to Muckross Abbey, perhaps past a herd of distinctive black Kerry cattle. Reach a line of lime and horse chestnut trees, go into them and turn right (N) as they reveal themselves as a most delightful formal avenue known as the Friars' Walk; follow the route of countless footsteps through history and walk toward **Muckross Abbey**. From the friary return to enjoy the enchanting view of the avenue of trees and turn right (NW) on to the main asphalt drive. At an asphalt path T-junction turn left (WSW) to follow the path signed towards Muckross House and gardens, which now runs through Monks' Wood.

Thought to be the site of the friars' garden, this wood is now a well-managed assembly of exotic trees and plants.

As the path emerges from the wood and comes close to the shore of **Lough Leane** turn right (SW) into more mixed woodland to follow the signs to Dinis Cottage and The Meeting of the Waters. At a cottage reach another path junction and carry straight on (SSW) past Arthur Vincent House (husband of Maud Bourne Vincent, mentioned later) on your right (north-west). Soon the route joins the **Arthur Young Walk**.

Where to look? At the engaging little spring, the birch trees with their roots submerged, the limestone glade or the profiles of Torc Mountain. Or perhaps to Mangerton, frequently swathed in delicate mist – a respectable mountain. Or the suggestive and potent forms of the yew trees as you pass through Reenadinna Wood – a unique natural yew wood growing on the carboniferous limestone.

After about 500 m emerge from Reenadinna Wood and continue along the path for another 400 m or so through an area of heath with grassland beyond, and as the tiny Doo Lough comes into view ahead, enter the Camillan oak wood which covers most of this peninsula. Then almost by surprise you encounter the shores of Muckross Lake.

By all means stray along the green lane toward the water's edge, where there is a small bench to rest, and listen to the waters burbling in and out of the rocks of the lake fringe and lapping on the shore, decorated with whin and bramble.

Pass a variety of information markers for the Arthur Young Walk and reach the old furnace. A curious little building; would you like to take a guess as to what it might be? So far I've read several differing accounts and none of them have anything to do with it being a furnace, but I wonder if the site nearby remains from the days of charcoal coppicing.

As you continue, discover that the asphalt becomes a virtue here; water frequently rushes across this narrow isthmus at the extreme tip of the Muckross Peninsula from Muckross Lake into Glena Bay (Lough Leane) and without it the route would be waterlogged and impossible to pass.

Cross the very neat Brickeen Bridge onto Brickeen Island. Continue through the oakwood and out on to the narrow asphalt pavement, where the waters of Muckross flow beneath the clappers of the causeway into an inlet from Glena Bay, to reach the drier shores of Dinis Island. Arrive at **Dinis Cottage** on your right and notice the map board for the park. Now continue along the pathway, bearing left; carry straight on following the signs indicating the exit to the Kenmare road at 1.5 km through oak and holly as the velvet-covered slopes of Torc now loom before you.

Reach the Kenmare road (N71) by a small parking area. To undulate your way across the northern slopes of Torc Mountain bear right (SW) and cross the road. Follow the broad track E for 30 yds. After the first bend (VARIATION A continues along the track) turn right (S) just before a large holly tree to follow the rocky path that looks as if it ought to be a stream, first as it zigzags S and then as it turns generally SW to head, between rhododendrons and brambles, for a clearing above a tiny col at about the 180 m contour and just discernible on the OS 1:50 000 scale map. Just as you appear to have gone in completely the wrong direction the path makes a turn left (SSE) to cross the col. Follow as it rises out the other side SE between the rhododendron bushes.

Don't miss the views south-west as you climb; as you rise try to look behind to the loughs and lakes of the south-west and the continuing view of the peaks in the west. I'm told that red deer sometimes roam Torc, although from my experience you are more likely to see feral goats. But in truth Torc is the main grazing area of red deer (Cervus elaphus), *the only herd in Ireland which has had a continuous existence since Red Deer arrived after the last Ice Age. However, what you are more likely to see are the smaller Japanese Sika deer* (Cervus nippon) *which are recognised by their white tail and rump, and are more common in the National Park woodlands.*

The path engages in some entertaining undulating as it rises and falls below the summit of Torc – undulating in this case means there are one or two boulders to scramble over, and entertaining means you definitely have to watch where you put your feet.

Begin to gather in the rewards of your ascent with the spectacular views over the lowlands to the north, eventually catching a glimpse of Ross Castle reflecting white in the sunlight.

Continue until you reach a small viewing clearing with a couple of wooden benches to help you see the church spire in Killarney in comfort. Go on to pass a small covered well and a dry stone front to a rock overhang which may offer some shelter in bad weather.

Still continue E, descending along the path, cross yet another delightful stream to continue on through the woods descending gently with another viewing platform and a bench.

As you proceed cross a number of small streams, then cross another stream by a tiny wooden bridge and continue down along the right (true) bank of the stream. Here mulch from fallen, only partially decayed leaves can mean you need to exercise care in descent. Pass a signpost off left to a viewing point and keep going down through the wood. At a vague path junction before a waterfall, turn sharp left (NE) (if you miss this left turn don't worry – just turn left (N) when you reach the track, which brings you to the connection with VARIATION B) into more woods and rhododendron bushes, a clearing and a shale track in a pleasant old plantation. Follow this E to a track junction and turn left (NNE) to join the old Kenmare road (now the route of the Kerry Way) and follow the direction of the sign to the car-park. After a few metres turn right (S) and descend the gravel path to a bridge over a stream and a concrete flow meter. Cross the bridge through the squeezer ENE, quickly reach a path junction and turn left (NNE) to the sound of the water falling and drumming below you.

Unfortunately the rhododendrons spoil your view of the water, although occasional viewing platforms offer some views of the waters and cascade.

Stay with the path as it descends the hillside, keeping close to the river most of the way. Descend a flight of steps to arrive at a viewing platform at the foot of the Torc Cascade.

The locals call this a waterfall, but with the volumes of tumbling water that fill the fall after heavy rains it is easy to see why the tourist promoters felt justified in calling it a cascade.

Pass through a pleasant glade as the water moves boisterously over pools and rocks and stay with the path by the river bank to reach a car-park with a toilet block and a National Park Information Office and display building.

Staying with the river, pass under the N71 Kenmare road through a small and engaging tunnel. VARIATION A rejoins the walk at this point. At a tarmac lane, fork left (W) following the right bank of the river. Pass through the kissing gates into the grounds of Muckross House and follow the driveway until you encounter, through the trees, the boathouses on your left.

As you walk along this drive don't miss the stunning example of the Monterey cypress, it must be over 30 m (100 ft) high with twenty-seven separate stands rising from the trunk. Fantastic! The rocky promontory beyond, called Dundag Point, and supporting the boathouses, may have been an iron age promontory fort; Dún Daghdha, the fort of Dagda (a mythological hero) or Dún an daig, the fort of wood. The carboniferous limestone supports an area of natural yew wood. An unsurfaced but pleasant path runs though the varied woodland close to the shoreline and is known as the Boathouse Trail.

This pair of boathouses, one wet and one dry with a fathom meter, would have kept boats wet, for ready use, and dry for long-term storage. The wet house is over a hundred years old and built with local red sandstone.

Before reaching a clearing turn right (E) and follow a gravel path through the ubiquitous rhododendron bushes, keeping to the left (NE) at a fork. Emerge on to a fine lawn and turn left (NNE) toward Muckross House.

You may now pretend that it is a Sunday in 1776 and that you and your host, Mr Thomas Herbert, are taking a constitutional stroll. The conversation has just drifted from a discussion of events in America to the 'wild prospects' of Muckross and the recent plantation of yew trees.

At the gravel track in front of the house turn left (NNW). Walk around the house, perhaps commenting to your host on the quality of the Portland stone and the various delights of his garden. Turn right with the gravel drive and arrive in front of **Muckross House**.

I am afraid that on entering you will be rudely awakened from your dreams; there is a minimal charge, which is necessary to continue the funding of the museum. Here you will find toilets, shops, a restaurant and all the other tourist paraphernalia. And a rather nice explanatory plaque of various birds that appear in the courtyard.

Carrauntuohill from Hag's Glen

From the main entrance take the driveway running through the open parkscape to continue generally N. At an asphalt crossroad turn right (E) and follow this drive as it runs towards Monks' Wood and climbs gently to meet the south-western end of the Friars' Walk you encountered earlier today. Turn left to descend amid the avenue of trees to the asphalt drive at Muckross Abbey. Turn right and return to your car.

THE COMMENTARIES

Muckross Abbey

Said to be the site of a much older establishment, the abbey was Franciscan until destroyed by

Cromwell. Strictly speaking, this is the Franciscan Friary of Irrelagh, and it is really a friary church not an abbey. The considerable set of buildings is regarded as one of the best remaining examples of the construction activity of the Franciscans in Ireland in the fifteenth century. A papal brief of 1468 notes that a building begun twenty years before was not yet complete, and other evidence, not least the building itself, shows that it must have been constructed between 1448 and 1475, probably under the patronage of the ruling MacCarthy Mor.

There is a simple church, a small sacristy and a cloister. Later the church was divided into nave and choir by inserting a tower, and a transept was added. Following the Dissolution of the Monasteries the friars struggled to retain attachment to the building in spite of harsh treatment and murder from landowners and army. An attempt at restoration made in 1626, as seen from the inscription in the north wall of the choir, seems to have been soon thwarted.

Adding an air of mystery are the yew trees, which I first came to see. One is planted at the centre of the cloister court; legend has it that it is an ancient tree and that the cloister was built around it. The Office of Public Works reports that it is rooted in the rubble of the building and so came later. I wonder if it is perhaps why so many chieftains, their clansmen and three of Kerry's poets sought to be buried here.

Lough Leane

It was across the waters of Lough Leane, one midnight in May 1558, that Lady Ellen MacCarthy, daughter and heiress of MacCarthy Mor, Earl of Clancar, was rowed to Muckross Abbey, there to marry her cousin Florence MacCarthy. Unfortunately Queen Elizabeth of England was planning a marriage for Lady Ellen that would result in MacCarthy lands falling under the control of the English Crown. The couple were arrested in July the same year and Florence imprisoned in the Tower of London. Later political manoeuvring allowed Florence his release, the recovery of his lands and the right to his titles MacCarthy Mor, Lord of Desmond (the kingdom around south Kerry and north Cork).

Arthur Young Walk

Which is exactly that. After breakfast with the owner of the estate, Mr Thomas Herbert, on 27 September

1776 Arthur Young, a sort of very well-known David Marshall (I should hope!), went for a walk to the Muckross Peninsula. Two hundred years later his notes are still published as a guide to this nature trail. Young notes that this is a new road.

Dinis Cottage

Landscaping was an essential accoutrement to the 'big house' and cottages were frequently designed as an 'incident' within the view. But the Herberts are also considered to have been progressive landlords and would have responded to such lectures as that given by architect Joseph Maguire to the Royal Dublin Society in 1867. Maguire's paper was entitled 'Healthy Dwellings for Labourers, Artisans and Middle Classes and Improved Structural Arrangements', and offered a dozen or so designs for improved dwellings. There are a number of houses on the Muckross estate that are probably products of this twin-themed ethos. Dinis may be one of them. The second cottage on the site, it was built as a lodge for entertaining visitors, in 1833, at a time when there was a Royal Commission of Enquiry into

the Conditions of the Poorer Classes in Ireland; and the riots in Belfast act like bookends around its construction.

Muckross House

What a grand place. There must have been some contrasting lifestyles here, as demonstrated by the recorded fates of the duly celebrated Thomas Herbert, owner of Muckross, and Rudolf Erich Raspe who worked as a miner in Herbert's copper mines. Raspe died of scarlet fever and is buried in an unmarked grave. Today he is recognised as the author of The Surprising Adventures of Baron Munchausen.

The house was built in 1843 for the MP for Co. Kerry. Portland stone was shipped from England and dragged over the mountains by cart, to add grandeur to the mock Elizabethan style. I think the ivy rather softens the strident pose of power and wealth the architecture was meant to convey, and the building is certainly more imposing in winter; I'm also not sure that the ivy is the best way to treat the stone.

Finally I think it worth noting that this estate was the original kernel of the Killarney National Park.

Yet another American bequest, the house and 11,000 acres were presented to the nation in 1932 as a memorial to Maud Bourne Vincent, who had received it from her parents as a wedding gift in 1910 and who died in New York in 1929. Now the house stands as a museum of Kerry folklife and offers some interesting exhibitions.

Surprisingly the gardens predate the house and are described by William Ockenden as early as 1760.

VARIATIONS AND ALTERNATIVES

A: A SHORTER WALK: Follow the walk for the first 10 km (6 miles) until you reach the Kenmare road (N71); Bear right (SW) and cross the road. Follow the broad track E through rhododendron woodland until the track drops to re-cross the N71. Follow the tarmac path to rejoin the original walk as it comes from Torc waterfall to enter Muckross Park, and so return to the start (11 km/7 miles, <2.5 hrs, Easy.)

B: A MOUNTAIN SOJOURN: TORC MOUNTAIN: Begin at the Torc Cascade car-park (MR V 966846). Follow the asphalt path (S) which leads up the Owengarriff river valley, past the Torc Cascade. Cross to the left bank at the bridge to follow the route of the old Kenmare road. Join here from the walk. Follow the old road past Torc to reach a right elbow in the river course which now runs from the south-east and Mangerton Mountain. Turn right to head NNE along the railway sleeper boardwalk eventually swinging right (NE) to the summit. Return the same way. (9 km/5.5 miles, ascent 500 m/1640 ft, high point Torc Mountain 535 m/1755 ft, <2 hrs, Moderate.)

C: EVENING AND AFTERNOON STROLLS: KILLARNEY DEMESNE: Go into the park at the entrance in Killarney opposite the cathedral (MR V 958906). There are a number of paths running to the shores of Lough Leane, Ross Bay, Ross Castle and Ross Island. Or follow

VARIATION B as far as the Torc Cascade, or the concrete water gauge and bridge, and just enjoy the woods of the old Bourne Vincent Memorial Park. All Easy.

Alternatively, this figure of eight makes use of the start and finish of the walk. Begin with the main route, and at the place indicated in the text, turn right (E). Turn right (SW) again at the next junction, follow a short length of path you have already walked and fork left and immediately right to follow the lakeside path to rejoin the main route at Muckross House. (5 km/3 miles, <2 hrs, Moderate.)

D: CARRAUNTUOHILL: For those of you wishing to climb Ireland's highest mountain. The classic route is undoubtedly the horseshoe along the peaks around Coumloughra Lough, but the *quick* ascent of Carrauntuohill lies through the Hag's Glen. I believe it was in Sean Ó Suilleabháin's book *Southwest* (New Irish Walk Guides) that I read that this glen records the most mountain accidents in Ireland. Remember that, if the weather and forecast is anything but good.

Start from the car-park at MR V 837873 and go SW on the track alongside the Gaddagh river. Pass along the spur between Loughs Gouragh and Callee into the heart of the glen and up on to the col. Turn right (NW) and follow the cairns to the summit.

Do this eight and a half times to climb the equivalent height of Mount Everest, and jog around Muckross a few times to get the trekking distance. (11 km/7 miles, ascent 900 m/2950 ft, high point Carrauntuohill 1039 m/3409 ft, 4 hrs, but allow 6, Strenuous.)

E: OTHER WALKING: There is probably more written about walking in Kerry than any other part of Ireland, especially Macgillycuddy's Reeks which contain the highest mountains in Ireland and lie to the west of this walk. For those with different tastes there are a number of short nature trails in the area of Muckross, for example the Old Boathouse Nature Trail (<1 hr) and the Arthur Young Walk (>2 hr), both signposted from in front of Muckross House.

| *From O'Sullivan Beare to the Copper Mines of Allihies*

So many of the 'beauty spots' of Ireland will fall into your lap. Not so the Beara Peninsula; you have to go and look for it. But, once found, I have no doubt that this particular combination of mountain, valley, island and sea will beguile you endlessly. For this is a landscape of imagination. Spend balmy summer Sundays at the foot of jagged rock and it might seem quite easily that you are in Provence; watch the shimmering peaks of Kerry above the silent white mists drifting across the Kenmare river bay and imagine yourself amidst far-off Asian mountains; or place yourself in the lives of those who have lived here, today or in earlier times – those who came before the peat and were perhaps just beginning to learn of metals, but left the wedge graves and standing stones, those who were willing to die in defence of this wild country, those who came to steal the copper ores from the earth, or berth their giant dreadnoughts in the waters of Bantry Bay.

Map: OSi 1:50 000 Discovery Series Sheet 83, Kerry (part) | *Distance: 16 km (10 miles)* | *Ascent: 2100 ft (640 m)* | *High point: Knockgour ridge 1200 ft (366m)* | *Naismith time: <4.5 hr* | *Difficulty: Challenging* | *Rescue services: 999* | *Garda: Castletownbere: 027 70002, Bantry (24 hours): 027 20860* | *Tourist information: Skibbereen: 028 21766*

ADVICE AND GRADING

For all but a short section early in the walk the route follows the **Beara Way**, created during 1993 and formally established in

1994. So, although this is graded as a Challenging walk, it is without real difficulty. You could probably undertake it in either direction and still feel you had saved the best until last. But interestingly, of all the walks in the book, this seems to be the one with the greatest variety of birds. So take your binoculars, for the birds and for full enjoyment of the stunning panoramic views before you. Finally you might consider combining the walk with a drive around the Beara Peninsula. As usual there are variations to suit other tastes, including a bog trotter's delight to the summit of Hungry Hill.

GETTING THERE

From Eyeries take the R575 Allihies road heading toward the prominent dome shape of Miskish Mountain (386 m/1266 ft), following the signs towards the Mass rock. One km after a cemetery turn L into a metalled bohereen with a sign for the Beara way in the bank. Follow this for a little under 2 km (1.25 miles), through a small group of houses and buildings (Inchinteskin), bearing R at a fork until you reach a narrow track on your left running at an acute angle to the boreen and marked by the distinctive COSPOIR waymark, a yellow figure on a black pillar, indicating the route of the Beara Way. Park your car off the road here (MR V 630483).

THE WALK

Leave your car and walk along the stony green lane (SE) with Miskish Mountain on your left and the northern bulge of Knockgour on your right, thus tracing a short portion of the Beara Way. Follow the track as it winds its way alongside and across the Travara stream and zigzags toward the top of the col ahead of you, lying between the two mountains. (Do not be tempted to turn left along the route of the Beara Way northwards

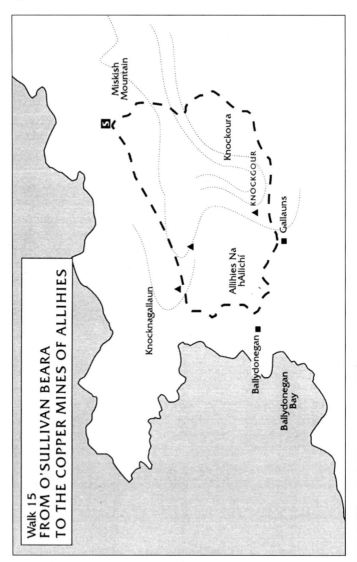

Walk 15
FROM O'SULLIVAN BEARA
TO THE COPPER MINES OF ALLIHIES

Miskish Mountain

Knockoura

Knockgour

Gallauns

Allihies Na hAilíchí

Knocknagallaun

Ballydonegan

Ballydonegan Bay

to Eyeries.) Just before reaching the top of the col, the track, heading roughly SW toward a gate, makes a sharp left turn to rise toward the crest. Stop at this point and read on.

You now have the choice of a small diversion to view the exposed capstone of a wedge grave, or to continue your walk which now runs along the Beara Way. If you choose to view the grave, continue on up the green lane to the crest of the saddle. Cross the fence by the large rustler's stile and reach the crest. *Here the playful antics of the martins compete for your attention with the view south-east to* **Bear Haven and Bear Island,** *and glimpses of the slopes of Hungry Hill and the start of the Caha Mountains off to the east-north-east.* Now follow the track left around a small outcrop until you see the remnants of the **wedge grave** ahead of you, SE across the wet bog. From the grave return to join the walk at the bend in the green lane.

At this bend the walk leaves the track and continues straight ahead (to go generally S) through a wooden forestry gate to join the Beara Way as it passes now through a Coillte Teo (State Forestry Company) plantation. From here on you may notice the occasional COSPOIR waymark.

The goldcrest must be the smallest bird in Ireland and Britain, smaller even than the ubiquitous little wren. But with its tantalising jizz and its bright orange/yellow poll, it is a delight to see. They are known to like coniferous trees and I'm sure I saw more than one as I worked my way through this plantation.

At a fork bear left (SSE) to reach the crest of the saddle, with more views of Bear Island, the headland of Muntervary and the waters of Bantry Bay; the scene of many a folk-song and folk-tale, with a history of families, flesh, and steel.

Descend through the forest and along the track with glimpses on your right of the ridge running from masted Knockgour north to the lesser summit of Knockoura. Do your best to traverse an exceptionally boggy section at a small tussocky clearing, picking the best dry line you can find. Cross a small stream and emerge from the trees as the track turns SW, to panoramic views. Cross the sheep wire and continue on through another forestry gate, fork left at a minor junction and follow the track to the S to descend into the valley. The small rocky knoll now on your left seems to be a favoured location for the **kestrel**. The road crosses and recrosses chattering streams, with miniature cataracts and small waterfalls. Finally pass ruined buildings on your right (south-west) before turning right (SW) on to an asphalt bohereen that crosses the ever-growing stream.

Tarmac walking is inevitable in Ireland unless you seek to walk exclusively on mountain or bog. For so many old tracks, which would have developed into footpaths elsewhere, served some minor community here and justified asphalt when it became available. But this is a quiet road serving only a few residents and in walking for this book, the only other creature I encountered here was a domesticated goose out for a midday ramble.

Pass through the townland of Knockoura, then as the road takes a 90° left turn, turn right (W) along an ageing metalled bohereen and head straight for the masts atop Knockgour, the mountain of the goats. The track climbing to the saddle between the mountain and the ridge can be seen as it rises into the trees.

As you reach the top of the saddle, 330 m (1083 ft) and the highest point on your walk, you may look north-north-east to the col you traversed between Miskish and Knockgour, and to the east-north-east to gaze along the Caha Mountains and the sentries of Maulin, Knocknagree and Hungry Hill that present themselves as guardians of the peninsula. Scramble to the nearest summit of the ridge on your left for a superb panorama eastwards and the chance to amble along the ridge aways southwards. To the south-south-west you may spot the signalling tower on Black Bull Head; there is a further tower on Dursey Island, which you may spot later, and a rather sad ruin on Bear Island. I assume these to be among the many that formed a chain along the west coast of Ireland, built in the early days of the Napoleonic conflicts (1790s) as a system of communication. Unfortunately even the most efficiently designed semaphore devices require clear weather. You may read of other such towers in Walks 8, 10 and 12.

There are also a number of Martello towers in the area; you may read about these in Walk 1.

Back on the track, I wonder how many pilgrims might have trekked across this spot. Ahead on the right a little up the slope of Knockgour, and now surrounded by Scottish Blackfaced sheep, is a holy well. Perhaps it earned its title from a visit by St Cloan (more later) and that was the source of its reputation for healing, or maybe the climb to this spot from the coastal plain on either side was an excuse for merriment and celebration, dancing and singing to the music of the fiddle on the flat fields below, and surely enjoying a little of the local mountain dew!

Continue W along the shale track with its rare views, as it moves down gently towards the parish of Allihies, until you reach another asphalt boreen where it bends on its way toward the summit of Knockgour; turn left (W) to sink with the road in the direction of the brightly coloured village of Allihies. Alternatively, at the junction, cross over the road and go straight ahead to descend directly towards the copper mines via VARIATION A. Or turn right to follow VARIATION B to the summit of Knockgour.

Having made the left turn on to the bohereen, you have arrived at Guala Hill (not named on the map); almost immediately on your left, some distance into the field, you may see a pair of standing stones. It is possible to follow a vague tread across the moor to these stones which, now leaning, still stand over a metre high, and appear to be siltstone or mudstone. Known also as gallauns, together with the dolmens, these and similar relics form some of the earliest evidence of human occupation in this peninsula, possibly dating from the early Bronze Age. Legend has it that two such stones mark the burial of two warrior heroes who lost their lives to each other at this spot. Whether gravestones, sites of communal activity or just 'signposts', such stones appear jumbled around the Beara.

Return to the bohereen and follow this road with its quickening views across the valley and to the mountainscape on your right.

The lush sheep-grazed grasses sprawled out above the bed of peat are scattered with tussocks of purple moor grass and other moorland plants; but the drain running alongside this valley shows the limits of the depth of this

Atlantic bog, as compared to the deep red bogs of the central lowlands of Ireland; though some would say that the turf was better here.

The distant peak to the north-east forms one of the sprawling fingers of the Slieve Miskish Mountains and is Knocknagallaun, which I assume to be 'the hill of the standing stones', though I have never spotted any there. Perhaps it is a little dramatic irony for the later occurrence of the ruins of the Allihies (Bearhaven) copper mines. The deserted engine houses stand like gallauns which creep to the edge of the village fields nestling amid the ragged outcrops and crags of the parish of Allihies.

The views remain as you descend; what I assume to be upturned and folded mudstone sediments, which now form this mountain ridge, stand in stark contrast to the turf-laden rounded contours of Knockgour and perhaps give some idea of what the land was like when the creators of the standing stones, dolmens and promotory forts first arrived.

Finally reach the T-junction in Kealogue (probably from Coill Og, young wood, though nothing remains these centuries on), and turn left (SW). At the fork immediately ahead keep right (SW).

Now pass a road on the left and immediately turn right (NW) into the wide waymarked entrance of an old boreen running between dry stone walls and offering a superb view of the mountain ridge ahead. This easy walking offers tantalising glimpses in varying directions as the green lane winds its way down through pastoral land. Cross the Ballydonegan River by a concrete bridge and begin to emerge from the valley with an impressive view of the strand on your left. This intimate little lane twists its way to a tarmac road where you turn right to reach the main village of the parish, actually called Cluin, but known to everyone as Allihies.

It was St Cloan who first brought the monks to this remote end of the peninsula, and some say it was he who gave his name to the village. But cluin *also means wet meadow, and anyone ambling in these parts will soon discover a few of those.*

Take the left fork into the village to pass a small information shed on your right. Rise up through the village (refreshments) and at a road junction fork right to follow the signs for Castletownbere

Allihies town

and the copper mines. Avoid the temptation to take a green lane on your left, instead stick with the tarmac and at another junction fork left to approach a pair of corrugated iron huts. Turn left into the wide road entrance immediately in front of the huts and swing right behind the huts, to follow the tarmac road towards the prominent ruin of the engine house.

Go through a modern gate, following the road and passing an old tailings dam on your right before turning left at a road junction.

As you close on this hillside look for a large black bird rising above the crags; in spring it might even be 'tumbling', flying upside down, or 'nose-diving'. This is the largest perching bird in Ireland, once regarded as a bird of ill-omen, and a harbinger of death, persecuted in the east and driven, like so many Celts, into the mountains here in the west: the raven. I saw bullfinches here too, carefully avoiding the raven's attention.

The road twists itself up the hillside and you are offered open views of the bay, the strand created from the mine tailings, and Bull and Cow Islands. Follow the road until it winds its way through the scarred hillside past the curious sight of dry stone walls built across spoil heaps, **Mountain Mine** on the right and reservoirs on the left. (The Beara Way waymarks may diverge from this route but will regain the track at the crest of the mountain ridge.)

Reach the crest of the saddle to a stunning vista towards the northeast.

A finger of land points out from the Beara tipped with the island of Inishfarnard, whilst beyond lie the hills of Kerry and Macgillycuddy's Reeks.

Follow the track, now chippings, stretched out ahead of you to the ENE, and entertain yourself with the view of distant mountains and the pattern of the fields on the northern coastal plain and the call of the larks in the heather. Spot the salmon fishery off the coast as you follow this stony green lane; ignore farm tracks off to the left and right but respect the occasional warning of mine shafts.

At MR V 599467 you may also spot the track off to the right that runs back up the hill towards the Mass rock. In the times of Roman Catholic oppression, senior members of the community, together with a priest, would find a site suitable for the parish community to worship in their chosen manner, away from the eyes of the Protestant authorities that would prevent them. A rock was a common object to gather around, and to act as a makeshift altar. I imagine a band of loyal look-outs, and the height of this spot would have given them fair warning of any approaching military. Today it seems popular with the stonechat, an attractive little bird with a squeaky little warble and resident in these parts.

Leave open country by a stile as Miskish once again comes into view and the road continues to run along the western spur of Knockoura. Continue to descend into the plain, the houses of Aughabrack ahead of you, in spring your route striking through a storm of wildflowers. The track joins a stream whose banks are lined with willow and furze. Reach a T-junction and turn right on to the tarmac lane (SE) to follow a left-hand bend and continue on NE to arrive at the start of your walk and regain your car.

THE COMMENTARIES

Beara Way

This route is the product of the work of the Beara Tourist Association who were able to secure agreement from the landowners for a concessionary way of 185 km (115 miles) around the Beara Peninsula. The route offers a number of opportunities for day walking and includes Dursey and Bear Islands. You can follow the route from the map, OSi Discovery Series Sheet 83.

Beara is known as a peninsula of bachelors, for so many young women have to travel to Cork and its environs to find work. So promoting the Way is part of a strategy to attract tourism to this oft-forgotten peninsula, a means to attract further trade. Ventures such as the Rally of the Lakes, which starts and finishes in Killarney, don't always bring revenue, whereas walking is perceived as environmentally friendly, bringing people to stay for several days and relax here.

Bear Haven and Bear Island

Bear Island, with the Gaelic name of An tOileán Mór (the big island) was once called Inysgraggy in a papal document of 1302. In more recent times it was a critical port of the British fleet, harbouring the super dreadnoughts of the British navy and so remaining a 'treaty port' after the partition of Ireland in 1922, even until as late as 1937. The moorland walking is pleasant here whilst Rerrin (Raerainn) offers a pleasant place to relax and take refreshment.

Knockgour from Church Cove

But perhaps the most famous story relates to the 'flight of the earls', a well-known tale in the history of the Irish/Gaelic resistance to the English. It is to the events that followed the defeat of Hugh O'Neill (Walk 6) at the battle of Kinsale (1601/2) that the 'flight' is often attributed. But here we are concerned with the story of a different hero. For after the battle, with the rout of the Spanish fleet and the defeat of Hugh O'Neill, Donal Cam O'Sullivan Beare was left with no alternative but to flee from the Beara Peninsula with his loyal band of a thousand followers and make his now famous march through Ireland to try to seek protection, arriving in Leitrim on 14 January 1603 with thirty-five followers left. And it was

here, from Bear Haven and the protection of Dunboy Castle, that they began, after Sir George Carew landed forces on Bear Island and began his siege of Dunboy Castle, finally capturing it in mid-June 1602.

Wedge Grave

Uprights and a capstone of several tons of sedimentary rock make a burial chamber that would then have been covered by rubble, to form a distinctive mound. And while this is not the most dramatic example, you do get the idea, and somehow it brings you closer to its origins than the more popular or well-known dolmens in other parts of Ireland. Certainly this land was peopled *before the growth of the bog, as can be seen by the depth of the grave, while the small islands of uncut turf that remain show the extent to which it has now been penetrated.*

The Kestrel

Unlike the hen harrier, merlin or peregrine falcons, which are few in number, the kestrel is perhaps Ireland's most common bird of prey. This small brownish bird is widespread throughout Ireland. In addition to a large population of residents, some also arrive here for a summer vacation, whilst migrants stop over, perhaps on their way to northern Africa, and yet others choose to come as winter visitors.

The bird can be recognised by its distinctive colouring of blue-grey head and tail and spotted chestnut mantle, its shrill call of kee-kee-kee-kee, *its manner of dropping sideways from its perch or of hovering stationary whilst searching for prey. And unlike the persecuted peregrine the activities of the kestrel are seen to help keep in check the populations of mice, rats, voles, insects and other life generally regarded by the farming and game community as 'pests'. Always it seems to be equally*

at home in farmland, in moorland, or above sea cliffs. Certainly there are fragments of all three habitats at this end of the peninsula; perhaps that's why the bird seems so common on this walk.

Allihies Copper Mines

I stand here with the strangest feeling, for I was born in an English village with five coal mines, surrounded by more villages with more mines. Then England experienced the biggest mine closure programme it has ever known. As if in shame, as if denying our right to mourn, the headstocks were dismantled, buildings torn down, the area levelled and slag heaps covered with grass and bushes as if to wipe out all memory of the loss. The old lived out their years in bewilderment at the destruction, their descendants torn from them, travelling in search of work; young families struggled in debt, crippled by the negative equity trap of the 1980s housing boom. To me the word 'ruin' speaks of more than just dilapidated buildings or rusting machinery. It speaks of people's lives, their homes and communities, their children's futures; of everything they had struggled to make good. And I think of Allihies and know at once why I see these ruins as both noble and grotesque.

Mountain Mine

These are the mines of Daphne du Maurier's novel Hungry Hill; *it often seems that reality is harsher than fiction. Mining was actually begun to the west sometime in 1812, by the Earl of Bantry and John Lavalin Puxley, a local Welsh landlord who rebuilt Dunboy Castle from the profits he made from these mines. Later came the open cast mining at this spot and other mines were built at Coominches and Kealogue.*

The north engine house, standing now like a giant weathered tombstone, bears an informative plaque which regrettably fails to mention the lot of the miners, or of the population of Ahillies once the mines were closed. I'm told the average life expectancy of a miner was thirty-two, compared to forty-six for those in other jobs. At forty-two I am still looking forward to a few more years.

VARIATIONS AND ALTERNATIVES

A: THE CAMINCHES VALLEY: I originally walked this route with the blessing of the farmer, but with no idea I might write about it later. So go with care and in ones and twos only. Essentially you want to drop in to the river valley and head WNW until you encounter the road.

Follow the walk until the spot marked in the text, below Knockgour and above the Caminches Stream valley. Cross over to the right and go over the old fence to the centre of the lea, toward the crest of the flat west-running spur, turn left (WNW) and pick up a bit of an old track (as the farmer described it to me.) Toward the end of the track turn left (W) and follow the path to the river. Using the available boulders, ford the Caminches river and follow the stony track W along the valley, to reach an asphalt road by a stone bridge over the river you have just crossed, and turn right (N). Alternatively you can seek the track and boreen marked on the OSi map, which will bring you to the same asphalt road, a little further north.

Follow the minor asphalt road through its twists and turns, ignoring two tracks running off to the right to rejoin the walk at the track entrance to Mountain Mine on your right (MR V 589455), by a pair of concrete buildings with corrugated roofs. Allihies lies off to your left. (Up to 13.5 km/8.5 miles, ascent 2000 ft/610 m, high point Knockgour ridge 1200 ft/366 m, <4 hrs, Moderate/Challenging.)

B: KNOCKGOUR: Not a difficult climb, and not especially interesting underfoot, but the views make it worth the effort, although you can drive all the way to the summit telecommunications tower. Park off the road at MR V 610444. Go up the asphalt service road, or up the open mountain. The service road leads to a bog road which traverses the ridge northwards if you feel inclined to walk the length of the mountain. (Up to 1.5 km/1 mile, ascent up to 600 ft/180 m, high point Knockgour ridge 1200 ft/366 m, >30 mins, Easy/Moderate.)

C: DURSEY ISLAND: Take the R572 W, stopping before plunging into the sea at Dursey Sound. Park here, (MR V 510419), check on the return times, take your picnic and close your eyes as you trundle across the terrifying sound in the tiny wooden box, no doubt built to encourage the islanders to attend Mass. Ramble around the island, respect the property and take your litter home. Or follow the route of the **Beara Way**, marked on the OSi map. (Up to 8 km/5 miles, ascent up to 1400 ft/425 m, high point Tower Hill 832 ft/254 m, <2 hrs, Moderate. Dursey Island Cablecar Co. (Cork County Council (027) 70017.)

D: HUNGRY HILL: From Adrigole take the R574 to the Healy Pass and the highest point of the road at the heart of the Caha Mountains (1000 ft/305 m); even the drive is a little adventure. Park your car either at Don's Mountain Cabin, at the side of the road before reaching the cabin, or off the road at the pass, or at the sharp right elbow on the approach (MR V 790530). Go SW and up on to the ridge and follow the line of the county boundary to the summit of Coombane, then SW to the summits of Derryclancy and Hungry Hill. Return the same way. (Up to 9 km/6 miles, ascent up to 1250 ft/380 m, high point Hungry Hill 2251 ft/690 m, Challenging.)

E: OTHER WALKING: Glengariff is a well-known walking area with a number of waymarked trails. Garinish Island is also popular. Less frequented is Bear Island, by Bear Haven where British dreadnought battleships were kept until 1938. There are two way-marked routes on Bear Island and these may be walked separately or may be linked together as one. There is also the **Beara Way**, marked on the OSi map. Ferries go from Castletownbere (Patrick Murphy (027) 75004).

| *Ireland's Inland Munro*
GALTYMORE AND GLENCOSHABINNIA

I have no belief that Mr Munro can be held resposible for the sins of those who followed him, when he made his list of mountains higher than 3000 ft. Perhaps metrication accompanying the OSi Discoverer Series maps will save Ireland from the immigration of the folly that goes by the name of 'Munro bagging'; I would hate to see the vague treads now present along parts of this mountain hammered into mud and motorway by anyone simply anxious to tick off another mountain on their 'Munro' superlist.

It was twenty-eight years ago that I climbed my first mountain with my father. I didn't know what a Munro was then, and I doubt my dad did either. I don't know how many such hills and peaks I've climbed since then, but I do know that this is one I thoroughly enjoyed. Not for the height, the kudos, the heritage or the flora and fauna, but just for the route itself, for the tremendous exhilaration of the walk. In a strange way it 'cradles' you, nurses you through its well-behaved wilderness, perhaps because its claim to fame is as Ireland's inland 'Munro'.

Map: OSi Discovery Series Sheet 74, Cork, Limerick, Tipperary, Waterford (1995) | Distance: 12 km (7.5 miles) | Ascent: 3500 ft (1070 m) | High point: Galtymore 3018 ft (920 m) | >4 hours | Difficulty: Challenging bordering on Strenuous | Mountain rescue service: 999 | Garda: Tipperary: 062 80670 | Tourist information: Tipperary: 062 80528

ADVICE AND RATING

The walk proceeds around a collision of green, Glencoshabinnia, which I guess to mean the valley at the foot of the peaks. To help you get a grasp of these peaks you may wish to make a short journey to a scenic viewpoint (MR R 886309) on the road to Tipperary that climbs over the hill Carrigeenina; and incidentally where the same road crosses the route of the Ballyhoura Way. From this spot you may see almost all of the route of the walk. If you are still new to trackless walking, this should help you work out where you are going. Take out the OSi map and study the lie of the land; try to determine the route you will be following over the hills.

If you do this to help you become clear about the route then there is no technical difficulty. It is really only the distance and the stiff ascents of Cush, Galtybeg and Galtymore that qualify this walk as Challenging. However, there is a danger presented by the lips of the corries in thick mist, and escape routes leaving the route of the walk should be considered carefully.

GETTING THERE

The start of the walk is by the bashful Clydagh Bridge (MR R 872280) on the Glen of Aherlow scenic drive parallel to, and south of the R663, running roughly east–west at the foot of the northern slopes of the Galtee mountains, in the historic Glen of Aherlow, with 'views like a geography lesson', as one writer put it. The bridge can be found by turning L off N24 10km N of Cahir, and by driving along this minor road, retiring 12 km (7.5 miles) out of Anglesborough from the south-west; and 8 km (5 miles) out of Rosadrehid from the east.

Once found, the bridge may be recognised by a small stone tablet bearing an eroded inscription and placed in the centre of its southern parapet. Park your car by the side of the road on an area

Walk 16
IRELAND'S INLAND MUNRO
Galtymore and Glencoshabinnia

GLEN OF AHERLOW

▲ KNOCKMOYLE

▲ 'CUSH'

Glencoshabinnia

L Curra

L Borheen

▲
SLIEVE-
CUSHNABINNIA

▲
GALTYMORE
MOUNTAIN

▲ GALTYBEG

▲
O'LOUGHNAN'S
CASTLE

▲
GREENANE

of land between the bridge and the small boreen to the south. This is the start of your walk, and directly to the south of you is the summit of Galtymore.

THE WALK

Leave your car and begin walking through the **Glen of Aherlow**, E along the road, over the bridge and past a farm track on your right (south), until you come to a boreen. Turn right (S) up this metalled way toward the fringes of the plantation of Stonepark;

pass a cottage and forestry entrances to rise up through the trees. Park at a widening of the road by an information board on the left. Cross a stile to follow a track rising towards the forest. At a sharp left-hand bend strike off right to the righthand corner of the forest and open moor.

Set off SSE across the flank of Knockmoyte and directly for the summit of Slievecoshabinnia ('Cush'). Take care as you cross the fences, and as you round the flank of Knockamoyte ascend slightly to take advantage of the spur which runs north-north-west from 'Cush' and which will help to ease your ascent and avoid a boggy section of moor below. Eventually reach the summit of 'Cush'.

The rewards begin arriving, even as you begin your climb, with enchanting views of the corries at the head of Glencoshabinnia, whilst from the summit of 'Cush' this handsome green amphitheatre strikes the perfect stage for the summits of Galtybeg, Galtymore and Dawson's Table, the north-running spur you will descend later in the day, and the conical hillock you will pass at the close of your walk.

To the west may be your first opportunity to glimpse the rolling hillsides of the Ballyhoura Mountains, and to the south-east the opportunity to look at the summits of O'Loughnan's Castle (a reported volcanic phenomenon) and Greenane running east from Galtybeg.

Aim now for Galtybeg which is SSW on a bearing of approximately 215° by descending along the southern spur of 'Cush'. Avoid scarring the mountain by eroding further the faint path that is beginning to develop. As you descend from 'Cush', perhaps taking time to admire the valley on your left, set between 'Cush' and the minor peak of Knockanstakeen, take care to navigate around the large steps in the slope created by a small rock outcrop and peat hags.

As you climb Galtybeg enjoy the sight of the pretty Borheen Lough in the corrie to your left. Quite where the name of the lough comes from I don't know. Perhaps a small road (bohereen) used the lough as a route marker from past days of booleying (later, and Walks 6 and 10), perhaps cattle (bo, a cow) were brought on a small road, to drink there.

Reach the col and cross it, aiming for the north-eastern spur of Galtybeg, and begin ascending. On the steeper sections of the ascent try using the steps created by the sheep grazing. It may make your ascent a little easier. The climb lessens as you reach the summit ridge.

Once you have achieved the small cairn at the end of the line of summit rocks you may collapse in a heap if you wish; however you must remember that you will need to recompose yourself for the ascent of Galtymore!

On a clear day you may gaze south-west over Coopers Wood and the An Óige youth hostel, once a hunting lodge, nestling secretly in the smooth valley, and across to the Knockmeal-down Mountains, geologically so similar to the Galtees, yet so very different in appearance, now revealing both the famous Vee Gap and the summit of Knockmealdown itself.

From the summit of Galtybeg head off W on an approximate bearing of 255° toward Galtymore. First descend toward the rim of the corrie below Galtymore. Arrive at the peat grough lying between the two mountains.

This is a fine spot to stretch out and relax, maybe have a cup of tea and wonder at the forces of nature that created this environment. The panorama to the north embraces one of the richest dairy-producing regions in the whole of Europe, and the hills forming the northern border of the Glen of Aherlow provide a variety of landscape features to hold your interest. Whilst the highest peak, Slievenamuck (1216 ft / 371 m), still retains evidence of early human occupation.

Cross any remaining groughs and keep to the dry line at the rim of the corrie, eventually turning away from the lip, to pass a small spring on your left, and climb to the summit of Galtymore.

As you climb the mountain look back and left at the whaleback summit of the southern spur of Galtybeg with its hags camouflaged and mysterious, running toward the peak of Knockeenatoung.

Reach the flat **summit of Galtymore** with its small cairn and partially destroyed concrete pillar (presumably a triangulation station), and carry on W along the broad ridge to a further cairn.

Galtymore in cloud

As you reach the summit, flattened areas of grass may testify to the way rain lashes the peak and washes over the surface of the land and down the hillside; scrubbing the lumps of conglomerate rock and boulders of ancient red sandstone as it flows.

From the second cairn continue W descending toward a prominent dry stone sheep wall which runs along the ridge above the the corrie which holds Lough Curra (Lake Corragh).

Enjoy the fine views of the lake as you descend. On a calm day it is possible to see the dramatic faces of the rock above, reflected in the lough's bible-black waters. But before you go down the hillside look to the west to enjoy the complex interlocking arrangement of peaks before you, or better still on a good day to relax on the summit of Galtymore, take out your map and identify the hills and valleys that surround you.

Aim to follow a route between the **sheep wall** and the rim of the corrie. Walking close to the wall does provide an easier line than traversing the open area of Dawson's Table, but the more interesting route is to stay around the rim of the corrie.

Whichever way you choose, eventually join the wall as it curves and reaches around the upper lip of the corrie. Then where the stone sheep wall rises up the hillside ahead of you (W) look for a route to continue taking you around the brim of the corrie and on to the prominent spur which runs northwards from the fringes of Dawson's Table. Follow the occasional sheep tread above the western shoulder of the corrie and make this final ascent on today's walk, taking the opportunity to look back at the heavily veined face of the ice-scarred rock, the summit of Galtymore and eastwards across the peaks of the Galtee range.

I have no idea of the depth of Lough Curra below you, but the waters look black and bottomless, the home of myth and magic. A curra *or* curragh *is a marsh, and I guess that refers to the northern fringes of the lough, for I have heard of no history of the better known alternative meaning to the word: a race course.*

Reach the crest of the shoulder and follow the edge of the corrie, heading N across the open moor of the spur as the view opens up before you. Begin to descend gently, leaving the rim of the corrie, to walk along the upper parts of the eastern brow of the spur or along the spine, as you choose.

Follow the rock-strewn spur in this generally N direction, descending gently, possibly passing a group of three cairns located near the nose of the spur on its eastern brow; until you arrive at a small outcrop on the more grassy lower slopes, at the nose of the spur. Turn right (E) here and descend towards a small but prominent knoll (conical hillock).

Something tells me that this must once have been a significant military spot; perhaps in the days of Donal Cam O'Sullivan Beare.

Pass around the north (left) of the knoll and bear left (N) to follow the line of a drain and small wall (with stakes) running N across open country and rough pasture. Soon pass sheep pens and reach the end of the ditch and wall. Turn right (E) through a gap in the wall and walk toward the forest and plantation. Although it is concealed as you approach, quickly reach a wooden gate, in the wall on your left (N). Turn left (N), pass beyond the gate and go along a muddy track. Moor becomes pasture and the boreen becomes green, as it is joined by other tracks from the left and right. Continue to follow the now metalled boreen as it passes homes, modern driveways and twists its way to join the Clydagh river and falls gently down the hillside to rejon the road close to the Clydagh Bridge, your starting point and hopefully your transport.

THE COMMENTARIES

Glen of Aherlow

A one-time wooded valley where saints and hermits lived and rebels and outlaws took refuge. A mile or two ahead in Ardane are the cross-slabs in the Kyles of St Berrihert, an English monk who came to Ireland after the Synod of Whitby (another good place to walk) in the seventh century. I'm told the saint also has a great holy well in the townland of Ardbane, to which, every February, pilgrims take a pebble from the running water and cast it into the well.

I must also mention one of the sadnesses of this glen; the lack of folk memory or oral tradition. For all that must have happened here there seems no community memory before 1881. In researching Walk 15 on the Beara Peninsula, I found people could tell me of virtually every place that Donal Cam O'Sullivan Beare had stopped on his epic march after the Battle of Kinsale (1601). He came through the Glen of Aherlow too, the Ballyhoura Way (COSPOIR LDWR) seeks to follow his trail, but there seems little knowledge here of the activities of Donal Cam O'Sullivan Beare and his ragged band. The Glen of Aherlow must have experienced substantial evictions.

Summit of Galtymore

Old Father Mole, the poet Spenser called this mountain, but the origin of today's name is not known. Perhaps Sliabh na Gcoillteadh, mountain of the woods. But it has also been called Slieve Grud, which might be a reference to the glen being marshy, Slieve Galton and Slieve gCrot, I know not why, and Sliabh 'Crotta Cliach', the Harps of Cliach; romantically perhaps. I think I read that it was T. J. Westropp, the antiquarian, who thought the streams of the mountain on the west end of the northern slopes appeared as the harp strings of the legendary harpist Cliu. But whatever, never ever call it 'Slieve Gawlty'! It's 'Gal' as in gallon; say it now, 'Galtea'. Which is about as close as we're going to get to the old local pronunciation of 'Gailthes' or 'Gylethes'.

Today the summit is adorned with various tokens, symbols and mementoes, as it has probably been for centuries. In addition to the cairns, close to the white cross mounted on the eastern face of one of the larger rocks forming the edge, is a bronze plaque, a memorial to James Blake and Richard Hayward. The white-painted cross carries no inscription, but look out across the glen, as you may do, from this commanding height.

Perhaps it was monks or warriors that erected the first cross here and perhaps the Celts placed their signs here too; but the forerunner of the present cross was erected in 1932 to

Bog asphodel

commemorate the 1500th anniversary of the landing of St Patrick, in Ireland. It, and the subsequent iron and stone crosses, fell victim to the pillaging of the Galtees weather. A 1950s photograph by W. A. Poucher shows a cross leaning against the concrete foundation. Today's iron Celtic cross I believe was put up in 1975, by the sons of the woman who still lives in the glen. She tells a brief but interesting tale of their struggles with the cross and a Land Rover.

Sheep Wall

You would wonder why a wall like this was built: what manorial whim or peasant necessity gave rise to the labour. Names of peaks like Greenane (summer dwelling place) tell us the hills were likely used for booleying (see Walks 6 and 10). And evidence shows that access was from the easier slopes of the south of the mountain rather than the way you have come. Families ran quite large herds of between twenty and forty cattle. In fact it seems to have been an almost total transhumance, akin to that found in the Alps. Those tending the cattle would plant potatoes and other vegetable crops by their huts and come down only to deliver butter and go for Mass. Although there does seem to have been a period when it stopped altogether when the landlord raised a seasonal charge of £3.00 per head of cattle, on a facility that had previously been free. Perhaps this was to get rid of the practice.

It does seem that the Galtees did escape much of the land war of 1881 probably because by that date Lord Kingsborough had already evicted anyone who had less than twenty acres on this side of the Galtees, and apparently rented the land to those who wished to build slate houses. This was certainly in keeping with the 'improvement' intentions of many landlords in the nineteenth century and the arrival of sheep seems very reminiscent of the activities of Mr John Adair (Walk 7) in the 1860s. The wall undoubtedly dates from that period.

VARIATIONS AND ALTERNATIVES

A: BLACK ROAD TO GALTYBEG: Take the bohereen (MR R 907176) N off the N8 which runs south of the Galtees from Michelstown to Cahir. Park just before it changes to a track. You may follow this over the slopes of Knockeenatoung towards Galtybeg, until it evaporates around the 2100 ft (640 m) contour. The mountain is yours, climb the last 800 m to the summit of Galtybeg. Return the same way. (8 km/5 miles, ascent 1475 ft/450 m, high point Galtybeg 2620 ft/798 m, >2.5 hrs, Moderate.).

B: THE GALTEE RIDGE: This is not a circular walk, so you will need to decide what to do about getting to/from the start and end. And it really only forms a route suggestion, you will need to plan your way on the map. The route keeps to the highest ground of the spine of the range and runs west to east, from Baurnaugurray farm (MR R 815222 off the R513) by the edge of a plantation to

Temple Hill, along Lyracappul, Greenane and Slieveanard and the final unnamed summit before descending through a plantation ride to reach the N24 which goes S to Cahir. (29 km/18 miles, ascent 4300 ft/1300 m, high point Galtymore 3018 ft/920 m, 8 hrs, Grade 6 – Difficult and then some. Stunningly rewarding.)

C: BANSHA WOODS: West of the N28, just north of Bansha and on the eastern slopes of The Steeple, are the Bansha Woods (MR R 934334). There are red squirrel here, so rare now in other parts of Western Europe, and Moor's Rock yields views of the three counties of Cork, Limerick and Tipperary, whilst the Coillte trail provides waymarked walking. Don't waste your time looking for the Aherlow Castle. It was a nineteenth-century pasteboard job now demolished. (6.5 km/4 miles, ascent 300 ft/100 m, <2 hrs, Easy.)

D: THE DEVILSBIT: To the north by Templemore is the Devilsbit Mountain. See walk 19D.

E: OTHER WALKING: In addition to the whole Galtee ridge other interesting walking abounds. To the north are the Slieve Felim and the Silvermine Mountains; to the west, the gentle pastoral landscape of the Ballyhoura Mountains; whilst the Knockmealdown Mountains lie to the south and Slievenamon and the Comeragh Mountains (Walk 17) are to the east. Not the tall towers of the western fringe, but fine places to be.

You will find helpful literature available on walking in the Ballyhoura Mountains, providing worry-free rambling in a pastoral landscape, something that a lack of footpaths or a right of way can make quite rare in lowland Ireland. The Ballyhoura Mountain Park holds woodland, rugged mountain, grouse moor and peat bog with an abundance of wild plants and berries, and an interesting assortment of wildlife from the natterjack toad to the peregrine falcon. Signposted off the R512.

| *Wilderness and Beauty in the Comeragh Mountains*

A WALK AMID WILD CORRIES

Silver rivers and glittering corries are set amid sandstone and shale in a mountain wilderness that rises steeply and without ceremony from the fields and hedgerows of the fertile plain below. This is a quiet retiring landscape that rarely trumpets its own merit or vies for prominence amongst the favoured rambles of walkers.

Maps: Comeragh Mountains, Nire Valley, Co. Waterford. Scale 1:25 000, 1992. OSi 1:50 000 Discovery Series Sheet 75, Kilkenny, Tipperary, Waterford (North) | Distance: 15 km (9 miles) | Ascent: 900 m (2950 ft) | High point: Fauscoum 800 m (2625 ft) | Naismith time: 4.5 hours | Difficulty: Strenuous | Mountain rescue service: 999 | Garda station: Clonmel: 052 77640 | Tourist information: Waterford: 051 875823 | Miscellaneous: The 1:25 000 map is published by Eileen Ryan (052 36141) and available locally

---

ADVICE AND GRADING

Lacking the sights and signs of commercial heritage, this route provides a captivating walk that offers an unusual blend of solitude and silence in the middle of wilderness and spellbinding views. It makes a comprehensive introduction to the two mountain ranges of the Monavullagh and the Comeragh and traverses their highest point, Fauscoum, the low blanket bog peak that takes its name from the 'wild corrie' to the south-east.

But it is definitely a walk for those competent with map and compass. If you are not and the mist comes down, you might face a long walk home, assuming you are not injured from a fall. There is no serious walking difficulty, but for the most part there are no paths and walking across bog can be a little tiring. Finally, there is steep descent into The Gap, which requires some care. The variations provide easier, quicker alternatives, and all in all, they are walks I really enjoyed.

GETTING THERE

The walk starts in the heart of the Comeragh Mountains deep in the Nire valley at the foot of Knocknaffrin. From Clonmel head for Harney's Crossroads (SSE), by taking the road signposted to the golf course. At the crossroads turn right (SSW) to join and follow the 'Comeragh Drive'.

As the road climbs close to the summit of a small hill on your right (Crocdubh, 440 m/1443 ft), the Comeragh ridge is clearly visible to your left, running north-west/south-east. Immediately on your left (east) and the most northerly peak is Shauneenabreaga at a modest 535 m (1755 ft), followed by Knocksheengowna (675 m/2215 ft) and the most prominent peak, Knocknaffrin (755 m/2477 ft).

After 5 km (3 miles) reach Birchell's Bridge over the River Nire. Turn immediately left (E), signposted to Hanora's Cottage and the Nire Lakes. Continue on for a further 4 km (2.5 miles), pass over Labartt's Bridge and by Hanora's Cottage, the school and the Nire valley church, and ignore the two roads off to your left. Then pass through a picturesque farmyard to reach a barrier at the end of the road in the townland of Knocknaffrin. Turn left into the car-park and park your car (MR S 278128).

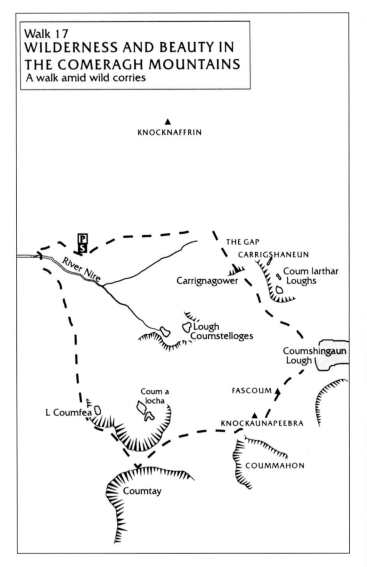

Walk 17
WILDERNESS AND BEAUTY IN THE COMERAGH MOUNTAINS
A walk amid wild corries

▲
KNOCKNAFFRIN

THE GAP
CARRIGSHANEUN

River Nire

Carrignagower

Coum Iarthar
Loughs

Lough
Coumstelloges

Coumshingaun
Lough

Coum a
locha

FASCOUM

L Coumfea

KNOCKAUNAPEEBRA ▲

COUMMAHON

Coumtay

THE WALK

Leave the car-park and return along the road (WNW) past a ruined cottage on your left. Continue on until a track and gate appear also on your left (not shown on some maps). Go through the gate and down the track (S) toward the River Nire. Enjoy the chaffinches playing in the furze as you reach the river, then cross by a bridge that appears to be made from an old lorry trailer chassis, begin to ascend and continue on upwards through a gate until the track peters out.

From here on there is no path and it is necessary to strike out generally S, aiming for the high ground ahead, to cross a tributary of the Nire and ascend Curragh Duff and the north-west shoulder of Coumfea. So cross the tributary at a point where it is joined by another small stream. Make use of the numerous boulders to cross and emerge on the other side heading due S toward the end of a fence ahead, which meets the minor stream now on your left.

As you ascend toward the skyline and the crest of this spur of Coumfea, look to the north-east to view 'The Gap' through which, 'fortune willing', you will pass later today. As you reach the ridge gaze at the topography that surrounds you: the Knockmealdown Mountains and the Galtees (Walk 16) to the west and north-west, Laghtnafrankee (VARIATION A) immediately to the north-north-west and to the north-north-east, the distinctive northern ridge of the Comeraghs (VARIATION C), and all of them the home of the disappearing **Irish hare***.*

When you are satisfied that you have reached the crest of the shoulder, head SW along the spine toward the broad flat summit, an area of groughs in the blanket bog marked by a very small pile of stones.

The mountain chain to your immediate south as you ascend this spur is, of course, the Monavullagh, and the summit of Seefin, with its little cabin, will be visible once you have made Coumfea. Seefin (Suidehe-Finn, Finn's

seat) is a common name among Irish mountains and tells you it is yet anoth-
er spot frequented by the warrior god Finn MacCool (Walk 5 and others),
possibly during his pursuit of the lovers Diarmaid and Grainne (Walk 9
and others).

However, as you approach Coumfea, you may choose to keep
to the left (east) of the more obvious line as this will bring you to
the rim of the cwm and reward you with views of Lough
Coumfea (west) and Lough Coumstillogue (east), destined to
make you draw breath at their beauty. As you pass by the first
(east) of the two loughs the summit of Coumfea then becomes visible to the south-south-west.

From this summit set off SW on a bearing of 140° or so, toward
the ridge on the skyline across a shallow col. After 800 m this
bearing will bring you to the lip of the back wall of Coumtay. To
get there, navigate your way to the right and then the left of the
upper reaches of two groughs, the first running north into Coum
a locha and the second running south into the Glenastuckaun
stream. Then pass along to the right (south-west) of a drain ahead
of you, so avoiding an area of bog to the north-east which runs
to the edge above Coum a locha. Arrive at the lip of Coumtay and
above the source of the river of the same name which flows hundreds of metres below you south-south-west to the coast at
Stradbally.

Take the time to savour this fine view of the coastal landscape, from
Helvick Head and the mouth of Dungarvan harbour east to Waterford and
the Wexford coast beyond. Then if you can tear your gaze away, look to
the east-north-east across the upper reaches of Coummahon above the
famous Mahon Falls, to search out the summit of your next objective
Knockaunapeebra, found at a map bearing of about 70°.

The driest route to Knockaunapeebra is now reached by walking a north-trending arc. Head NE along the broad flat ridge
toward, but falling short of, the peak immediately to your north-
east (Coum a locha at 750 m / 2444 ft, MR S 295108), then traversing due E toward the summit of Knockaunapeebra, and eventual-

ly ESE to meet the river above Foilanprisoon where the water begins tumbling downwards and plays tunes among the rocks and you may enjoy the landscape and views above the Mahon Falls. Of course if summits are irresistible to you, there is no reason why you shouldn't make for the rounded cap of Coum a locha and then go generally ESE.

Now head ENE to ascend to the summit of Knockaunapeebra. This is a rare old hill, as they say in Ireland and there is no easy way up. You may prefer to ascend by picking a zigzag route to allow you to contour your way up to the summit, but of course if you're super fit you'll experience no difficulty in racing straight to the top and arrive at two piles of stones at the summit.

The two cairns allow you to identify this peak easily. On a fine day you might take your boots and socks off here, waggle your toes and enjoy the view. Even on a summer Sunday you can have this summit to yourself – I guess that's the value of what looks to be a difficult climb lying a little off the beaten track. Get a clear view of the Helvick Head and the Waterford and Wexford coasts, and catch a glimpse of the houses in Furraleigh below.

Leave Knockaunapeebra and head NE for the summit of Fauscoum (800 m/2625 ft, MR S 317105) the highest point in the Monavullagh–Commeragh range, picking your way through the groughs on the intervening col as you do so. As the contours begin to flatten out pick your way through the exposed areas of shales and groughs as the summit pile of stones comes into view. When you reach the cairn enjoy the 360° panorama.

Wild or Wilderness Corrie (Fauscoum), this summit too takes its name from a neighbouring corrie, south of Coumshingaun. It is now possible to head roughly N to follow the spine of the plateau. After periods of heavy rain this plateau becomes almost unnavigable. There are great areas of exposed peat that have now been this way for more than twenty years. They are regularly washed by the rains and appear almost like black sand upon a wave-washed beach with a curious stepped effect where the liquid mass has advanced forward, and you dread a thunderstorm. And I am reminded that bog-burst stories number well among the accounts of Ireland's natural disasters (Walk 6). Better then to take the route along the back wall of Coumshingaun and fortune may bring you sight of the **peregrine falcons** that soar above the cliffs there.

From the summit of Fauscoum go north of due E to arrive above the southern shoulder of the **Corrie Coumshingaun**. Take care as you approach the corrie lip, turn left (N) and follow the path around the corrie rim. Do not follow the path all the way to Stookanmeen, the prominent north shoulder of Coumshingaun. But as the plateau on your left falls to meet the path and a small edge of stones comes into view (which looks as if it has been arranged deliberately for some garden centre), turn NW away from the corrie to head toward the summit of Coum Larthar (MR S 311122). This is best achieved by heading slightly left (W) of the bearing crossing the upper reaches of the Uisce Soluis, the water of light, and then making use of the shale bedded groughs to aid you in your climb to the moonscape **summit of Coum Larthar**.

Continue on toward the Comeragh ridge as you begin to gently descend toward an assembly of boulders that appears to be a small peak. This is actually an optical illusion. The 'peak' rises no more than 3 m above the surrounding land, but in fact forms the top of a very steep escarpment known as Carrignagower (the Goat's Rock). So proceed with caution, take your time and pick your way through and down the mountainside very carefully, as if you yourself were the goat in question, taking care to avoid the steep drop of several metres, below the centre of this outcrop of rocks. Of course if you've a mind for something approaching difficult there is great pleasure in it.

As you descend the escarpment aim for the highest point in the col which is off to your right (toward the north) as though you were going to join the path that rises up the edge of the ridge to Knocknaffrin, before you. Then as you reach the foot of the escarpment look out for a sheep tread running NW across the col toward the track which passes through The Gap. As the sheep path begins to peter out before you reach the head of the track strike out across the heather, picking up a faint tread that leads the last few metres to the track in **The Gap**.

At the track turn left (W) to follow the path marked by a series of stakes. After reaching the final crest in the undulating path (a spur of Knocknaffrin) turn left (SW) off the staked path to follow an obvious footpath which leads down towards two stakes, a tourist sign to The Gap, the car-park and your start.

THE COMMENTARIES

The Irish Hare

Not your common or garden 'town' hare (brown hare, Lepus capensis) found throughout most of Europe, this is the ramblers' hare (the mountain hare, Lepus timidus). It has shorter ears, but longer legs, to propel the more heavily built body. The tail is almost all white and the body brown with a noticeable blue tint, but its coat can change colour. It is not unusual to see the white or Arctic hare on some Northern European moorland tops in winter, but is this really the same as the Irish hare and does the local variety really turn white in winter? This is the question. There seems to be some argument about it, and I don't know the answer, but I've seen the white hare many times, and I most definitely did see a very whitish hare on Valentia Island, in early spring after a long cold spell. So who knows?

One thing is for sure, Ireland was the only European country where the mountain hare occupied the lowlands, but now it is becoming rare especially here, because the mountains rise straight from the lowland plain and have no foothills to offer shelter or act as a 'no man's land'.

Peregrine Falcons

In a society where we seem to care little about the impact of organophosphates on farm labourers and even less about the unquantified impact of defoliants on children who play near woodland, it is hardly surprising that the indiscriminate use of pesticides, and the selfish practice of egg collecting, have almost caused the extinction of

Looking from The Gap

the superb peregrine falcon. But because of the efforts of those that care, it does seem to be returning to the Irish landscape and you may see it on several of the walks in this book. Occasionally I even mention it, but obviously not the nest sites.

You may spot one when walking around an area of escarpment and crag. Larger than any other falcon (43 cm) in Ireland and Britain, it has a distinctive moustache and can be seen soaring and circling on the thermals. But you will have to be quick to catch it in a stoop; it has been measured in a dive, travelling at more than 100 miles an hour.

Corrie Coumshingaun

Geographers consider it one of the
finest European examples of a corrie, a rounded depression — in this
case more than 300 m (1000 ft)
deep — hollowed out of the bedrock
by the irresistible scrapings of ice
gathering at this point to start the
life of a glacier, probably during the
last Ice Age some 10,000 years or
so ago.

You may notice that all corries
face north or east, away from the
strongest sunlight. The debris
around the lower rim of the corrie,
which now captures the black lough,
remains from the final melting of the

glacier. And none of this explanation should detract from the mystery you may discover in the place!

Summit of Coum Larthar

Actually this summit has no name, but for convenience, following the practice of others before me on this plateau, I have borrowed the name of the neighbouring corrie, as was done with Coumfea, Fauscoum, Coumtay and others. In this case I beg indulgence, for this corrie (to the east) has another local name, Boola, a reminder of the once common practice of transhumance, for it means a milking place for cattle and probably refers to the use of the moor above the corrie for summer grazing (see Walks 6 and 10): perhaps this summit had better be called Boola.

It is dotted with isolated hags that may add to the strange and mystical appearance of these mountains, already fostered by the tops and corries. But no doubt the geographer sees a broad gently rounded summit strewn with shattered boulders which I imagine bear witness to the freeze-thaw action of the quaternary period, now thought to be equally important as the action of ice, evidence of which surrounds you and is so obvious in the corries like Coumshingaun.

For the rambler in us Knocknaffrin and the Comeragh ridge come into view. As you proceed across the summit you arrive at what is best described as a small assembly of slightly larger boulders, and as you descend you may enjoy the open views of the Nire valley backed by the Knockmealdown and Galtee Mountains. As your view opens to the north, enjoy the taunting profile of Slieve Mahon, the mountain of the women, and a story for another day; the locals have a saying for the occasions it is draped in mist.

The Gap

This 'Gap' has its own more interesting Gaelic name, Beal barr an bealach, the mouth at the top of the journey, or the way. And the track also has a name, Bóthar na socraidhe, the road of grief. For it was along this track that people carried their dead to be buried, from along the Nire valley and beyond over to Rathgormuck. One can only guess at the quality of the mourning the journey would have offered them. Whatever, the way now gives you *generally firm going under foot and the opportunity to relax and stretch out your legs on your way back to the car. So as you amble along look out for the curious gusts of tiny whirlwinds that whip up the dust from the road and tracks. Called*

sioth gaoithe, fairies in the wind, they seem quite common in this valley and seem to be suitable companions for the human train bearing their coffins through this sometimes serene valley.

VARIATIONS AND ALTERNATIVES

A: EASY VIEWS FROM LAGHTNAFRANKEE: A quick ascent with brilliant views, some say the best in Ireland. Park on a tarmac area at a right turn, south of Harney's Crossroads (MR S 265187). Take the boreen WSW. At a junction cross the road ahead, go on to the moor and keep heading generally SW up the centre of the wide long eastern spur until you reach a shelf and the summit comes in sight. Return the same way. (4 km/2.5 miles, ascent 100 m/330 ft, high point Laghtnafrankee 521 m/1709 ft, >1 hr, Easy.)

B: A WILDERNESS STROLL: There are three. From the car-park for the walk, follow the route in reverse direction into The Gap. Return the same way or via the track in the valley. (5 km/3 miles, ascent 200 m/655 ft, >1 hr, Easy.) Or from the car-park at the Mahon Falls (MR S 315080), signposted from the R676 (T56), take the well-maintained path alongside the river to the foot of the falls, or along the river, or both. (2 km/1.25 miles, 0.5 hrs, Easy.) Finally follow VARIATION D as far as the loughshore and back (take a picnic). (3 km/2 miles, ascent 250 m/800 ft, >1 hr, Easy.)

C: KNOCKNAFFRIN RIDGE: From Glennanore (MR S 260143) take the track NE to the summit of Knocksheegowna, turn right and head SSE over the summit of Knocknaffrin but not quite into The Gap, before turning right again to head NW along the countours of the mountain and let the path lead you back to Glennanore. (12 km/7.5 miles, ascent 630 m/2067 ft, high point Knocknaffrin 755 m/2477 ft, <4 hrs, Strenuous.). Reverse the route and add it to the end of the walk for a superb day. (27 km/17 miles, ascent 1530 m/5000 ft, <8.5 hrs, Difficult.)

D: LOUGH COUMSHINGAUN: The circuit of the lip of the corrie begins with a path running W from the R676 (T56) at MR S 350116, to the shores of the lough. Then back SE to zigzag up to the knife-edge spine of the south shoulder of the corrie. Follow the path up the shoulder, heading N around the lip of the back wall and E as far as possible down the north shoulder, past the lough, before turning S to pick up the path back to the road. (7 km/4.5 miles, ascent 655 m/2150 ft, high point corrie back wall 775 m/2543 ft, <3 hrs, Challenging.)

E: OTHER WALKING: In addition to the walking amid these mountain ranges, the Knockmealdown and the Galtee (Walk 16) Mountains are only a short distance away. There is pleasant lowland walking to be found around the River Suir and in East Waterford. COSPOIR's long distance Munster Way passes through Carrick-on-Suir and Clonmel.

| WALK 18 | *A Day Out from Dublin on a Barrow River Ramble* |

Rising in the old red sandstone of the Slieve Bloom Mountains, the stately Barrow abandons the blanket bog and the youthful waterfalls to cross the midland plain and head south, through a wide and open valley between the Wicklow Mountains and the Castlecomer plateau, to find the sea at Waterford harbour. A broad placid stream, it glides between rich agricultural banks, through meadow and pasture, fields of barley and sugar beet, past a plethora of signals of human occupation. A route of ancient importance connecting the heartlands of Ireland with the sea.

Maps: OSi 1:50 000 Discovery Series Sheets 55, Kildare, Laois, Offaly, Wicklow, and 61, Carlow, although not strictly necessary | Distance: 17 km (11 miles) | High point: the river basin runs around 60 m (200 ft) above sea level at this point | Naismith time: >3 hours | Difficulty: Easy | Emergency services: 999 | Garda: Athy: 059 863 1669, Carlow: 059 913 1505 | Tourist information: Portlaoise (for Athy): 057 862 1178; Carlow: 059 913 1554 | Miscellaneous: Iarnród Éireann (Irish Rail): 01850 366222, www.irishrail.ie

ADVICE AND GRADING

This is the easiest key walk in the book, but offers a reasonable length, and I think is best relished on a spring or early summer day, or perhaps in the heat of late August when the pastoral image can be at its most powerful. Botanists and bird-watchers, novice and expert alike, can expect to be excited and entertained. And for

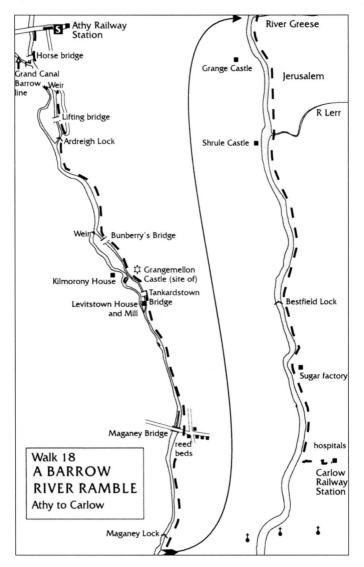

Athy Railway Station

River Greese

Horse bridge

Grange Castle

Jerusalem

Grand Canal
Barrow
line

Weir

Lifting bridge

R Lerr

Ardreigh Lock

Shrule Castle

Weir   Bunberry's Bridge

✡ Grangemellon
Castle (site of)

Kilmorony House

Tankardstown
Bridge

Levitstown House
and Mill

Bestfield Lock

Sugar factory

Maganey Bridge

reed
beds

hospitals

Carlow
Railway
Station

Walk 18
A BARROW
RIVER RAMBLE
Athy to Carlow

Maganey Lock

the rest of us it's a place to relax and to picnic; there are plenty of pleasant spots to stop. There is no difficulty in way finding, the route being a short walk from the two railway stations to the tow-path alongside the left bank of the river. The variations offer the chance of a town walk or varying lengths of riverside stroll.

HOW TO GET THERE

This walk and some of the variations are easily undertaken as a day trip from Dublin on the train. Buy a return ticket to Carlow. Depart from Heuston Station in Dublin and alight at Athy (1 hour). Return to Dublin from Carlow (1 hour 15 mins). You can vary this journey to follow the towpath to Muine Bheag (Bagenalstown). If you go by car, park at Carlow railway station and catch the train to Athy to begin your walk, or park at Muine Bheag if you are feeling ambitious.

THE WALK

Leave the railway station and take the main road (Boherboy/ Leinster Street) E into the centre of **Athy**. At the crossroads pass the town square on your left (south), dominated at the far end by the **Old Town Hall**. Continue along toward the **Cromaboo Bridge** and the large tower house which guards it.

It is not known when or by whom White's Castle or the White Castle of Athy was built, but it is thought that the proprietors of this manor erected a fort at the site of this famous ford sometime in the thirteenth century. In fact the importance of the Barrow as a barrier to armies, and as a major river highway for travel and trade, is echoed along its length by the presence of so many castles, mottes and tower houses.

Do not cross the river but turn left (S) at the bridge and walk along the asphalt and grass toward the distinctive cloistered corn exchange on the bank of the now stately Barrow. Keep to the right (west) of the building and continue along the asphalt pad along the left (east) bank of the river.

Built in 1862 in Jacobean style, this corn exchange functions today as the courthouse and both district and circuit courts are held here. Until the creation of a modern drainage scheme, this whole area would flood regularly and I've no doubt that the river in spate has threatened proceedings occasionally. There is even a photograph showing ice floes floating underneath the Cromaboo Bridge. Just north-east of Athy, off the Dublin road, is a knoll with the revealing name of Gallows Hill. I guess that for at least some visitors to Athy's earlier courts, that was their next and final ramble.

Athy is a major junction of the Grand Canal and the River Barrow and ahead is the Horse Bridge, made with gentle inclines, rather like a modern motorway slip road, to ease the ascent for the horses. It was built originally in 1796 with six arches, and reconstructed in 1927 with four, to cope with an increased water flow. The bridge was needed to let men and horses move from the Ardreigh canal towpath, which you are about to walk upon, to the Grand Canal towpath, the oldest organised transport system in the country. At times the flood of water between these arches has been so great as to sweep away men and horses. The rail bridge, coming after, was built to carry coal from the Wolfhill Collieries off to the west.

Pass beyond the horse and rail bridges to reach the first of a number of river weirs and the start of the Ardreigh Cut. By the time you reach the old lifting bridge and a decaying canal wharf, a remnant of the old mill here at Ardreigh, the track has become a boreen and you may divert left here for VARIATION B1. As the boreen turns left (east) away from the river, follow the path which keeps close to the canal bank, to the right of the white house, and arrive immediately at a set of lock gates as the canal and footpath rejoin the **River Barrow**. Continue on to reach a weir at the start of another lateral canal known as the Levitstown Cut.

Pass Bunberry's single-span stone canal bridge, which always reminds me of Bunbury, Algy's conveniently sickly 'friend' in Oscar Wilde's play The Importance of being Earnest. *Isn't that what you're doing now — skiving off the usual responsibilities of twentieth-century life — Bunburying?*

The lifting bridge – Ardreigh cut

Stay with the left bank (canal on your right) and pass a green lane off to your left (east) which runs to the R417 and which you may take for VARIATION B2. But the walk continues on under another stone bridge and past the ruins of Kilmoroney House, on your right, and the site of Grangemellon Castle off to your left.

A short distance after the bridge, peer through the branches of the hedge on your left (east) and notice the far wall of the field and the curious arches. I assume this to be the site of fifteenth-century Grangemellon Castle, bought for a home in 1766 by Colonel 'Handsome Jack' St Leger, ten years before he established the famous English classic horse race. Did I hear you exclaim **'Gordon Bennett'**? *What a perfect link to another race!*

Soon the canal and towpath come close to the road (R417) and a small community, and pass under the Tankardstown Bridge. Immediately after the bridge there is direct access to the road for VARIATION B3. Pass another small group of cottages, farm buildings and a small lifting bridge: a curious contraption that is made to lift horizontally by winding a handle. Head along the track toward the disused grey block of Levitstown Mill.

Now a home for crows who squawk incessantly, Levitstown Mill thrived on the river bank for more than 150 years until it was gutted by fire on 14 March 1942; they say the fire was a spectacular sight, visible for miles around. Some of its foundations are said to be built upon oak piles driven into the bed of the river. Now overtaken by more modern technologies, it was obviously not considered worth rebuilding. I assume the turbine now humming the rhythm to the raucous melody of the crows provides electricity for local use or for the national grid.

Pass the Levitstown lock gates and along the path to the end of the Levitstown Cut. For the next mile or two the path and river meander through a pleasant pastoral scene and the walk provides an interesting variety of birds and blossoms. Pass another small quay by the elongated navigation island and reach the Maganey Bridge. For VARIATION B4, go on to the road through the gate in the wall on your left (east-south-east) before the bridge. Otherwise pass under the bridge and continue along the towpath toward the Maganey Lock, cut around the gently roaring weir.

Maganey has a handsome eighteenth-century bridge with seven stone arches and sculptured niches that span the river. With but a short walk to the Maganey (Maigh Geine) Crossroads, this may also make a pleasant detour for light refreshment, from either the grocery store or the Three Counties public house, named after the nearby meet of the counties of Loais, Kildare and Carlow. Then you may rest and gaze to the south-west at the rising land of the Castlecomer plateau, which like much of Ireland, in contrast to the rich arable soils of the south-east, provides mainly rough grazing and is now being progressively afforested.

About 400 m (0.25 mile) after the lock, the towpath crosses a well-concealed bridge, built to help the towing horses cross the River Greese, now well canalised and flowing into the Barrow from the east. After times of heavy rain the Barrow here shows obvious signs of carrying the flash rainwater delivered from upstream and from the Greese; debris can be hanging around the banks on bushes and trees several feet above its summer level. A little further downstream across on the west side is the site of yet another tower house, Grange Castle, sitting on the banks of the River Guillic. It was across from this site that one spring day I met a fisherman who had cycled the towpath from Carlow. He told me he was fishing for trout and had caught one or two that morning, but actually fishing here is a bit of a mystery and I really should have been there the Monday before, when he caught a 30 lb pike with a 4 lb trout in its mouth! But 'that's the way of it', as they say here. Perhaps it is because this townland is known as Jerusalem.

The path continues on to reach another island at the mouth of the River Lerr, rushing in from the east with its mouth again spanned by the brick arch of a towpath bridge built to carry the horses. The footpath running east on the right (north) bank of the Lerr offers VARIATION B5.

Once past the Lerr and the island in the Barrow at its mouth, you may look back again over to the west bank and the Elizabethan castle of Shrule that once figured prominently in the history of King's and Queen's counties.

Arrive at another cut where for more than 400 m (0.25 mile) the canal, bypassing the substantial rumbling weir, kisses the Barrow along a narrow ridge of shrubbery, before arriving at Bestfield Lock.

Ahead to your left (south-south-east) are the buildings and tower of a sugar-processing factory. The sugar beet processed here arrives from as far away as Wexford, right across the south to Tipperary. Certainly not an attractive feature of the landscape but an important part of the local economy, providing much needed jobs and a view soon forgotten.

Pass the works and go under the pipeline to join a gravel path; as you round the gentle right bend in the river, the nineteenth-century spire of the seventeenth-century (1630) St Mary's Church signposts the buildings of **Carlow**. As the towpath leads you into the fringes of the town pass a walled cemetery on your right (east) to reach an open area, known as the Old Graves. For VARIATION C into Carlow continue along the towpath. Otherwise leave the river here by turning left (E) along the fork in the pad to put the pork and bacon warehouse on your right (south), and follow the path as it winds left and right through the town park, now named after another literary son of Ireland, playwright George Bernard Shaw. Pass the swings and slides and emerge through the gates on the far side of the park, into Grave Lane (a name not much loved by the residents). Walk along this short lane to reach the (R417) Athy road.

Shaw is celebrated for his connection with Carlow, not least for his presentation to the town of the building which now houses the public library and which formerly served as a vocational school.

Cross directly over the road through a gateway and pass a small disused gatehouse into the grounds of St Dympna's Hospital. Of the three paths forking ahead, take the one on the extreme right which passes between the wall on your right and a line of trees on your left. Emerge past the crescent shape of the Sacred Heart Hospital on your left, on to the Dublin road (N9). Go straight across the road, veering right (SW) toward Carlow to take the first turn left (E) into Railway Road. Pass by the schools to head toward **Carlow Railway station**, directly ahead.

Athy

THE COMMENTARIES

Athy

The River Barrow divides the lands to the east and west, from the Slieve Bloom Mountains to the south coast seashore. And with limited opportunities for river crossing, Athy owes its origins to command of a strategically important ford across the river. Many battles were fought for possession of this ford, with one led almost 1900 years ago by King Aodh of Munster, who was injured and fell, but who gave his name to the place: Ath Aoi or the ford of Aodh. Or, as a few Irish-speaking people would have it, Bailleata-aoi, the town of the ford of Ae.

But the early foundations of Athy were in the thirteenth century with the two monasteries: that of the Crouched Friars and the Dominican Abbey. At numerous times after that, various warlords would sweep down on the startled inhabitants, put them to the sword and burn the place to the ground; 1308, 1315, 1546, 1650 and 1798 are prominent examples.

Old Town Hall

The Old Town Hall, having given way to the high-tech architecture of the council building on Standhope Street, now houses the library and a museum, having also served, since 1947, as the first national headquarters of Macra na Feirme (young farmers' clubs). A founder and the first secretary was Stephen Cullinan, a local teacher. The organisation lists an impressive number of achievements and its fiftieth anniversary was celebrated in 1994 when the President of the Republic, Ms Mary Robinson, unveiled the monument in the town square.

The town hall was originally built in 1752, probably from a design by the notable Richard Castle. Castle was of German origin and changed his name from his native Cassel to suit his new home. The refurbishment by Kildare County Council was undertaken in 1976. However, the bell hiding in the cupola was originally the bell of the former Protestant church and was made in 1682, whilst the final curiosity remains the town hall clock. It is wound up each day by the local librarian, and the works can still be viewed if one asks nicely. But beware if the librarian takes a holiday: the clock stops.

Cromaboo Bridge

Stand still, fill your lungs with pure Irish air and hail the war cry of the Desmonds ... or is it the Fitzgeralds ... 'Crom-a-Boo!' Have all about you scattered in terror and bewilderment? Well, perhaps you'd better practise further downstream!

It's known that a stone bridge stood on this site as early as the sixteenth century. But the first bridge, perhaps the ford of Aodh, was probably made from wicker wattles, later followed by a construction of timber, with its continuing importance leading to a building in stone. It is the intriguing inscription this bridge bears, rather than its architecture, that stirs the rambler's interest and tells us the date it was built: 'Foundation stone laid by his Grace Robt. Duke of Leinster 23 May 1796. Contract: Sir James Dulehanty Knight of this Trowel.' This refers not to an appointment by the monarch of England but to excellence in his trade as a mason, a practice of appreciation not unknown at the time.

River Barrow

The route of the Barrow below Athy is now almost deserted although once it formed a prosperous commercial way. In the seventeenth century the river was made navigable for 'modern' traffic by dredging and building weirs above the rapids and shallows every two or three miles. Each weir leads obliquely across the river into the mouth of a bypass or lateral canal which carries boats and barges past the unnavigable section. This is the longest lateral canal on the navigation and extends for 3.2 km (2 miles). But many of the weirs are long and exposed, one reason why the river is treated with such great respect by boatmen; there is no forgiveness for a lapse of concentration here. Cuts, or canalised sections, were built along the Barrow at least as early as the sixteenth century, to provide a means around natural and man-made cataracts and weirs. Many mills and maltings took advantage of the canalised sections to drive water wheels and use the effective transport offered by the Barrow to Waterford, Shannon and the west coast, and eventually via the Grand Canal to Dublin.

Gordon Bennett

It was in the locality of Athy that the famous Gordon Bennett Motor

Race was held in 1903. Bennett was an American paper millionaire and a great patron of motor racing and balloon racing. The course, but apparently not always the cars, followed a figure of eight on the roads hereabouts. In order to protect the inhabitants the cars were led through the towns by a cyclist. However, at Mass the previous Sunday local people were advised to keep their livestock and fowl off the roads and to hide behind the trees along the route to protect themselves from these dangerous inventions. Wise advice as Europe becomes more car-crowded.

Graiguecullen Bridge

If you continue on by the Barrow to reach the N81, you arrive at the road which runs over the bridge variously called Graiguecullen Bridge, Barrow Bridge and Town Bridge, although when it was rebuilt in 1815 it was renamed Wellington Bridge, presumably to mark Wellington's victory at Waterloo. Now it is named after the community of Graiguecullen, found to the west of the Barrow and forming part of the greater Carlow.

Carlow (Ceatharlach)

Even in the eighteenth century Carlow was still called by its old name Catherlough or Ceatharlach. Earlier still it was written Ceithiorlach, meaning the quadruple lough. Or should that be written Cathair loch, meaning lake-fort? Both names are perhaps connected with the large area of lough, pool and swamp that existed at the confluence of the Rivers Barrow and Burren, around the site of the present ruins of Carlow Castle. This Norman construction of the thirteenth century was accidentally destroyed in 1814 by a doctor who used gunpowder on the building when trying to convert it into a hospital. What Cromwell didn't manage …

Carlow is now a cathedral town of the Roman Catholic diocese of Kildare and Leighlin; the Cathedral of the Assumption, constructed between 1929 and 1933, was one of the first built after Catholic emancipation.

Carlow Railway Station

The station was designed as the terminus to the Dublin–Carlow line by Sir John MacNeill and dates from

1845. Its yellow brick and Jacobean style have a certain charm and make it a pleasant place to wait for a train to Athy or Dublin. Together with the courthouse in Athy they form a pair of bookends to the walk. Today the line continues south through Kilkenny to Waterford.

VARIATIONS AND ALTERNATIVES

A: SHORT WALK: ATHY: Turn this into a town walk. Follow the walk through Athy along the river to the horse bridge. Cross the bridge and turn N away from the canal to follow the path running parallel with the right bank of the Barrow, toward the modern (1965) Dominican church. Pass the church and follow Convent Lane to Duke Street and turn right to return to the Cromaboo Bridge. (2.5 km/1.5 miles, 30 mins, to as long as you like, Easy.)

B: VARYING THE LENGTH: Join the walk by the Athy courthouse and follow the route until you reach a boreen (by a dilapidated lifting bridge) which runs alongside the River Barrow. By a COSPOIR yellow waymark, turn left (E) to the R417 Athy–Carlow Road. Turn left again (N) and walk along the road back to Athy. VARIATIONS B2–5 are described in the text. (Variable between 3 km/2 miles and 13 km/8 miles, 30 mins up to 3 hrs, Easy.)

C: INCLUDING CARLOW: For a stroll through Carlow, follow the walk but do not turn left through George Bernard Shaw park, rather stay with the towpath, through the urban fringe, until you reach the bold **Graiguecullen Bridge**. Turn left here and follow the N9 into Carlow. (20 km/12.5 miles, 4 hrs, Easy.)

D: MUINE BHEAG (BAGENALSTOWN): You may extend the walk by continuing on through Carlow, along this exceptionally beautiful stretch of river to Bagenalstown and return to your car in Bagenalstown or by train to Dublin, Athy or Carlow as suits. (32 km/20 miles, 6.5 hrs, Easy, but long.) Alternatively you may walk just the stretch from Carlow to Bagenalstown, as suits you. (14 km/9 miles, <3 hrs, Easy.)

E: OTHER WALKING: The walk follows part of the COSPOIR long distance trail the Barrow Way, which runs along the towpath for 109 km/68 miles. Details of this route can be obtained from COSPOIR. The Carlow Chamber of Commerce also produces a Walking Tour and Tourist Guide to Carlow Town, which offers a pleasant introduction to the place.

WALK 19 | *Slieve Bloom Mountains and the Heights of Ireland*

It is true that as you approach this land of undulating heath and bog, now quite heavily forested, the highest point, that half-munroe of Arderin, hardly raises itself above your eyeline. But this compact group of hills gives birth to two of Ireland's most noted rivers and, without surprise, to a long-standing reputation for astonishingly rapid floods which probably gave rise to the following ancient writing about a Slieve Bloom well:

> …if anyone gazes on it, or touches it, its sky will not cease to pour down rain until mass and sacrifice are made at it. (*Historia Brittonum* of Nennius; Todd 1848; Feehan 1979)

A minor exaggeration perhaps; but here is one of the few places I have experienced that peculiar phenomenon of water running uphill. One December morning whilst ambling up the bohereen over Bull Bog and towards Monicknew Bridge, after a night of incomparably heavy rain (that is, except in comparison with the day after – which was even worse), my head bowed towards the horizon, the river coursing over the asphalt was actually running, at a most alarming rate, straight uphill towards me. Of course it was an illusion created somehow by the route of the bohereen up the flanks of Monicknew Glen and the height of the hedges there. But it was only by making myself very conscious of my footfall that I convinced myself that I was slowly climbing and that the water running toward me was actually going downhill. This phenomenon continued for several hundred metres as I progressed up the glen. Safe as it is, it can be a very disorienting experience after a few minutes, creating the strangest sensation in your stomach.

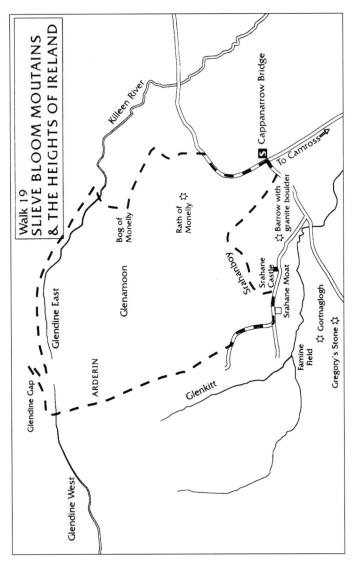

Walk 19
SLIEVE BLOOM MOUTAINS
& THE HEIGHTS OF IRELAND

Killeen River

Cappanarrow Bridge

S   To Camross

Bog of Monelly

Rath of Monelly ☆

☆ Barrow with granite boulder

Glenamoon

Strahanboy

Srahane Castle

Srahane Moat

☆ Gortnaglogh

Glendine East

Famine Field

Gregory's Stone ☆

ARDERIN

Glenkitt

Glendine Gap

Glendine West

So with the highest peak around 500 m, and a reputation for torrential rain, there might be times when the place is more suitable for ducks than mountaineers. But I can't think of any place worth visiting that doesn't have its occasional down side, and I've known rainfall elsewhere that would make Arderin seem a desert. So give these mountains a chance. Let yourself discover the prodigious variety within the landscape: the rare combination of habitats and the plants and wildlife supported there. You may discover Slieve Bloom truly is unique.

Maps: OSi 1:50 000 Discovery Series Sheet 54, The Slieve Blooms. Laois and Offaly County Councils, 1:40 000, Slieve Bloom Environment Park | Distance: 11 km (7 miles) | Ascent: 430 m (1400 ft) | High point: Arderin, 527 m (1734 ft) | Naismith time: <3 hours | Difficulty: Challenging | Rescue service: 999 | Garda: Mountrath: 057 873 2236, Borris in Ossory: 0505 41122 | Tourist information: Portlaoise: 057 862 1178, Mullingar: 044 48650 | Miscellaneous: Slieve Bloom Environment Park Visitor Centre, Birr: 057 912 0029 | Further reading: Feehan, John, The Landscape of Slieve Bloom, *Blackwater, Dublin, 1979*

ADVICE AND GRADING

This is a pleasant ramble offering a satisfying combination of pastoral landscape, wild moorland and the flora and fauna of plantations set within muted glen. Throughout the route there are features and places to rustle your curiosity and urge your reflection. Perhaps the best times to visit are in May and August, when you may walk without the rain and the colours dance before you. The alternatives and variations provide for other walks around Slieve Bloom and the Devilsbit Mountain.

GETTING THERE

From Port Laoise take the N7 W to Mountrath and then minor
roads W to Camross, which lies to the south-east of the Slieve
Bloom Mountains and the summit of Arderin. From Camross follow the signs to the Glendine Forest, W over the Delour river and
then NW for 2.75 km (1.75 miles) to reach a sharp left bend in the
road with a right turn over the old stone Cappanarrow Bridge.
Before reaching the bridge there is an area of grass verge where
you may park (MR N 263966).

THE WALK

Leave your car and walk NW toward the road junction and the
Cappanarrow Bridge. Do not cross the bridge, but turn left and
follow the signpost to Glenkitt (SW) along this minor road. Walk
up the hill for about 150 m (500 ft), pass a modern bungalow and
turn right into a farm lane. (After heavy rain parts of this route can
be very muddy. For a drier route, go past the farm lane and follow the tarmac over the rise to a road junction and turn right to
regain the route at a farm track a little past Srahan Castle, MR N
246967.)

Ignore the track on your left and carry straight on through a
gateway to undulate along the lane, through pasture land, past
farm buildings and directly toward the rounded profiles of the
spurs and glens of Arderin. At a second set of buildings and
before a gate, the track turns left (SW), passes through a gateway
and degenerates into a very muddy path. Endure this for a few
hundred metres as you walk along the foot of the south-eastern
slopes of a very prominent **esker** to reach a more frequently used
and marginally less muddy farm track. Go through the gateway
around a bit of a slurry pond and past some modern farm buildings on your right (north) and down the track as it swings right
(N) through the working farmyard. Continue W through the

farmyard and farm gates and follow the track as it turns SW to cross a small concrete bridge over a stream.

On your right (north), a short way up the stream toward the mouth of Glenall (Glen Aille, perhaps meaning glen of the cliff) and at the north-eastern end of a second esker, is a killeen (cillín). *Roughly meaning small or 'lesser' church, a* cillín *is the site or enclosure of a monastic settlement or building, itself probably established on or near the site of a more ancient Gaelic holy place. Such places have since been used as a place of burial for unbaptised children or even strangers of unknown origin or religion. And it is perhaps the religious connection that has given birth to the most commonly heard explanation of a ballaun, a bowl shape hollowed into a fragment of stone. There are a number of ballauns in the Slieve Bloom Mountains, including one at this* cillín *and another close by the Rath of Monelly that we pass later. Others can be found on the Aran island of Inis Oírr, (Walk 12). Looking a little like a giant mortar, ballauns were long thought to be early Christian fonts, but it is quite likely that they were made before the Christian invasion and were used for grinding grain.*

Go through a second set of gateposts and S along the unfenced track across the open pasture to reach the asphalt bohereen at the heart of the township of **Srahanboy** and turn right. (If you took the drier alternative along the roadways, regain the main route here.)

*A short detour made by turning left (E) along the bohereen will bring you to the slight remains of **Srahan Castle**, while on your left (south) as you walk along the decaying asphalt, hiding behind the hedge, visible through the gaps and a gate is the Srahane Moat. Well, what do you think this ancient earthwork is? Local tradition says it was a safe place to herd cattle, when the communities hereabouts were under attack. Possibly – I'm open to other suggestions.*

Stay on the remains of the tarmac boreen, ignoring a track off to the left and at a second junction ignore the signs into Glenkitt and turn right (NNE) with the gently rising lane.

Ahead on your left (slightly west of north) now you may see the Heights of Ireland, or rather the long south-running spur of Arderin, which you are about to traverse.

Follow the boreen left as it passes between some recent buildings, go through a gate to a track junction and fork left (NW). Follow the firm track through a second gate to reach a third gate by a left turn (west-south-west) in the track.

As you rise up the track you may clamber on to the lower moor on your right, to view the lazy-bed ridges (Walks 4 and 12), similar to those at Gortnaglough, which remain from the days before the starvation of 1848. You are now on the long southern spur of Arderin (MR N 239973) with the wide round summit NNW of you (338° true), whilst below you to the east and south, cultivation ridges remind us of the lost occupation of these mountains.

Do not go through the gate, but leave the track and strike out NW up the gentle slopes of the open mountain. Cross the stream, which flows into Glenall past the *cillín* you may have visited earlier. Leave behind the enclosure on your left (west) and make for the wide crest of the sometimes wet, tussocky and peaty spur that will take you NNE across the blanket bog to **the summit of Arderin**.

The aim now is to join the Slieve Bloom Way which runs generally east–west through the Glendine Gap.

So from the summit head NNW (map bearing: 348°) continually descending into the highest point in the col (the Glendine Gap), down the final steeper slope and through the scattered trees of the plantation. Scramble 30 m or so out the other side of the col, generally N, to reach a road, and the Slieve Bloom Way.

And it is probable that for centuries the only track across this 23 km (14 mile) stretch of mountains ran through this gap called Glendine (gleann doimhin, deep glen). Lloyd Praeger, the botanist, found the spot rewarding in other ways. In his book The Way that I Went *he recalls his ascent to Arderin as one of the wettest days he had ever had. But in a gulley in this col he discovered both the rare Welsh Poppy (Meconopsis cambrica) and Wilson's Filmy Fern (Hymenophyllum Wilsonii), and so considered his 'modest' 60 km (37 mile) walk of that day to be worthwhile.*

Toward Arderin from Camross

Turn right (E) and follow the road descending around the contours of the unnamed high ground at 484 m above you and above the infant Killeen River on your right (south). Make a right U-turn (SW) at a junction to follow the track as it descends to the rushing stream and waterfall. Now stay with the track across the stream as it turns a sharp left (E) and begins to follow the long flank of the eastern spur of Arderin, keeping the Killeen river on your left (north becoming north-east).

Glendine East is quite unlike other valleys in these mountains; the U-shape profile of the valley, the striations scraped into the bedrock and the hanging valleys, perhaps clearer on the northern side of the glen, all betray this as a glaciated valley. Its floor and sides were sculptured by the action of ice, perhaps flowing down from the edge of an ice sheet running north from the summit. But as you descend, gazing in wonder at this place take the time to look carefully for the flashing wings of the dipper as you near the stream.

Make a long progressive descent until the track bottoms out at a car-park area amid Sitka spruce and Lodgepole pine, and then undulates gently for a while before beginning to climb slowly into an area of maturing plantation.

Most of the new forests of the Slieve Bloom date from 1911 and 1926. The conifers are quite varied, but as you will see descending Glendine East, Sitka spruce proved very successful, along with larch and Lodgepole pine.

Ramblers, environmentalists and others frequently complain about insensitive planting by forestry authorities, right across Western Europe. Summit planting destroys a beautiful view, and riverside planting destroys the fragile dingle habitat, whilst the restriction of light to the forest floor produces a poorer show of flora and fauna than a natural deciduous wood; except perhaps for fungus. And notable here, on the edges of the woods, is the distinctive Fly agaric (Amanita muscaria), straight out of a fairy tale with its bright crimson cap with white spots. Actually the spots are the remains of the disappearing white cap as the fungus matures. In the days before fly-paper, CFCs and aerosol sprays, people would break fragments of mushroom into a bowl of milk and let it stand overnight, until the poison had seeped into the liquid. Then during the day they would place the bowl near the centre of the room, where the aroma would attract flies who would alight on the 'soup'. The taste organs on their feet cannot recognise the poison. The flies would eat and die, keeping the cooking or eating area free from their infections.

Eventually reach a T-junction. Do not follow the marks for the Slieve Bloom Way which goes left (north-east) across the River Killeen, but re-enter the plantation by turning right (ESE) past the sign for Glenamoon (Gleann na Mumhan) and between two gate pillars. Ignore the minor track now on your left (south).

Before continuing you may wish to look at the Slieve Bloom Way board, which you will find on the left of the track toward the river. J. B. Malone is remembered for his creation of the Wicklow Way as well as for his writing and broadcasting. His countryside descriptions gave hours of pleasure not only to ramblers but to those unable to venture out into the remaining wilderness. As you may see from the map, the whole route of the Slieve Bloom Way is some 77 km (48 miles), but VARIATION A *provides some ideas on walking the whole of the way in manageable portions.*

Quickly reach another junction with a small forestry cabin. Fork left along the rising track through a pair of wooden gates and into an area of new plantation to turn left (SE) on to a vague path.

As you turn, an area of new plantation across the track and to your right now covers the **Bog of Monelly**, *resting on a small shelf on the long curving eastern spur of Arderin, cut by the River Killeen in the east and the Glenamoon now out of sight in the west.*

The footpath follows a decayed bog road, with mature plantation on the left (north-east) and fresh plantation on the right (south-west). This little-used green road grows stronger as it rises to meet an old white-painted wooden gate at the edge of the plantation.

On your right (south-west), now completely hidden by trees, across the crest of the spur, is a ring barrow. I spent a pleasant time with the farmer here as we roamed around on tractor and on foot, discussing life in these

Glendine forest at dusk

hills and searching for this barrow, looking over the Rath of Monelly *(which lies ahead) and studying a ballaun near the edge of the field. These mountains are full of fascinating artefacts teasing you as to their origin and the lives of those who have left them for us. Certainly there are many circular burial mounds, or barrows, in these mountains. The earliest, from the Bronze Age, might be 4000 years old, whilst this particular barrow, I think, is from the Iron Age which means it is probably around 2000 years old, give or take a century or two.*

Continue to descend the sometimes wet, but clear green road, as the character of the walk changes yet again and we begin to return to the pastoral landscape with supremely beautiful views to the east and south. Pass a farmyard on your left (north-east) as you reach asphalt, keep on around a sharp right turn past another farm.

Pass a short track on your right (west). From the gate at the end of the track, westwards you may see a clump of trees set in the field beyond, which together with gorse and whin dress the Rath of Monelly. Was this the ancient fort of Mumhan aileach from the time when the men of Leix drove back the army of Momonians who may have built this rath? Whatever, now it is steeped in myth and tales of fairies, and rewards a brief detour later.

Finally reach the end of the lane and turn right (SW) on to the asphalt road. This is soon joined by the Glenamoon river on your right as you pass by a tarmac track and descend gently alongside an area of heath and fen. Soon reach the attractive stone **Cappanarrow Bridge** and the end of this engaging walk.

THE COMMENTARIES

Esker

The world of geology has gained this name from the Gaelic eiscir *roughly meaning a sandhill. So when, on your Irish travels, you encounter a place called* eskragh *or* eskeragh *you'll know it is a place of eskers.*

This long, sinuous, steep-sided, narrow-crested ridge, which consists of cross-bedded sands and gravels, was laid down by glacial meltwater either at the retreating edge of the ice sheet or in an ice-walled tunnel. No one is certain, but the general consensus of opinion is that they run at right angles to the retreating edge of the melting ice and that the materials were deposited by meltwater streams flowing through or below the ice. A similar feature called a drumlin can *be found in Walk 6 in the Sperrin Mountains. The excavation to create a flat area for the modern farm buildings, found towards the western end, provides you with a chance to see the composition of the esker at first hand.*

Srahanboy, Srahan Castle

It was a local man, Eaton Thomson of Srahane, who in 1933 found the Glenkitt javelin head now in the National Museum in Dublin. Made of chert, it was discovered in the blanket bog north of you between Glenkitt and Glenall. Unlike the bogs of the lowlands, blanket bog may contain centuries of history in no more than a metre of peat. However this is not a rough piece of flint but a beautifully crafted head and tang about 9.25 cm long, so that in this case the find suggests that before the formation of blanket bog, Neolithic man was at least a visitor to these mountains.

Should you take the short diversion you may discover the remains of Srahan Castle on the left of the boreen. With walls a metre thick, the castle once measured 12 m by 7 m, but regrettably now only a small fragment remains. I assume that like so many, it suffered at the hands of Cromwell. Certainly in 1641 a Catholic family called Connor lived in the castle and owned much of the land hereabouts.

South-west from Srahan Castle, around 1.5 km distant, beyond moat, fen and river, is the township of Gortnaglough, site of the cultivation ridges of a famine field and of Gregory's Stone (see Bog of Monelly).

The Summit of Arderin

As you make this climb, the slopes of Glenkitt fall away to your left to greet the tiny wisps of dew which rise from the treeline of the plantation and confirm the valley in its Gaelic name Gleann Ceath, glen of the mists. The turf blanketing the old red sandstone and lying beneath your feet supports an extraordinary diversity of plant and animal life, as does other blanket bog, much of which supported the populations thriving here before the famine. Even the humble heather Calluna vulgaris was used to make brushes and brooms, or stems were woven together to make baskets, whilst whole heather provided twigs for both thatching and bedding. Other species will be easily recognised: tussocks of purple moor grass, the featherbed moss of bog cotton and, naturally, a starring plant amid the cast on the moor, sphagnum moss (not for use on your garden).

The summit itself is a past centre of Druidic custom, perhaps because of the quite extraordinary view of the landscape of fifteen counties of Ireland, said by Baldwin (1819) to be the richest and most extensive in Ireland.

Other fragments of human presence can be found in old references to the Wolf's Road which ran along the crest of these mountains from the Glendine Gap, whilst below a little into Glendine West is the site of the fairy thorn known as the Criochan Thorn. Here people gathered on Height Sunday, the last day in July, where they presumably danced and made merry to the sound of the Uilean pipes, and showed some kind of thanks to the fairies responsible for the thorn. Otherwise I suppose it is possible that the thorn is an old marker showing the route across these mountains, as is the tradition elsewhere in Ireland.

Bog of Monelly

The bog, now partially forested, was once the home of a famous Irish rapparee. Dispossessed of their rights and lands by the Cromwellian campaign of the late 1640s and the dishonest administration that followed, three Costigan brothers, heirs of one of the oldest tribes in the area, turned rapparees; and it was here amid the Bog of Monelly and the surrounding woods that they took their refuge. By 1654 two of the brothers had been captured and executed, but Gregory Costigan was able to continue his exploits and evade capture for a few more years, until finally he was betrayed by his godson, made drunk in a local shebeen in Glencora. Passing through

Gortnaglough, presumably on his return to Monelly, Gregory was shot and beheaded by soldiers, on the stone that still bears his name. It is said that he was a local hero and that his treacherous godson was torn apart by his neighbours.

Cappanarrow Bridge

For those who have the time to stay, there is an interesting history to the roads, pathways and passes of these mountains, from the ancient days of the Celtic bó thar, a wide cattle track, and the old Irish slighe, which was probably no more than a general direction, to roads constructed in the years after the famine such as The Cut, running over the mountains to the west. This stretch of road you are now walking along also dates from that time, while the earlier, older road ran on the higher ground a little to the south, where it can still be seen. So I would guess the bridge is of similar vintage (1850). An attractive, homely bridge, it is, like so many local bridges, an appealing example of the local stone-building skills.

VARIATIONS AND ALTERNATIVES

A: SLIEVE BLOOM WAY, IN EASY STAGES: It is possible to split the whole of the Slieve Bloom Way into shorter circular walks. For example, to enjoy the Way as it traverses Glenbarrow, the most beautiful of all the Slieve Bloom glens: start from the lower car-park in The Cut (MR N 299036), go S to join the Way at Monicknew. Turn left (E) and follow the Way anti-clockwise to return to The Cut. Go over the hill (S) to return to your start and car. (24 km/15 miles, ascent 600 m/1975 ft, high point Clarnahinch Mountain/Ridge of Cappard, 450 m/1476 ft, 6 hrs, Difficult.) Alternatively you may follow the longer route to the west in a clockwise direction, then to shorten that, turn off the Way right, on to the R440 (on road or moor) to rejoin the Way at the Letter Cross Roads and complete your clockwise return: to The Cut.

B: AN EVENING STROLL: (MR N 209046) A forest park walk by the Camcor river by the Coneyburrow Bridge. (3 km/2 miles, <1 hr, Easy.)

C: THE CUT (AN GEARRADH): (MR N 299036) If you have felt deprived of grouse, here is your chance to make up for it. Here in the plantation is Sitka spruce and lodgepole pine planted more than fifty years ago, whilst blanket bog still covers the the tops of the mountains, and together these habitats provide a homeland to a variety of wildlife, including (I am told) wild deer. Wander where you will. (Distance, ascent and time as you please, Easy to Challenging.)

D: DEVILSBIT: A few miles to the south-west, close by Templemore and the Timoney standing stones, is the defiant Devilsbit Mountain. Start from MR S 044730 and head NE up the clear path, past the Marian cross, to scramble the final few metres to the flat summit and triangulation pillar. Return the same way. (5 km/3 miles, ascent 800 ft/245 m, high point 1577 ft/481 m, 1.5 hrs, Moderate.)

E: OTHER WALKING: There are a number of forest parks in the region of the Slieve Bloom Mountains, and both the tourist information offices and the Environment Park visitor centre will advise you on what else is available. There is, for example, a short heritage trail around Mountmellick, walks around the Tara Bog, and the towpaths of the Grand Canal. Finally, dedicated bog trotters with transport at each end of the mountains might like to traverse the tops, heading NE from Nealstown roughly following the county boundary then heading E from Wolftrap Mountain to Carnahinch Mountain (wear your gaiters!).

| *Ancient Knowledge and Secret Places*
GLENDALOUGH, THE RETREAT OF MONKS

There can be few more impressive ways to come upon Ireland than to arrive by ferry across the Irish Sea into Dublin or Dun Laoghaire. Or few pursuits more pleasant than to make your way down to Marlay Park in the suburbs of Dublin to begin the gently undulating walk south, over the Dublin hills, among the Wicklow Mountains and into the Vale of Glendalough.

Maps: OSi 1:50 000 Discovery Series Sheet 56, Wicklow, Dublin, Kildare (part). The Office of Public Works makes a nominal charge for its leaflet on Gleann dá loch (Glendalough), which contains a useful 1:25 000 scale colour map, covering the area of the walk and variations | *Distance: 17 km (11 miles)* | *Ascent: 660 m (2165 ft)* | *High point: 698 m (2290 ft)* | *Naismith time: 6.5 hours* | *Difficulty: Strenuous* | *Mountain rescue service: 999* | *Garda: Rathdrum: 0404 46206* | *Tourist information: Wicklow: 0404 69117* | *Miscellaneous: Wicklow Mountains National Park Office: 0404 45656; Glendalough Visitor Centre: 0404 45325; St Kevin's Bus Service, Dublin: 01 281 8119*

ADVICE AND GRADING

A Strenuous walk with Easy, Moderate and Difficult variations. The route offers an increasing contrast of wilderness and wildlife with ancient human occupation. Winding past the bleak homes of feral goats and herds of red-like deer, and the soaring flight of the

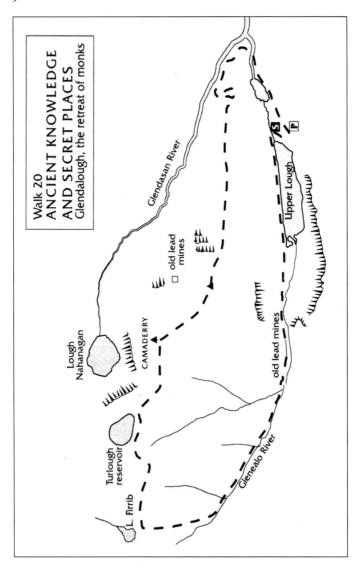

Walk 20
ANCIENT KNOWLEDGE
AND SECRET PLACES
Glendalough, the retreat of monks

Glendasan River

old lead
mines

Lough
Nahanagan

CAMADERRY

Turlough
reservoir

L. Firrib

Glenealo River

old lead mines

Upper Lough

P

peregrine, the mountains slowly reveal the scars of human occupancy since St Kevin sought silent retreat here.

Today the landscape is offered new protection and interesting exposition since the whole of the walk is located within the **Wicklow Mountains National Park**. A visit to the Park Information Centre and the Glendalough Visitor Centre will help you interpret what you see.

GETTING THERE

Glendalough lies less than 48 km (30 miles) south from the centre of Dublin. A bus service runs from Dublin through Bray but will only leave you time for one of the shorter walk variations, unless you stay over in the area.

Car drivers might like to approach along the route from the west taken by St Kevin more than 1500 years ago and now recognised as the old pilgrim road. From the N81 at Hollywood (holy wood, where St Kevin blessed the trees), turn east and follow the R56 ESE over the Wicklow Gap. Before descending into Glendasan, on your right (south) catch a view of Tomaneena (Tuaim An Aonaigh, which I am guessing means tumulus at the marsh), now named Turlough Hill by the ESB to celebrate its artificial summit; and pass the site of a causeway, unusually now raised above the bog and known as St Kevin's Road. The respectable hill of Camaderry, featured in the walk, remains on your right (south-west) as you descend the glen past the remnants of old metal ore works. Finally at the foot of the glen reach a T-junction and turn right (W). Pass the first major car-park and Glendalough Visitor Centre on your left and continue around left and right corners that take you over the bridge of the Glendasan River. Now stay with the road for another kilometre or so as it penetrates deeper into the vale, to reach the car-park, toilet block and parkland picnic site, at the upper lough. This belongs to the

National Park and there is a charge. Park your car here (MR T 127968).

Start with a gentle walk through the Vale of Glendalough. Leave your car and return to cross the Glenealo river by the stone bridge. Turn left (W) on to the bohereen and almost immediately pass a stone cross beyond the dry stone wall on your left (south). At the first left bend, continue straight ahead (W) past the double wooden gates, along a well-maintained track, which runs above the shore of the upper lough. *Called the Miners' Road, this must have been built originally to give access to the lead mines further up the valley.* Remember to turn right for VARIATION C.

Calm days come often in this valley. The water of the lough behaves as a mirror and reflects the opposite bank and the slopes of Spink; reflections of the clouds above can appear to be hundreds of feet below you, as though you were walking along the side of some Alpine peak. And it becomes clear what inspired St Kevin to seek to retreat here. The wood on your right (north) serves as a home to sparrowhawks and long-eared owls, whilst the pine woods found generally around the Upper Lough offer shelter to red squirrels. As you pass beyond the lough, towards the large alluvial fan of the Glenealo river, look for herons. For of all the places in Ireland where I have observed them fishing, it is here that they seem most undaunted by my presence as they hunt amid the reed beds.

Pass through a broken gateway and by a redundant stile to reach the small spoil heaps, ironmongery and tailings reservoir of **old lead mines**. As you reach the decayed buildings of the mining village the track evaporates into the spoil, but you will regain it in due course. As you reach the river turn right (N) and follow the left bank around a meander to cross an agglomeration of large boulders and regain the track which now greens up and zigzags its way up the slope alongside the river.

Notice the subtle changes in the landscape as you rise up this valley. I have found the mutilated carcasses of frogs along this path, possibly the work of kestrels, which I believe I may have seen hereabouts, although their jizz was very un-kestrel-like and I mistook them for some other bird. The park wardens tell me that stoats and feral mink are also quite common around here and that the frog carcasses may be their work. So keep your eyes peeled, you may be in for a treat.

On the left, ahead on the slopes of Lugduff, are more abandoned mines; the area is known to the locals as Van Diemen's land because it was considered to be such a desolate place. Lugduff may have originally been Barnelogdduffe, and probably meant 'the high point by the black hollow'. If, like me, you have begun to develop an interest in the names given to the landscape in Gaelic, you may already be familiar with words like aran, *a corruption of* fearann *meaning land, or with* inis, innis *or* inch *meaning island. But* inis *is also used to describe a water meadow or low-lying ground by a river. Hence* inis *is the name used by local shepherds to describe this area of land on your left, below Van Diemen's land on the right bank of the river.*

As you approach another spoil heap sited on the opposite bank of the river, the track begins to wane. Do not be tempted to cross to the green lane evident on the right bank (your left) but continue with one of the threads of path running alongside the left bank and giving enchanting views of pools and cataracts, until you reach a major tributary and the beginnings of the upper reaches of the Glenealo valley.

It is possible to follow this (NW) and after 700 m branch off right (NNE) along a second tributary to ascend directly to the summit of Camaderry, but you would have denied yourself the chance to taste just a little of the wilderness of these tops and a strong chance of spotting the **herds of deer** *or the wild goats that frequently roam here; the glen is also dotted with glacial erratics of granite and schists.*

As you rise in the valley notice the dark-looking spur marked by crags, which signals the most north-westerly point of the long smooth profile of

Lugduff on your left (south). And look to the north for the artificial intrusion of the Turlough reservoir and the south-east lobe of Tomaneena shown on the map at a height of 681 m.

As you progress up the valley listen for the raucous call of the peregrine falcon now returning to Wicklow and look for the tell-tale white rump of the dipper inches above the water, flying speedily away from you up the course of the stream.

The route can now become quite wet so stay with the path alongside the left bank of the Glenealo river, as it inclines progressively towards the NE and its source. Please do your best not to add further to the threatening erosion by widening the path unnecessarily. After 2.5 km (1.6 miles) reach a second tributary, a narrow fast-flowing stream that rather surprisingly cuts two large deep meanders before slowing into the Glenealo.

Cross the tributary and head generally N (map bearing 348°). You will see the rounded profile of a spur (MR T 055984) which, in plan, runs like a deformed shepherd's crook from Conavalla on your left (west). This high ground lying between the diminutive Lough Firrib and the south-west lobe of Tomaneena (shown at 681 m, north-north-east), is your next objective. To reach this, strike out straight for it across the open mountain seeking an easy ascent, initially on the grassy patches between the tussocks of ling and bell heather then switching to the faint livestock treads, and the water drainage groughs that grow ever deeper as your climb becomes more gentle.

If you prefer, it is possible to reduce the traverse across open mountain by continuing along the river bank for a kilometre or so, toward the source of the Glenealo, to reach another small tributary before striking out east to the high ground. And if the fancy takes you, you could continue on from the tributary on a map bearing of 346° to reach Lough Firrib itself, and regain the walk by going east, then south-east along the ridge.

Pass through an area of isolated peat hags, continuing N-wards on the higher ground but perhaps favouring the eastern edge of the hags in mist, to reach the high ground and a change in direction.

From Spink to Camaderry and Upper Lough

To the north-west you will see the moor above Lough Firrib, to the north Fair Mountain and to the east the Turlough reservoir and the summit at 681 m, the south-western lobe of Tomaneena, which forms your next objective.

Head E into the highest point of the saddle making use of convenient groughs, perhaps picking up a path heading E/SE out of the col heading a little to the right (south) of the distinctive nose outcropping ahead of you, then running toward and past a second prominent outcrop. Follow the path as it crosses a broad flat rocky summit, past a fenced-off quarry, to reach a track serving the small weather station and mast on your right (south). Turn left to head generally NE toward Turlough Hill.

The contrasting profiles of the artificial banks of the Turlough reservoir and the smooth natural lines of Camaderry are quite striking.

Before reaching the asphalt of the Turlough service road, cut right (NE) across waste ground to join a path on the moorland side of the prohibiting perimeter fence and follow this to the spur running from the south-east end of the reservoir. To the east-south-east is the summit of Camaderry. Leave the path and the fence and head into the saddle to describe a south-bending arc through the peaty wilderness. In my experience this is not as wet as the previous saddle, haghopping is unnecessary and a dry route is soon found through the groughs.

Notice how the milky-green, perhaps dehydrated, sphagnum moss still clings tenaciously to the caps of the peat hags, held together by the roots of the ling. The wide groughs penetrate to the rock beneath and the shattered fragments of quartzite, schists and conglomerate all provide evidence of the mineralisation of the bedrock at some time in the land's geological past. This no doubt encouraged the early prospecting and the eventual establishment of the mines.

As you emerge from the saddle look for a narrow but distinctive path running generally E towards the summit. Arrive at a small collection of large granite boulders now crowned with lumps of quartzite and generally regarded as the summit of Camaderry. From the collection of rocks follow the path SE along the ridge toward a secondary summit.

Leave the summit and the views of Fair Mountain, Tonelagee (backside to the wind) and the Wicklow Gap and pass through an area of hags, perhaps made eerie by the silver glow of sunlight piercing the mist that sometimes embraces the mountain. *Below, on the slopes to the north-east, are the remains of more lead mines and later, on the flanks of the great spur running south from Tonelagee, you may see the tailings fans of other workings, prominent on the mountainside.*

Arrive at a cairn of assorted boulders and stay with the path (E) as it becomes quite distinct and continues to descend the eastern spur of the mountain. After a little less than 1.5 km (1 mile) you will be descending the more gentle slopes of a lower shoulder. Here your route diverges from the path on a fainter tread and you will need to take care that you do not miss it. Look for a tread that forks off to your left and heads towards the left hand end (north) of the few remaining trees of an old strip plantation, which runs across your way. The path remains close to the spine of the spur and becomes more prominent as it is joined by other threads from your left.

It is important to gain this route, as a large field of bracken lies before you and following the footworn path is the easiest way through. When the bracken is at its full height, it becomes difficult to identify any possible navigational aids such as large boulders, enclosure walls, earth banks or a forestry turntable, that may be present on your map. Should you find yourself passing through the remains of the strip plantation and beginning to descend SE, stop, turn left (N) and traverse through the bracken along the line of the plantation trees until you encounter the path and turn right (E).

However, you may choose to stay on this south-east running path. It quickly turns south to descend directly back to the car-park entrance, following a clear path down the steep flanks of the spur. It is an enjoyable descent, but it does need care, and should definitely be avoided in the wet, unless you want to descend on your bottom! There is also the tempting glitter of gold under foot. But don't be fooled, it's only iron pyrites!

Continuing on the route proper, there are now fine views of Derry Bawn Mountain and the ridge to Mullacor across the Vale of Glendalough to the south-east, and across to Brockagh Mountain and Brockagh East, north-east ahead of you. In spring and autumn, the uniform green of the distant plantations bursts into a revealing contrast of colours, to delight even the jaded eye, as the consistent foliage of spruce and other evergreens provides a canvas to the strident yellow of the European larch and the firecrest russet of its Japanese cousin. And in winter and summer the seasonal cloaks of the multitude of deciduous trees give infinite variety as every plant and tree works to transform the rugged desolate tops into the tranquil sheltered valleys.

Towards Spink across Lower Lough

But keep an eye on the bracken too, for as you pass there is doubtless a timid but plump little woodcock, with its distinctive long beak, sneaking through the fronds; it occurs to me that, although their religious order demanded they consume only meagre fare, this curious little bird must have been a delicacy enjoyed by the monks through the centuries.

Another 500 m after the plantation, reach a long-disused forestry track and turn left (NE). There now follows a series of eight right and left bends and elbows, as the track zigzags down

the spur. The eighth and final bend is a right elbow and the junction here is easily missed if you are in a rambler's reverie. But this is not a problem; VARIATION C arrives up from the right to this point, and if you are lost, just take the directions from there.

At this last right elbow, leave the track by going straight on, to descend over a hump along a path toward the summit of Brockagh East Top across Glendasan. The path leaves the plantation to reach a fence, turn left (N), descend gently into Glendasan scrambling over a small rocky protuberance. Immediately turn left toward a wide track and enter another plantation, eventually heading NW along the path. Go into a dark section of trees, and quickly reach a dry stone wall. Turn right (NE), descend to a gravelled boreen running alongside the Glendasan River, and turn right (SE) again.

Notice the river deepen as you near a silt dam. Crystal clear on most days now, I would imagine that the river was once heavily polluted by the tailings and the heavy metal deposits from the mines further up the glen, and there is probably still a need to trap silt brought down in times of storm and flash flooding.

At a bend, reach a single-storey house and gain sight of the majestic **round tower**. Continue on to the tarmac road and turn left (E): at the bridge turn right (S) off the road and through the gateway, into the **monastic enclosure**. Take the first right (W) and have a close look at the round tower. Then turn left and pass by the cathedral and the eighth-century cross of St Kevin. To your right (west) is the Priest's House. Continue ahead, descend steps, and pass (south) the church called St Kevin's Kitchen with its distinctive belfry tower. Go through the two steel kissing gates, over the Glenealo river by the wooden bridge and turn right (W) to join the **Wicklow Way** and follow the green road signposted to the Upper Lough.

*Ahead of you before the turning right is the **deer stone**. I understand the green road is probably eighteenth-century, though the Way may have an older history. Certainly it was used a century later by pilgrims performing the stations of the cross on St Kevin's Day, 3 June (Walks 3 and 8). On your right across the river you may see the ruins of St Mary's Church before arriving close to the shore of the Lower Lough, once called Loch ná Péiste because it was thought to be home to a water monster. On your left are cliffs of mica schist, the original sedimentary rocks of the area, baked by the heat of molten granite, ten times hotter than boiling water.*

Pass through a delightful birch wood interspersed with sessile oak, ignore a footpath running off to the right to the car-park and continue on a little further to reach the Wicklow Mountains National Park Information Office in a small cottage. If the centre is open go in; you will be assured of a welcome. Otherwise turn right (NW) and pass through parkland on your way back to the car-park.

The walk has not yet revealed all its treasures. The woodland here is home to a variety of small birds, including the attractive little long-tailed tit, and to your left (west) are ancient stone crosses and a caher of unknown origin and age. Actually, Hall's map of 1842 shows a second, larger, caher close to the site of the present car-park. Various suggestions place the date of these monuments from early Christian to Iron Age; not a lot of difference! And finally, the land on which you are standing is perhaps the most recent geological feature of the area. Once several feet below the water of the lough, as the water level fell in antiquity, it revealed this large alluvial fan, created from the silt deposited by the waters that cascaded down the Poulanass (the pool of the waterfall) Waterfall from the slopes of Derry Bawn (whitish oak wood), Lugduff and Mullacor (a round summit, or Mullaghmor meaning great summit).

THE COMMENTARIES

Wicklow Mountains National Park

Basically these mountains have been folded, baked, boiled and scraped and, to preserve what they have become, were established as Ireland's fourth National Park in 1991. This core area around Glendalough is being expanded to take in most of the central uplands of the Wicklow Mountains, including the source of the river of which Dubliners are so proud, the Liffey, and the almost unique mountain blanket bog around Sally Gap to the north. The visitor centre offers interpretations of what you see of the mountains, their formation and their present appearance.

Old Lead Mines

It is reckoned to be 400 million years, a tenth of the age of the earth itself, since the huge molten bubbles of the Leinster granite forced their way up into the mudstone and sandstone rocks laid gently on the sea-bed more than 100 million years before. The sediments were baked into new metamorphic rocks. As the granite cooled and cracked, in rushed more molten matter, boiling off thousands of gallons of water and cooling the residue to the mineral-bearing rock, so eagerly exploited during the eighteenth and nineteenth centuries. During that time, the Glendalough workings became the largest in Ireland, vying with mines in the neighbouring Glendasan and Glenmalure. Mainly mining for galena, the ore bearing lead, they also processed commercial quantities of copper and zinc, though the smelting was undertaken elsewhere above Shankill in Dublin and later in Cardiff in Wales. I can't imagine what the miners' life was like, but no doubt it was hard and short. The Derbyshire expression for lead mining, 't'owd man', probably says it all. Thankfully for us, the commercial value of these mines has long since evaporated and the valley is progressively reclaiming its own.

Herds of Deer

If you are unlucky enough not to spot deer in either the Glenveagh or the Killarney National Parks, perhaps this walk will reward your perseverance, for it is estimated that there are more than 5000 deer amid this mountain chain. The shy immigrant sika seek the shelter of the plantations while the native red deer prefer to roam the open wilderness, and frequent areas such as this. To be correct, they are actually red-like. Unlike in Killarney, the native red deer became extinct during the first half of the eighteenth century; they were reintroduced at a later date and then cross-bred with the smaller sika deer. This plantation-loving breed was imported to the Powerscourt estate, from whose deer park it originally escaped during the troubles of the 1920s, through damaged water gates over the River Dargle, and again when the park was abandoned in the 1940s. There are thought to be a hundred or so deer around Glenealo, probably moving in several groups, though you may spot individual red-type stags during rutting.

Their eyesight is not particularly good and the limited movement of a lone walker is unlikely to startle them into a canter into the distance. If you have a pair of binoculars, or a monocular as I favour, you may have an opportunity to observe them at leisure. This would not have been the case, I imagine, with their territorial predecessors, the Great Irish Deer.

Wandering in herds across Northern Europe and Siberia, these are renowned as the largest of all Eurasian deer. The males stood 1.8 m (6 ft) at the shoulder with antlers spreading more than 4 m (nearly 14 ft). Luckily for the lone rambler, their heyday was around 11,000–12,000 years ago. Actually the antlers are thought to have been quite frail and used for aggressive or territorial display to rivals. Like me, they were probably vegetarian, browsing on the scrubland of the tops, their antlers preventing the older males from entering the extensive woodlands that began to develop from 10,000 years ago.

Turlough Hill Power Station

The original Gaelic name of the hill and its anglicised descendant have already been explained. The name Turlough, used by the ESB, comes from the Gaelic and refers to those lakes that disappear at various times during the year, found in the west and parts of the north. This is really a giant battery, a means of storing energy. The water in this artificial lake arrives by pipe and pump through the middle of the mountain, using electricity during periods of excess production. It is drawn from Lough Nahanagan, which will remain out of your sight, in its dramatic rocky black corrie, but can be found, a kilometre to the north-east and almost 250 m below. In times of peak demand the water is allowed to flow down again, through turbines, to generate electricity. I hate the artificial contours created by this hilltop reservoir, but at least the power station is well concealed beneath the mountain, the electricity transmission station hidden from view, and there is no nuclear waste to contend with.

Round Tower or Cloigtheach

These are a unique emblem of Ireland, significant of the early Celtic monastic life. The first written reference to a round tower comes in 950 AD and the general period of their construction is reckoned to be between the tenth and twelfth centuries, which I think must make them among the earliest mortared buildings in the British Isles. This particular tower had its conical cap reconstructed in 1876, supposedly from the original stone, restoring it to its original height of 33 m (108 ft). The doorway is more than 3 m (11 ft) from the ground and entry would have been by wood or rope ladder. The six internal floors were also of wood connected by ladders. Their purpose is not certain but it's thought that they served as a landmark, as a refuge in times of siege, and as a belfry. Apparently the monks would hang out of the four uppermost windows, facing the cardinal points of the compass, and ring hand bells. This was most probably the function of the belfry attached to St Kevin's Kitchen, which you will see shortly. There was a third round tower, to the east, at the site of the Trinity Church, but these remains were destroyed by winds some time in 1818.

Monastic Enclosure

Ireland's importance in European affairs began well before her entry into the European Community in 1972. Glendalough was once a major centre of European learning, and with the formation of a national park that meets the requirements of the World Conservation Union, it might be argued that things have come full circle.

The enclosure marks a monastery founded by the acolytes of St Kevin (528–619 AD) in the sixth century and according to Peter Harbison it was one of the most famous religious centres in early Christian Ireland. The deaths of its abbots and illustrious monks, the raids of the Vikings and later the Normans are recorded in old Irish annals, and the enclosure is reputedly hallowed by earth from Rome.

The stone monuments from the eighth to the twelfth centuries are scattered across the floor of the valley and probably represent only a small fraction of the buildings that existed in its heyday; these would have been built mainly of wood and thatch, wattle and daub. A full account of the place is given in the excellent visitor centre, which you can find by turning left (E), and crossing the River Glendasan; just ask directions from one of the many visitors.

The Priest's House, twelfth-century, is probably the tombshrine of St Kevin, whilst the cathedral, the largest church in Glendalough, probably dates from the eleventh century, although some references consider it to be much older. St Kevin's Church, or

Kitchen, I find one of the most interesting buildings because of its stone roof. The belfry was probably added later. St Mary's Church, the most westerly building of this group, may be seen from the green road and is possibly one of the oldest buildings, dating from the tenth century.

Deer Stone

The Deer Stone is a ballaun (Walks 12 and 19) and is said to have been used to gather the milk from a white hind or a doe, depending on whose story you prefer, to feed a royal fosterling of St Kevin. I wonder where the name really comes from. I recall being told of 'deer stones': significant sites where some species of deer stag would leave the herd and choose a spot to challenge its rivals. This spot would be used, possibly for centuries, by successive bucks; strangely, such sites would often have importance for humans, and have been or

become sites for gallauns, standing stones, and later for religious worship. Reputable water diviners claim they can detect a meeting of forces within the earth at these points. Of course this is all rather fanciful and probably has nothing to do with the name, but I thought you might find it intriguing.

The Wicklow Way

The Republic's first COSPOIR-sponsored long distance trail, opened in 1981, and something of a memorial to J. B. Malone (Walk 19), who conceived the route. Also called Sli Cualann Nua, an ancient route from the days of Tara, the Way enters Laragh via an old Mass path, follows this green lane to Lugduff Brook and climbs to the summit of Mullacor, on its way from Marlay Park in Dublin to Clonmel in Co. Carlow. Five days for a fit backpacker.

VARIATIONS AND ALTERNATIVES

A: GLENEALO WATERSHED: A bog trotter's treat, with fine views most of the time, and navigable by the experienced even in mist, with the security of a convenient escape into Glenealo once west of easting MR T 080. From the car-park go S to the green road and follow the Wicklow Way to the summit of Mullacor. The

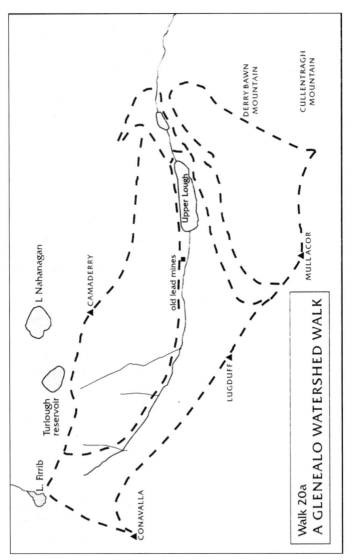

DERRY BAWN MOUNTAIN

CULLENTRAGH MOUNTAIN

L Nahanagan

CAMADERRY

Upper Lough

old lead mines

MULLACOR

Turlough reservoir

LUGDUFF

L. Firrib

CONAVALLA

Walk 20a
A GLENEALO WATERSHED WALK

waymark posts will aid your ascent. Ignore the route shown on the preliminary edition of OS map Sheet 56. Now follow the ridge NW over Lugduff to the north-east spur of Conavalla (MR T 044980). Go NNE/NE to Lough Firrib. Then staying with the high ground, head ESE and drop into the saddle at MR T 057985 to join the walk. (21 km/13 miles, ascent 885 m/2900 ft, 8 hours, Difficult.)

B: A FINE VIEW: From Lugduff Spink over the Vale of Glendalough. This impressive finger of rock runs east from the summit of Lugduff and towers over the Vale of Glendalough. A number of forest tracks and paths run up the Spink from the car-park. Follow the white waymarked path over a footbridge with signs for Poulanass waterfall. A hundred metres after the waterfall join a forest track, turing right. At the second bend take the white arrow path on R up a sleeper stairway to Spink. (Up to 6 km/ 4 miles, ascent up to 300 m/1000 ft, 90 minutes, Moderate.)

C: A FAMILY RAMBLE: Begin by following the walk alongside the Upper Lough until you reach a pair of disused semi-detached cottages on your right. Almost immediately turn right (NE) on to an old forestry track. Follow this as it declines into a footpath, and yields the kind of views that can make you sigh. At an obvious path junction (a left elbow in the track), turn right to rejoin the walk. (5 km/3 miles, ascent 85 m/280 ft, 90 minutes, but allow 2.5 hours, Easy.)

D: A PLEASANT STROLL: Both the start and finish of the walk provide easy walking in sensible shoes. The loughside stroll at the start of the walk is likely to be less busy than the green lane to the monastic enclosure. You could form a circular walk by taking the road from the car-park to the monastic enclosure and join the walk at the gateway. (There is no climbing and the circular walk is about 4 km/2.5 miles, an hour or so, but take as long as you want, Easy.) There are also 2 km and 4 km waymarked trails starting from the National Park Information Office.

E: OTHER WALKING: The Wicklow Mountains are the Dublin ramblers' playground. There are a number of books and pamphlets on walks, trails and access routes in the area; those written by David Herman provide a variety of rambles. The **Wicklow Way** is described in the commentaries.

Appendix 1 | Rambling Safely

GOING WALKING

Apparently the United States army once wrote a manual on walking, actually instructing their soldiers on how to put one foot in front of the other. Eventually they threw it away after GIs kept tripping over their own feet, trying to follow the instructions in the manual. Whoever was in charge finally accepted that walking is either something you do, or don't do, and if you're a GI, you probably do! But wisely, they kept their other manuals on getting fit, going equipped and finding the way.

I'm sure these manuals must have included such gems as, 'It's a good idea if you know where you're going, before you begin.' So at least read the route instructions given in the text. With all but the easiest walks, trace the proposed route on the OS map, at least with your finger, if not with a pencil. If this is a new skill, start with the easy walks and use the route sketch given with the key walks; this will help. Look at the OSi or OSNI map carefully; try to interpret the contours, get a feel for the topography and some idea of the landscape in which you will be walking. Is it mountainous or flat, inland or coastal, is it very boggy with lots of groughs and tiny streams, are the contours close together indicating that the ground is steep, are there lots of escarpments or cliffs? Use the key to become familiar with the map symbols and use the walks as a chance to practise using your compass and map-reading skills.

If it is mountainous or difficult terrain, look for possible escape routes: ways off the top of the mountain, below the fog or out of other danger, which will lead you to a safe route such as an asphalt road. Or even for short cuts to get you back safely should you suddenly feel that you've had enough for one day. Make sure that you carry any phone numbers you may need in case of emergencies, and that you have any necessary travel details such as bus or train times. If you are new to walking, don't overstretch yourself, or your companions. It takes time to get fit, at least six weeks of regular walking. Don't push it too soon, use the graded walk options in CHOOSING YOUR WALK to help you choose appropriate walks as you progress.

Tell someone where you are going, leave a security message. By all means make a note of your route and give it to them; quote the number of the walk in this book if you wish. Tell them what time you expect to be back, and to notify the police or garda if you don't return. Of course, if you decide to stop off for an evening meal on the way home, don't forget to notify them that you are down safely. I for one have been up a mountain in winter in the dark on more than one occasion because someone went home without cancelling their security message.

Even though it causes a few laughs, because I walk alone so often I admit to taking a mobile phone. You'd be surprised at where they work. I even made a call for assistance once when I injured myself in the Sperrin Mountains.

Use the checklist at the back of the book to make sure you have the basic essentials: your map and compass, a whistle, a torch, rainwear and spare clothing. Use last page to make your own list and just give it a quick check each time you go for a walk. These are not big jobs and will help free you, your family or companions from any worries, allowing you a greater opportunity to enjoy your day.

FINDING A MAP REFERENCE

There are very few signposts on the hills so that once you are away from the built environment, map references are a great way of finding a place on the map, and of telling it to someone else.

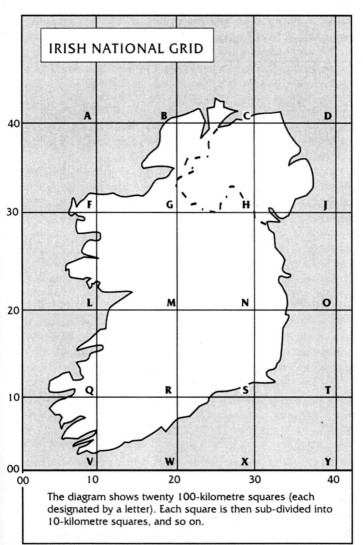

The diagram shows twenty 100-kilometre squares (each designated by a letter). Each square is then sub-divided into 10-kilometre squares, and so on.

This is especially true in Ireland as there are so few footpaths or footpath signs. The system of map references is not difficult and is easily understood once explained. That is why they are used in various parts of the walk descriptions: in ADVICE AND GRADING, to identify the location of a viewpoint, in GETTING THERE, to indicate the start of the walk, and, of course, occasionally in THE WALK, to assist in route finding. They are not the only way used to identify a location, but they do help if you want to be exact, or to double-check a place.

Here is an example map reference: MR O 285378. Imagine a map of the whole of Ireland. Now over it place a large grid of squares as in the diagram opposite. This is called the National Grid. Now you can see that if you start at the bottom left-hand corner and count, first the lines from left to right, and then from the bottom upwards, you may give a pair of numbers as a reference to a square in the grid. The two numbers would refer to the bottom left-hand corner of the square they represented. For example, Dublin is in square 300200 (square O).

In fact these large grid squares are referred to by their grid letter, but the same principle of the two numbers is used to identify points within each grid square. So now we know that our reference O 285378 is to be found in square O.

Sheet 16 of the Republic of Ireland Ordnance Survey half-inch scale (1:126 720) map covers square O. Unfold the map. A little to the right and beneath the centre of the map you will see the crossing of the main grid lines 300 and 200 and in red the characters S T N and O, marking the names of the grid squares. In the newer 1:50 000 scale Rambler series the letters are marked in blue, and of course the area covered by the map is not so large. On the bottom of Sheet 16 find the 300 grid line marked 00 in red, and follow it eastwards (right) until you reach 20. This is the first figure in your grid reference, 2. Then continuing eastwards count off 8 of the smaller dividing segments. This is the second figure in your grid reference, 8. Still continuing eastwards, imagine that the next segment, between marks 8 and 9, is divided into ten, and count off 5. Mark it with a pencil. This is the third figure in your grid reference, 5. Now we have MR O 285, and Howth is somewhere along that vertical line running up the map from the point you have identified. This reference is called the easting and is always written first.

Now on the left-hand side of the map find the 200 grid line marked oo in red and follow it northwards (up) until you reach 30. Now count off 7 segments, and imagine the following segment to be divided by ten, and count off 8. Again mark it with a pencil. This is called the northing reference and where this horizontal line crosses your vertical easting you will find the summit of the Ben of Howth. Congratulations. Now how high is it?

So in finding or making a reference first you check the grid letter, then you go across the map, from the left side; and then up the map from the bottom edge. This practice is the same for both the old imperial standard maps and the newer metric series for the Ordnance Survey offices of both the Republic of Ireland and Northern Ireland. Practise with the map references given in the different walks, and collect your own map references to record your activities on a walk.

USING YOUR MAP AND COMPASS

A summer stroll along the River Barrow (Walk 18) hardly needs a compass. You simply make sure you are on the correct bank and follow the river. But I am frequently surprised to meet people in the hills who neither carry a compass nor seem to know how to use one.

And yet a compass means freedom: freedom from tracks and paths; freedom from relying on friends who know the way; freedom to explore that distant skyline or find that hidden clough. Freedom to go where you will. And because the skill is easy to acquire and simple to practise, that freedom is open to anyone who can walk. It is also a freedom born of security, because together with using the map, using the compass will always help to get you home.

Modern protractor compasses are ideal. They combine a clear plastic base plate with a magnetic needle damped in a fluid, and are simplicity itself to use. To take a bearing from map to compass hold your map flat and somewhere secure, then: First mark the two positions on your map: one, your present position and two, the place you want to go, your objective. Draw a line between the two. Then estimate the bearing; that is, guess the angle between the vertical grid lines (grid north) and your pencil bearing line, measuring clockwise. This will act as a check later.

Second, place the long edge of the compass along the pencil bearing line you have drawn with the arrows on the compass base plate pointing towards your objective. Third, turn the circular compass housing until the lines and arrow on the bottom of the circular housing (orienteering lines) are parallel to the vertical grid lines on the map. Read off the bearing on the circular bezel at the index mark on the centre of the base plate. Check this against your estimate, it will make sure that you do not have the compass pointing back to front!

Good; you may now make one small adjustment to improve the accuracy of your bearing. On the edge of your map will be a diagram of three arrows under the title 'North Points'. This will tell you the extent of magnetic variation. For example, the OSNI 1:50 000 series Sheet 13, for The Sperrins, says, 'Magnetic north was 8°2' west of grid north ... in 1984. Annual change ... is about 12' east.' In other words, the magnetic needle of our compass does not point to exactly the same north as the grid lines on the map, but to a few degrees further west. And because of an annual change of about 12 minutes east (there are 60 minutes in a degree) by 1989, five years later, it would have been 7°29', and ten years later, in 1994, 6°29'. If this variation were less than 2 degrees we could ignore it, but as it is, we need to make an adjustment to ensure we walk in the right direction, or spot the correct landmark. But this is no problem. The compass needle points west of grid north ($6°29'$ in this case), therefore our compass bearing will be $6°29'$ short of the true reading, and we must add this to the bearing we took from the bezel at the index mark. Taking an example from Walk 6 in The Sperrins, a map bearing quoted in the text was $238°$, therefore our magnetic bearing must be $244°29'$, in 1994. Rotate the compass bezel $6°29'$ anti-clockwise and the job is done.

Finally hold the compass flat, in front of you, away from any metal objects that may deflect the needle. Now rotate the whole compass and base plate together, or yourself, until the needle is parallel to the orienteering lines on the bottom of the circular housing, and the red head of the needle is pointing to N on the compass bezel. The lines and arrow on the base plate now show the direction of your objective. Carefully check it again, then go for it.

Taking a bearing from the landscape to the map (resection) to determine your own location, is simply a matter of reversing the procedure. Find an object in the landscape that you feel you can identify on the map: a church, a distinctive peak, a confluence of two rivers. Point the base plate at the object in the landscape, allow the needle to settle and rotate the bezel until the orienteering lines run parallel with the needle and the red tip of the needle is pointing to N on the bezel. Read off the bearing at the index mark, and this time subtract the magnetic variation, by rotating the bezel the required amount clockwise ($7°29'$ in our example). Now place the compass on the map with the edge of the base plate touching the feature you have taken your bearing from. Keeping the edge of the base plate at that point, rotate the whole compass until the orienteering lines of the circular compass housing run parallel to the vertical grid lines of the map, and N on the bezel points to N on the map. Now draw a line from your chosen landscape feature along the side of your compass base plate. Your position lies along this line. Repeat the procedure with other landscape features that you can identify on the map, and if you extend the lines far enough, they will cross. If you've been accurate, three or more lines will all cross at the same point. That is your approximate position.

There are many outdoor and walking handbooks that will help you develop your skill with the compass, and exploit it to the full. Practise at home, on days out, and when you go on these walks. And once you have that skill – trust it. If we follow our instincts we are more likely to behave like lemmings than bats or birds. Ignore the appeal of your 'sense of direction', or anyone else's for that matter, and place trust in your skill and the compass.

Occasionally, to aid route finding, or to help orient you amid the wilder parts of the landscape, I have given map bearings. For example, in Walk 7 on the ascent to Slieve Snaght, you emerge on to a ridge in a gulley, and the summit of Slieve Snaght is 1000 ft higher and out of view across granite moorland. The bearing given in the route instructions should help you orient yourself and choose a route to Snaght. Don't forget to adjust for magnetic variation, and safe navigation!

PARKING YOUR CAR

From Malin Head to Mizzen Head is how the Garda Síochána (the Irish national police force, meaning guardians of the peace) describes its geographical area of responsibility; and the advice it offers for the protection of your car and its contents is echoed by the Northern Ireland Police Service.

Whilst Ireland has one of the lowest crime rates in Europe, the two police forces do advise you not to take unnecessary risks with your property, particularly portable goods such as cameras, binoculars and other outdoor equipment. Here is some of the advice they give:

- Always lock your car, even if unattended only for a short period.

- Never leave the keys in the ignition.
- Close all windows and lock all doors.
- Use a steering wheel or other mechanical immobiliser.
- Park in authorised car-parks when they are available.
- Never leave property in your vehicle. However, if you cannot avoid this, then lock it in your boot, transferring the goods before parking, and preferably out of general view.
- Do not attempt to 'disguise' property with a coat or other article.

The police make the point that most thieves are opportunists and are looking for an easy target, and that following this simple advice will make sure your day out is memorable for all the 'right' reasons. However, just in case, the telephone number of the local Garda or police station is included with each walk.

Appendix 2 | Almanac of High Places

Lugnaquillia is the highest Irish mountain outside of Kerry. Brandon is the highest mountain outside of Macgillycuddy's Reeks. Brandon is higher than Lugnaquillia, but of course it is in Kerry. Errigal is higher than Snaght in Glenveagh, which is lower than all of them, but still one hell of a walk over Rocky Cap from the Poisoned Glen. Slieve Donard is the highest mountain in Northern Ireland. It isn't a Munro, but its 2780 ft do actually rise from sea level. And Glenariff

HILL OR MOUNTAIN	RANGE	COUNTY
Anglesea	Cooley Hills	Louth/Down
Arderin	Slieve Bloom Mnts	Laoise
Benbreen	Twelve Bens	Galway
Benbulbin	Benbulbin	Sligo
Bencollaghduff	Twelve Bens	Galway
Bencorr	Twelve Bens	Galway
Bencorr Beg	Twelve Bens	Galway
Bengore Head	coastal	Antrim
Bengower	Twelve Bens	Galway
Benlettery	Twelve Bens	Galway
Ben More	Achill Island	Mayo
Ben of Howth (Black Linn)	coastal	Dublin
Bignian, Slieve	Mourne Mnts	Down
Black Mnt	Cooley Hills	Louth
Camaderry	Wicklow Mnts	Wicklow
Carnavaddy	Cooley Hills	Louth
Carrauntuohill	The Reeks	Kerry
Carrignagower	Comeragh Mnts	Waterford
Carrignabinnia	Galtee Mnts	Tipperary
Cathair na mBan	coastal	Inis Oírr
Chimney Rock Mnt	Mourne Mnts	Down
Clermont	Cooley Hills	Louth

isn't a mountain at all. So I have to tell you that I don't care. The long continuous ascents of mountains in other parts of the world would dwarf them all. That isn't what matters. What matters is how much pleasure it gives you to be there. I've lost track of the number of miles I walked to research this book, but I've never lost track of the phenomenal pleasure it has given me. I never have counted the number of Munros I might have climbed or judged a walk by the number of feet I've ascended. But the beauty or serenity of more than one place has brought tears to my eyes, put a lump in my throat or left me overwhelmed and breathless, and some of them are in this book.

All mountain heights are given in metres first, and then in feet.

HEIGHT	WALK NO.	MAP REFERENCE
428 m (1404 ft)	2B,2C	J 104176
527 m (1729 ft)	19	S 232989
694 m (2277 ft)	11A	L 782515
526 m (1726 ft)	9,9A,9B	G 692463
698 m (2290 ft)	11A	L 799530
712 m (2336 ft)	11	L 811522
582 m (1909 ft)	11	L 816533
114 m (374 ft)	5C	C 972458
666 m (2185 ft)	11A	L 782506
580 m (1903 ft)	11A	L 775495
277 m (910 ft)	10A	F 549045
172 m (563 ft)	1E	O 286377
747 m (2451 ft)	3,3A	J 320234
510 m (1673 ft)	2A,2B,2C	J 099156
700 m (2297 ft)	20,20A	T 081981
466 m (1529 ft)	2A,2B,2C	J 112141
1039 m (3409 ft)	14D	V 803844
720 m (2342 ft)	17	S 311122
778 m (2549 ft)	16B	R 850240
65 m (212 ft)	12,12A,12C	L 981021
656 m (2152 ft)	3,3B	J 364257
447 m (1466 ft)	2B,2C	J 099171

HILL OR MOUNTAIN	RANGE	COUNTY
Conavalla	Wicklow Mountains	Wicklow
Coshabinnia, Slieve	Galtee Mnts	Tipperary
Coumalocha	Comeragh Mnts	Waterford
Coumfea	Comeragh Mnts	Waterford
Coum Larthar	Comeragh Mnts	Waterford
Cove Mnt	Mourne Mnts	Down
Croaghaun	Achill Island	Mayo
Crockalough	Antrim Hills	Antrim
Dart Mnt	Sperrin Mnts	Tyrone/L-derry
Derryclare	Twelve Bens	Galway
Diamond Hill	Connemara	Galway
Donard, Slieve	Mourne Mnts	Down
Dunmore Head	coastal	Dingle
Errigal Mnt	Errigal Range	Donegal
Errisbeg	Connemara	Galway
Fauscoum	Comeragh Mnts	Tipperary
Foye, Slieve	Carlingford Mnt	Louth
Foxes Rock	Carlingford Mnt	Louth
Galtybeg	Galtee Mnts	Tipperary
Galtymore	Galtee Mnts	Tipperary
Greenane	Galtee Mnts	Tipperary
Hungry Hill	Caha Mnts	Cork
King's Mountain	Benbulbin	Sligo
Knockaunapeebra	Comeragh Mnts	Waterford
Knocknarea	Knocknarae	Sligo
Knockgour	Miskish Mnts	Cork
Knocknaffrin	Comeragh Mnts	Waterford
Knocksheengowna	Comeragh Mnts	Waterford
Laghtnafrankee	Comeragh Mnts	Waterford
Lamagan, Slieve	Mourne Mnts	Down
League, Slieve	coastal	Donegal
Leahan	coastal	Donegal
Lough Firrib	Wicklow Mnts	Wicklow
Lyracapul	Galtee Mnts	Tipperary
Lugduff	Wicklow Mnts	Wicklow

HEIGHT	WALK NO.	MAP REFERENCE
734 m (2408 ft)	20A	T 039972
643 m (2109 ft)	16	R 893262
755 m (2477 ft)	17	S 295097
729 m (2392 ft)	17	S 281095
770 m (2526 ft)	17	S 311122
655 m (2149 ft)	3	J 336271
668 m (2192 ft)	10,10B	F 555059
402 m (1319 ft)	4C	D 207234
619 m (2031 ft)	6,6B,6E	H 606964
677 m (2221 ft)	11	L 815510
445 m (1460 ft)	11B	L 732571
850 m (2789 ft)	3,3B,3C	J 358277
96 m (315 ft)	13C	V 305982
752 m (2466 ft)	7B	B 929209
301 m (987 ft)	11C	L 698402
800 m (2625 ft)	17,17D	S 317104
589 m (1932 ft)	2B	J 169120
384 m (1260 ft)	2B	J 137139
793 m (2600 ft)	16,16A,16B	R 890241
920 m (3018 ft)	16,16B	R 878240
870 m (2636 ft)	16B	R 924241
690 m (2251 ft)	15D	V 761497
467 m (1532 ft)	9,9A,9B	G 704442
735 m (2411 ft)	17	S 312096
327 m (1073 ft)	9D	G 625345
366 m (1200 ft)	15B	V 615450
755 m (2477 ft)	17C	S 284155
675 m (2215 ft)	17C	S 277167
521 m (1709 ft)	17A	S 235184
704 m (2310 ft)	3	J 329260
601 m (1972 ft)	8,8A,8B	G 543781
432 m (1418 ft)	8A	G 519802
650 m (213 ft)	20,20A	T 049988
827 m (2712 ft)	16B	R 845231
657 m (2215 ft)	20A	T 072954

HILL OR MOUNTAIN	RANGE	COUNTY
Lugduff Spink	Wicklow Mnts	Wicklow
Lurigethan	Antrim Hills	Antrim
Minaun Heights	Achill Island	Mayo
Mount Eagle	coastal	Dingle
Mullaghcarn	Tyrone Hills	Tyrone
Mullacor	Wicklow Mnts	Wicklow
North Tor	Mourne Mnts	Down
O'Loughlan's Castle	Galtee Mnts	Tipperary
Ravens Rock	Carlingford Mnt	Louth
Rocky Mnt	Mourne Mnts	Down
Rocky Cap	Derryveagh Mnts	Donegal
Sawel Mnt	Sperrin Mnts	Tyrone/L-derry
Shelmartin	Howth/coastal	Dublin
Slieveard	Tyrone Hills	Tyrone
Snaght, Slieve	Derryveagh Mnts	Donegal
Sturrakeen	Galtee Mnts	Tipperary
Temple Hill	Galtee Mnts	Tipperary
Tomaneena	Wicklow Mnts	Wicklow
Torc Mountain	Killarney	Kerry
Tower Hill	Dursey Isl	Cork
Unnamed summit	Cooley Hills	Louth

HEIGHT	WALK NO.	MAP REFERENCE
350 m (1148 ft)	20B	T 106958
385 m (1263 ft)	4,4C	D 227356
403 m (1322 ft)	10C	F 670027
515 m (1692 ft)	13,13A,13B	V 335989
542 m (1778 ft)	6E	H 510809
664 m (2167 ft)	20A	T 092939
679 m (2198 ft)	3,3A	J 317245
739 m (2425 ft)	16B	R 910240
457 m (1499 ft)	2B	J 149132
525 m (1722 ft)	3,3B	J 351252
579 m (1900 ft)	7	B 933156
678 m (2224 ft)	6,6B,6E	H 618972
168 m (550 ft)	1,1C	O 275376
419 m (1374 ft)	6E	H 488785
683 m (2240 ft)	7,7A	B 924149
503 m (1650 ft)	16B	R 961262
786 m (2579 ft)	16B	R 831220
680 m (2231 ft)	20,20A	T 063983
535 m (1755 ft)	14B	V 955839
254 m (832 ft)	15C	V 472404
454 m (1489 ft)	2B,2C	J 103165

Appendix 3 | Lexicon

abha, abhainn, avon, ow, owen, river, stream
ath, atha, anna, river crossing, ford
ayle, ail, aille, faill, cliff
baile, bally, settlement, village, town, townland
beag, beg, small
bó thar, bóthar, bother, cattle track, road
bothairin, bohereen, boreen, bohreen, little road
buaile, booley, from milk, summer pasture
caede mille fáilte, a hundred thousand welcomes
carraig, carrick, a rock
cill, kill, a small church or monastic site, religious cell
clogher, stony place
cnoc, crock, knoc, a hill
coill, kyle, kill, wood
cúm, coum, coire, corrie, cwm, cauldron or hollow
dainséar, danger
dún, dun, fort or fortified site
derry, oak.
drum, small hill or raised ground, a ridge of rock
drumlin, a small hill, a feature of glaciated landscapes, made from the moraine of retreating ice sheets
dubh, black
eisc, esk, eiscer, esker, steep rocky gulley, or famous glacial phenoenon
eas, waterfall
fáilte, welcome
fearann, farran, farn, arran, land
fionn, finn, white, clear
fraoch, freagh, heather, heath
gallan, gallaun, gallun, standing stone
garbh, garrif, garra, rough or rugged
greuch, greagh, greugh, marsh, wet land
inbhear, inver, enner, river mouth

inse, water meadow

innis, inis, inch, ennis, oilean, island

lis, liss, a fortified field, usually for animals

lough, lake

lyre, lear, ladhar, fork of mountain spurs

mac, son

maum, madhm, high mountain pass

mona, peat, peat bog; hence Bord na Mona, the Peat Board

mór, more, big, great, large, important

mullagh, mullach, a summit

O', grandson

ought, ucht, breast of a mountain

oughter, higher, upper

páirc, park, field

potín, poteen, the native – an illegally distilled spirit

ra, rath, raheen, an earthwork, probably settlement

reask, riasc, risk, a marsh

ros, ross, a promontory of land, wood, or a copse

skerry, skerrig, skellig, craggy rock

slane, turf spade

sliabh, slieve, mountain, land unfit for agricultural use

tholsel, tolsel, the old administrative building of a town

teampull, church

tobar, tober, tobber, holy or magical well, or both

tóchar, causeway across a bog

trá, beach

uisce, water

Appendix 4 | Places to Go, People to See, Things to Do…

International calls

With certain exceptions if you wish to dial to the Republic from the UK or vice versa you must dial as follows: international code + country code + area code (without the first 0) + the number. For example, to dial from the Republic to the British Mountaineering Council in the UK, you would need to dial: 00 44 161 273 5835.

The international exchange code in both countries is 00. The country code for the UK is 44 and the country code for the Republic of Ireland is 353. However if you wish to dial into Northern Ireland (only) from the Republic simply dial 048 followed by the local number you require, omitting the province wide 028 area code. For example, to call the Northern Ireland Tourist Board in Belfast, from anywhere in the Republic, dial: 048 9024 6609.

Transport – Irish Republic

IARNRÓD ÉIREANN
(IRISH RAIL)
Connolly Station
Dublin 1
01850 366222, www.irishrail.ie

BUS ÉIREANN (IRISH BUS)
59 Upper O'Connell Street
Dublin 1
01 873 4222, www.irishbus.ie

BUS ÁTHA CLIATH
(DUBLIN BUS)
59 Upper O'Connell Street
Dublin 1
01 872 0000, www.dublinbus.ie

AER ÁRANN
(Flights to the Aran Islands including Inis Oírr)
Minna, Inverin
(Connemara)
Co. Galway
091 593 034,
www.aerarannislands.ie

HAPPY HOOKER
(DOOLIN/INIS OÍRR FERRY)
The Pier
Doolin
Co. Clare
065 70 74455

Transport — Northern Ireland

NORTHERN IRELAND
RAILWAYS
Information Centre
East Bridge Street
Belfast BT1 3BP
028 9089 9400

ULSTERBUS TRAVEL
CENTRE
Europa Buscentre
Glengall Street
Belfast BT12 5AH
028 9033 7006

Maps

EASONS
40 Lower O'Connell Street
Dublin 1
01 858 3800

STANFORDS
12–14 Long Acre
London WC2E 9LP
020 7836 1321,
www.stanfords.co.uk

IRISH ORDNANCE SURVEY
National Map Centre Ireland
34 Aungier Street
Dublin 2
01 476 0487, www.irishmaps.ie

TIM ROBINSON'S FOLDING
LANDSCAPES
available from: Kenny's Bookshop
High Street
Galway
091 562 2793, www.iol.ie/kennys

ORDNANCE SURVEY OF
NORTHERN IRELAND
Sales Department
Colby House
Stranmillis Court
Malone Lower
Belfast BT9 5BJ
028 9025 5755, www.osni.gov.uk

Insurance and related advice

MOUNTAINEERING COUNCIL
OF IRELAND
Sport HQ, Joyce Way
Parkwest Business Park
Dublin 12
01 625 1115,
www.mountaineering.ie

BRITISH MOUNTAINEERING
COUNCIL
177–79 Burton Road
Manchester M20 2BB
0870 010 4878,
www.thebmc.co.uk

Information for ramblers and tourists — Irish Republic

BORD FÁILTE ÉIREANN
(WELCOME BOARD OF
IRELAND)
Baggot Street Bridge
Dublin 2
01850 230 330,
www.ireland.travel.ie

London office:
Ireland House
150 New Bond Street
London W1Y 0AG
020 7766 9920

Belfast office:
53 Castle Street
Belfast BT1 1GH
028 903 27888

Derry office:
44 Foyle Street
Derry BT48 6AT
028 7136 9501

IRISH SPORTS COUNCIL
21 Fitzwilliam Square
Dublin 2
01 240 7700,

Information for ramblers and tourists — Northern Ireland

NORTHERN IRELAND
TOURIST BOARD
Main office:
47 Donegal Place
Belfast BT1 5AD
028 9024 6609,
www.discovernorthernireland.com

Dublin office:
16 Nassau Street,
Dublin 2
01 679 1977

London office:
24 Haymarket
London SW1Y 4DG
020 7766 9920

SPORTS COUNCIL OF
NORTHERN IRELAND
House of Sport
Upper Malone Road
Belfast BT9 5LA
028 9038 1222, www.sportni.net

There are also Bord Fáilte and Northern Ireland Tourist Board offices, or 'All Ireland' offices, in all European capital cities, the Nordic countries, New York, Toronto and Sydney.

Appendix 5 | Rambling Checklist

Use this list to jog your memory when you are preparing to go for a walk. Try to get a sensible balance between going with nothing and taking the kitchen sink, bearing in mind the nature of the walk and the weather you are likely to encounter. Use the blank page to make a note of your own bits of kit that you might use occasionally, depending on the circumstances. And have a good day – I'll look for you!

- Get a weather forecast.
- Leave a note with a responsible person detailing your walk. Quote the walk in the book if it's appropriate.
- Map.
- Map cover.
- Compass.
- Whistle.
- Torch.
- *Best Walks* guidebook.
- First-aid stuff (in case you cut your finger on a drink can).
- Favourite snack for extra energy, fruit, chocolate or suchlike.
- Something to drink (yes, yes, I can imagine, but remember the dangers of alcohol).
- Extra clothes (if needed):
  pullover; hat, for sun, rain or cold; gloves; scarf; spare socks; jacket
  (and all that other stuff you don't think you really need until it turns out to be too late to go back for it, and you end up cold or wet or both!).
- Rainwear, gaiters and boots.
- Money (coins for call boxes when dialling other than 999, or for catching the bus back home).
- Phonecard.
- A comfy bag or sack to put it all in.
- And finally all those sensible things that all the best books tell you to take.

Achill 158, 162-73, *164*, 183, 190

Index